Quest

Second Edition

2

 **Listening and Speaking**

Laurie Blass

 **McGraw-Hill**

Quest 2 Listening and Speaking, 2nd Edition

Published by McGraw-Hill ESL/ELT, a business unit of The McGraw-Hill Companies, Inc. 1221 Avenue of the Americas, New York, NY 10020. Copyright © 2007 by The McGraw-Hill Companies, Inc. All rights reserved. No part of this publication may be reproduced or distributed in any form or by any means, or stored in a database or retrieval system, without the prior written consent of The McGraw-Hill Companies, Inc., including, but not limited to, in any network or other electronic storage or transmission, or broadcast for distance learning.

ISBN 13: 978-0-07-325330-5 (Student Book)
ISBN 10: 0-07-325330-8
  2 3 4 5 6 7 8 9 VNH/PCC 12 11 10 09 08 07 06

ISBN 13: 978-0-07-326961-0 (Student Book with Audio Highlights)
ISBN 10: 0-07-326961-1
  2 3 4 5 6 7 8 9 VNH/PCC 12 11 10 09 08 07 06

ISE ISBN 13: 978-0-07-110430-2 (International Student Edition)
ISE ISBN 10: 0-07-110430-5
  2 3 4 5 6 7 8 9 VNH/PCC 12 11 10 09 08 07 06

Editorial director: Erik Gundersen
Series editor: Linda O'Roke
Production manager: Juanita Thompson
Production coordinator: James D. Gwyn
Cover designer: David Averbach, Anthology
Interior designer: Martini Graphic Services, Inc.
Photo researchers: David Averbach, PoYee Oster

International Edition ISBN: 0-07-110430-5
Copyright © 2007. Exclusive rights by The McGraw-Hill Companies, Inc. for manufacture and export. This book cannot be re-exported from the country to which it is sold by McGraw-Hill. The International Edition is not available in North America.

McGraw-Hill

www.esl-elt.mcgraw-hill.com

The **McGraw-Hill** Companies

ACKNOWLEDGEMENTS

The publisher and author would like to thank the following education professionals whose comments, reviews, and assistance were instrumental in the development of the Quest series.

- **Roberta Alexander,** San Diego Community College District

- **David Dahnke,** North Harris College (Houston, TX)

- **Mary Díaz,** Broward Community College (Davie, FL)

- **Judith García,** Miami-Dade College

- **Elizabeth Giles,** The School District of Hillsborough County, Florida

- **Patricia Heiser,** University of Washington, Seattle

- **Yoshiko Matsubayashi,** Kokusai Junior College, Tokyo

- **Ahmed Motala,** University of Sharjah, United Arab Emirates

- **Dee Parker and Andy Harris,** AUA, Bangkok

- **Alison Rice,** Hunter College, City University of New York

- **Alice Savage,** North Harris College (Houston, TX)

- **Katharine Sherak,** San Francisco State University

- **Leslie Eloise Somers,** Miami-Dade County Public Schools

- **Karen Stanley,** Central Piedmont Community College (Charlotte, NC)

- **Diane Urairat,** Mahidol Language Services, Bangkok

- **Pamela Vittorio,** The New School (New York, NY)

- **Anne Marie Walters,** California State University, Long Beach

- **Lynne Wilkins,** Mills College (Oakland, CA)

- **Sean Wray, Elizabeth Watson, and Mariko Yokota,** Waseda International University, Tokyo

Many, many thanks go to Marguerite Ann Snow, who provided the initial inspiration for the entire series. Heartfelt thanks also to Erik Gundersen and Linda O'Roke for their help in the development of the second edition. I would also like to thank Dylan Bryan-Dolman, Susannah MacKay, Kristin Sherman, and Kristin Thalheimer, whose opinions were invaluable. Very special thanks to Pamela Hartmann, whose hard work and dedication continually inspired me throughout the development of this book.

TABLE OF CONTENTS

Quest: The Series

Quest Second Edition prepares students for academic success. The series features two complementary strands—*Listening and Speaking* and *Reading and Writing*—each with four levels. The integrated *Quest* program provides robust scaffolding to support and accelerate each student's journey from exploring general interest topics to mastering academic content.

Quest parallels and accelerates the process native-speaking students go through when they prepare for success in a variety of academic subjects. By previewing typical college course material, *Quest* helps students get "up to speed" in terms of both academic content and language skills.

In addition, *Quest* prepares students for the daunting amount and level of listening, speaking, reading, and writing required for college success. The four *Listening and Speaking* books in the *Quest* series contain listening and speaking strategies and practice activities centered on authentic recordings from "person on the street" interviews, social conversations, radio programs, and university lectures. Listening passages increase in length and difficulty across the four levels.

The *Reading and Writing* books combine high-interest material from newspapers and magazines with traditional academic source materials such as textbooks. Like the *Listening and Speaking* books, the four *Reading and Writing* books increase in difficulty with each level.

Quest Second Edition Features

- New *Intro* level providing on-ramp to Books 1-3
- Redesigned, larger format with captivating photos
- Expanded focus on critical thinking and test-taking skills
- Expanded video program (VHS and DVD) with new lecture and updated social language footage
- Test-taking strategy boxes that highlight skills needed for success on the new TOEFL® iBT
- New unit-ending *Vocabulary Workshops* and end-of-book academic word lists
- Teacher's Editions with activity-by-activity procedural notes, expansion activities, and tests
- Addition of research paper to *Reading and Writing* titles
- EZ Test® CD-ROM-based test generator for all *Reading and Writing* titles

Quest Listening and Speaking

Quest Listening and Speaking includes three or four distinct units, each focusing on a different area of university study— anthropology, art, biology, business, ecology, economics, history, literature, psychology, or sociology. Each unit contains two chapters.

Chapter Structure

Each chapter of *Quest 2 Listening and Speaking* contains five parts that blend listening and speaking skills within the context of a particular academic area of study. Listening passages and skill-development activities build upon one another and increase in difficulty as students work through the five sections of each chapter.

Part 1: Introduction

- Thinking Ahead – discussion activities on photos introduce the chapter topic.
- Reading – a high-interest reading captures students' attention and motivates them to want to find out even more about the chapter topic.
- Discussion – speaking activities check students' understanding and allow for further discussion.

Part 2: Social Language

- Before Listening – prediction activities and vocabulary preparation prepare students for the listening. Strategy boxes provide students with practical strategies they can use immediately as they listen to conversations.
- Listening – a high-interest conversation (available in video or audio) between students on or around an urban university campus allows students to explore the chapter topic in more depth.
- After Listening – comprehension, discussion, and vocabulary activities not only check students' understanding of the conversation but also continue to prepare them for the academic listening activities in Parts 4 and 5.

Part 3: The Mechanics of Listening and Speaking

- Chapter-specific pronunciation, intonation, language function, and collocation boxes equip student to express their ideas.
- Content-driven language function boxes are followed by contextualized practice activities that prepare students for social and academic listening.

Part 4: Broadcast English

- Before Listening – prediction activities and vocabulary preparation prepare students for listening to a short passage from an authentic or simulated radio program.
- Listening – a high-interest authentic radio interview allows students to practice their listening skills and explore the chapter topic in more depth.
- After Listening – comprehension, discussion, and vocabulary activities not only check students' understanding of the interview but also continue to prepare them for the academic listening in Part 5.

Part 5: Academic Listening

- Before Listening – prediction activities and vocabulary activities prepare students for listening to an authentic academic lecture.
- Listening – an academic lecture written by university professors allows students to practice their listening and note-taking skills. One lecture in each unit is delivered via video.
- After Listening – comprehension activities allow students to use their lecture notes to answer discussion questions.
- Put It All Together – a longer speaking activity provides students with the opportunity to connect all three listening passages and give a short presentation on the chapter topic.

Teacher's Editions

The *Quest Teacher's Editions* provide instructors with activity-by-activity teaching suggestions, cultural and background notes, Internet links to more information on the unit themes, expansion black-line master activities, chapter tests, and a complete answer key.

The *Quest Teacher's Editions* also provide test-taking boxes that highlight skills found in *Quest* that are needed for success on the new TOEFL® iBT test.

Video Program

For the *Quest Listening and Speaking* books, a newly expanded video program on DVD or VHS incorporates authentic classroom lectures with social language vignettes.

Lectures

The lecture portion of each video features college and university professors delivering high-interest mini-lectures on topics as diverse as animal communication, personal finance, and Greek art. The mini-lectures run from two minutes at the *Intro* level to six minutes by Book 3. As students listen to the lectures they complete structured outlines to model accurate note taking. Well-organized post-listening activities teach students how to use and refer to their notes in order to answer questions about the lecture and to review for a test.

Social Language

The social language portion of the videos gives students the chance to hear authentic conversations on topics relevant to the chapter topic and academic life. A series of scenes shot on or around an urban college campus features nine engaging students participating in a host of curricular and extracurricular activities. The social language portion of the video is designed to help English language students join study groups, interact with professors, and make friends.

Audio Program

Each reading selection on the audio CD or audiocassette program allows students to hear new vocabulary words, listen for intonation cues, and increase their reading speed. Each reading is recorded at an appropriate rate while remaining authentic.

Test Generator

For the *Quest Reading and Writing* books, an EZ Test® CD-ROM test generator allows teachers to create customized tests in a matter of minutes. EZ Test® is a flexible and easy-to-use desktop test generator. It allows teachers to create tests from unit-specific test banks or to write their own questions.

SCOPE AND SEQUENCE

Chapter	Listening Strategies	Speaking Strategies
UNIT 1 GLOBAL BUSINESS		
Chapter 1 **Doing Business Internationally** • Social Language: Conversation about negotiation • Broadcast English: Radio program about global business ethics • Academic English: Lecture on global business	• Listening for an Anecdote • Listening for Examples • Using Graphic Organizers • Previewing: Having Questions in Mind • Listening for the Meaning of New Words and Phrases • Taking Lecture Notes • Organizing Your Notes • Listening for Differences	• Finding a Cultural Informant • Taking Turns • Discussing Survey Results • Asking for Confirmation • Confirming Understanding
Chapter 2 **Social Services Around the World** • Social Language: On the street interviews about how to solve the problem of poverty • Broadcast English: Radio program about social services in the U.S. • Academic English: Lecture on welfare systems in Sweden	• Listening for the Gist • Listening for Numerical Information • Listening for the Meaning of New Words and Phrases • Taking Notes: Abbreviations and Symbols • Listening for Causes and Effects	• Predicting • Compromising • Making Eye Contact • Asking for Permission • Giving and Refusing Permission

Mechanics of Listening and Speaking	Critical Thinking Strategies	Test-Taking Strategies
UNIT 1 GLOBAL BUSINESS		
• Asking for Confirmation • Confirming Understanding • Reduced Forms of Words: Verbs Followed by *to* • Expectations: *got to, have to, supposed to* + Verb	• Exploring Implications and Consequences • Predicting • Making Connections	• Listening for the Meaning of New Terms
• Asking for Permission • Giving and Refusing Permission • *Yes/No* Questions • Reduced Forms of Words: Questions with *-d* + *you* • Answering *Do/Would you mind if . . .?*	• Making Inferences • Taking Notes: Abbreviations and Symbols	• Listening for Numerical Information

Chapter	Listening Strategies	Speaking Strategies
UNIT 2 ART		
Chapter 3 **Art Themes and Purposes** • Social Language: Conversation about art from the 1960s and 1970s • Broadcast English: Radio program about artist George Segal • Academic English: Lecture about pop art	• Review: Using a Culture Informant • Listening for the Meaning of New Words and Phrases • Taking Notes: Images • Taking Notes: Using Key Words	• Describing Art • Trusting Your Instincts • Forming and Expressing an Opinion • Asking for and Giving Clarification
Chapter 4 **Ancient Greek Art** • Social Language: Conversation about ancient Greek pottery • Broadcast English: Radio program about ancient Greek sculpture • Academic English: Lecture on ancient Greek art	• Understanding Time Abbreviations • Listening for Time Periods • Using Phonetic Symbols • Getting the Main Idea from the Introduction • Taking Notes: Timelines	• Correcting a Misunderstanding • Interpreting Time Periods • Giving a Presentation from Notes • Requesting an Explanation
UNIT 3 PSYCHOLOGY		
Chapter 5 **States of Consciousness** • Social Language: On the street interviews about dreams • Broadcast English: Radio program about one theory on why we sleep • Academic English: Lecture on sleep and dreaming	• Understanding Scientific Terms • Listening for Topic Change Signals • Distinguishing Between *Can* and *Can't*	• Avoiding Impolite Questions • Asking Questions • Keeping the Audience in Mind • Avoiding Answering Questions

Mechanics of Listening and Speaking	Critical Thinking Strategies	Test-Taking Strategies
UNIT 2 ART		
• Asking for Clarification: General • Asking for Clarification: Specific • Giving Clarification • *Wh-* Questions • /I/ vs. /i/ • Noun Phrases for Types of Art	• Identifying Impressions or Opinions • Thinking Creatively	• Forming and Expressing an Opinion
• Requesting an Explanation • Understanding Interjections • /θ/ vs. /s/ • Time Phrases with Ordinal Numbers	• Acquiring and Applying Background Information • Predicting	• Listening for Time Periods
UNIT 3 PSYCHOLOGY		
• Avoiding Answering Questions • *Can* vs. *Can't* • Verbs Ending in *-ed* • Verb Phrases with Prepositions	• Interpreting Symbols • Separating Fact from Theory	• Listening for Topic Change Signals

Chapter	Listening Strategies	Speaking Strategies
Chapter 6 **Abnormal Psychology** • Social Language: On the street interviews about fears • Broadcast English: Radio program about paranoia • Academic English: Lecture about anxiety disorders	• Understanding the Meaning of New Words: Medical Roots • Listening to a Lecture Introduction • Taking Notes: Using a Chart	• Asking Questions after a Presentation • Asking for Information Over the Phone • Asking Someone to Hold
UNIT 4 HEALTH		
Chapter 7 **Addictive Substances** • Social Language: Discussion on secondhand smoke • Broadcast English: Radio program about smoking as a gateway drug • Academic English: Lecture about nicotine addition	• Understanding Sarcasm • Understanding Latin Terms • Taking Notes: Numbers • Listening for Comparisons	• Listing Reasons • Agreeing and Disagreeing • Expressing an Opinion
Chapter 8 **Secrets of Good Health** • Social Language: On the street interviews about health tips • Broadcast English: Radio program about obesity • Academic English: Lecture about maintaining good health	• Guessing the Meaning of Proverbs • Using Context to Distinguish Sounds	• Making Comparisons • Giving Constructive Criticism • Giving Advice

The Mechanics of Listening and Speaking	Critical Thinking Strategies	Test-Taking Strategies
• Asking for Information Over the Phone • Asking Someone to Hold • /ɛ/ *vs.* /æ/ • Asking for Help: *I'd like* + Infinitive or Noun Phrase	• Interpreting Figurative Language • Paraphrasing	• Interpreting Figurative Language
UNIT 4 HEALTH: MEDICINE AND DRUGS		
• Agreeing and Disagreeing • Degrees of Agreement/ Disagreement • Expressing an Opinion • Reduced Forms of Words: *a* and *of* • The Language of Smoking	• Evaluating the Source of Information • Brainstorming	• Listing Reasons
• Giving Health Advice • Health Advice • Degrees of Advice • /θ/ vs. /t/	• Making Comparisons • Predicting	• Making Comparisons

Welcome

Quest Second Edition **prepares students for academic success.** The series features two complementary strands—*Reading and Writing* and *Listening and Speaking*—each with four levels. The integrated Quest program provides robust scaffolding to support and accelerate each student's journey from exploring general interest topics to mastering academic content.

New second edition features

- New *Intro* level providing on-ramp to Books 1-3

- Redesigned, larger format with captivating photos

- Expanded focus on critical thinking skills

- Addition of research paper to *Reading and Writing* strand

- New unit-ending *Vocabulary Workshops* and end-of-book Academic Word List (AWL)

- Expanded video program (VHS/DVD) with new lecture and updated social language footage

- EZ Test® CD-ROM test generator for all *Reading and Writing* titles

- Test-Taking strategy boxes that highlight skills needed for success on the new TOEFL® iBT

- Teacher's Editions with activity-by-activity procedural notes, expansion activities, and tests

Captivating photos and graphics capture students' attention while introducing them to each academic topic.

U N I T 1

GLOBAL BUSINESS

Chapter 1
Doing Business Internationally

Chapter 2
International Economy

Listening Strategy

Listening for Topic Change Signals

Speakers often use signals in lectures. These are words and expressions that help you to organize your notes. Some signals let you know when the speaker is going to change the topic. Here are three types of topic-change signals:

1. Speakers sometimes move away from the topic when giving a lecture. This is called a **digression.** They often give the audience a signal when they do this.

   Examples: By the way, we will have a test next Thursday.
   That reminds me, don't forget to read Chapters 3 and 4 by Monday.

2. Speakers also signal the audience when they return to the topic.

   Examples: As I was saying, the most important feature of . . .
   Getting back to what I was saying, this feature . . .
   Moving on, the feature we want to pay attention to is . . .

3. In addition, speakers sometimes signal the audience when they are going to introduce the next subtopic of the lecture.

   Examples: Now let's take a look at the reasons for . . .
   Let's turn our attention to the reasons why . . .
   This brings us to the topic of . . .

B. LISTENING FOR TOPIC CHANGE SIGNALS Listen for signals like the ones in the box above. Write the signal in the blank and indicate the purpose of each one: moving off the topic, returning to the topic, or introducing a new subtopic.

1. Signal: _____   Purpose: _____

2. Signal: _____   Purpose: _____

C. TAKING NOTES: USING AN OUTLINE Listen to the lecture. It's in four sections. You will listen to each section twice. Fill in as much of the outline as you can. Don't worry if you can't fill in everything. (You'll listen to the whole lecture again in Activity D.) Remember to use key words and abbreviations.

150   **UNIT 3** Psychology

Listening and Speaking Strategies guide students to develop effective academic listening and note-taking skills.

Three high-interest listening selections in each chapter introduce students to the general education course content most frequently required by universities.

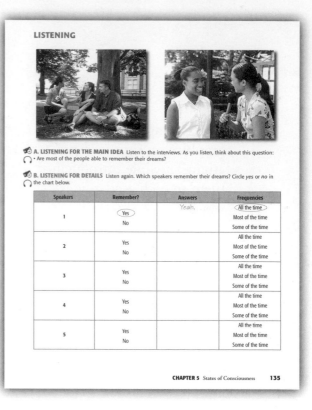

LISTENING

🎧 **A. LISTENING FOR THE MAIN IDEA** Listen to the interviews. As you listen, think about this question:
• Are most of the people able to remember their dreams?

🎧 **B. LISTENING FOR DETAILS** Listen again. Which speakers remember their dreams? Circle *yes* or *no* in the chart below.

Speakers	Remember?	Answers	Frequencies
1	Yes No	Yeah.	All the time Most of the time Some of the time
2	Yes No		All the time Most of the time Some of the time
3	Yes No		All the time Most of the time Some of the time
4	Yes No		All the time Most of the time Some of the time
5	Yes No		All the time Most of the time Some of the time

PART 5 ACADEMIC ENGLISH What Is Good Health?

BEFORE LISTENING

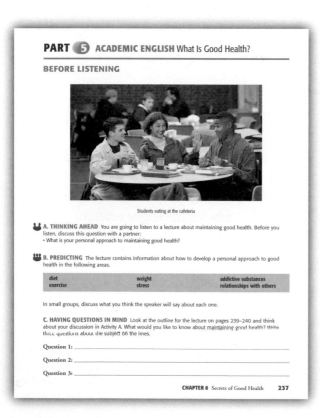

Students eating at the cafeteria

👥 **A. THINKING AHEAD** You are going to listen to a lecture about maintaining good health. Before you listen, discuss this question with a partner:
• What is your personal approach to maintaining good health?

👥 **B. PREDICTING** The lecture contains information about how to develop a personal approach to good health in the following areas.

diet exercise	weight stress	addictive substances relationships with others

In small groups, discuss what you think the speaker will say about each one.

C. HAVING QUESTIONS IN MIND Look at the outline for the lecture on pages 239–240 and think about your discussion in Activity A. What would you like to know about maintaining good health? Write three questions about the subject on the lines.

Question 1: _____

Question 2: _____

Question 3: _____

Gradual curve in each chapter from social language, to broadcast English, and then academic listening supports students as they engage in increasingly more difficult material.

• In Part 1, you read about a common dream theme, flying. In the interviews, Speaker 4 describes a dream about snakes, another common dream theme. What are some more common dream themes and symbols?

Write some common dream themes and symbols in the chart below. Then discuss possible interpretations for each. Think about psychological, cultural, and common sense interpretations. Write your ideas in the *Possible Interpretations* column.

Dream Themes/Symbols	Possible Interpretations
Flying	Desire for freedom, desire to travel
Snakes	

B. INTERPRETING DREAMS In the same small group, create a **dream scenario** (description). Use typical dream themes and symbols from your discussion in Activity A. Make your group's dream as fantastic, strange, or scary as you want. Use your imagination. Write it down or write enough details so that you can describe it later.

Then choose one group member to describe the dream to the class. As you listen to each group's dream, take notes.

Next, in your small group, use your notes to interpret each group's dream. Refer to the chart you made in Activity A for interpretation ideas.

Discussion, pair-work, and group-work activities scaffold the students' learning process as they move from general interest to academic content.

UNIT 1 VOCABULARY WORKSHOP

Review vocabulary that you learned in Chapters 1 and 2.

A. MATCHING Match the words on the left to the definitions on the right. Write the correct letters on the

_____ **1.** bargain

_____ **2.** charitable organizations

_____ **3.** CEOs

_____ **4.** lobbyist

_____ **5.** nurtured

_____ **6.** reforming

_____ **7.** self-sustainability

_____ **8.** stance

_____ **9.** subsidies

_____ **10.** whistle-blower

a. chief executive officers

b. a person who represents the interests of an organization

c. negotiate

d. a person who tells others when he or she sees employees behaving unethically

e. organizations that provide free services to help people

f. attitude

g. the ability to take care of oneself

h. helped to grow

i. changing

j. government money that helps people to work harder or produce more

B. TRUE OR FALSE? Read the statements below. Circle *T* if the sentence is true. Circle *F* if the sentence is false.

1. If you pay the asking price, you pay the first price that the seller gives you.   T   F

2. In a homogeneous culture, people from many different cultures live together.   T   F

3. If you defied your parents when you were young, you did what they wanted you to do.   T   F

4. Vocational training helps people to prepare for nonprofessional jobs.   T   F

5. People who have a strong work ethic believe in hard work.   T   F

6. If you lay a person off, you are giving him or her a job.   T   F

7. If you are fluent in Spanish, it means that you cannot speak it at all.   T   F

8. If you are a determined person, you are strong-willed.   T   F

9. If you donated something, you expected people to pay you for it.   T   F

10. In a free enterprise system, there are a lot of government controls on businesses.   T   F

Unit-ending *Vocabulary Workshops* reinforce key unit vocabulary that also appears on the High Frequency Word List.

Expanded video program for the *Listening and Speaking* titles now includes mini-lectures to build comprehension and note-taking skills, and updated social language scenes to develop conversation skills.

Audio program selections are indicated with this icon 🎧 and include recordings of all lectures, conversations, pronunciation and intonation activities, and reading selections.

Teacher's Edition provides activity-by-activity teaching suggestions, expansion activities, tests, and special TOEFL® iBT preparation notes

EZ Test® CD-ROM test generator for the *Reading and Writing* titles allows teachers to create customized tests in a matter of minutes.

UNIT 1

◯◯ GLOBAL BUSINESS

Chapter 1
Doing Business Internationally

Chapter 2
Social Services Around the World

CHAPTER 1

Doing Business Internationally

Discuss these questions:
- Look at the picture. Is the meeting formal or informal? Explain your answer.
- What clothing is inappropriate for a business meeting?
- Which rules of behavior are the same everywhere? Which are sometimes different?

Greeting

Tipping

Business entertaining

Giving gifts

A. THINKING AHEAD You are going to read some advice on business **etiquette** (manners) in New Zealand. The author wrote this advice for Americans who do business overseas.

Before you read, look at the chart on page 5. Discuss with a partner whether you think New Zealanders are likely to be the same as or different from people in your culture. Put a check (✓) next to your answers.

Example: In my culture, you do not tip. I think it's different in New Zealand. I think you tip there.

Situations	Same	Different
Tipping (e.g., a taxi driver or at a restaurant)		
Greeting businesspeople whom you don't know well		
Being on time for a business appointment		
Places where people entertain business guests (e.g., at home, in a restaurant)		
Appropriate gifts for a businessperson to bring to someone's home		
Appropriate conversation topics		

B. READING Read about business etiquette in New Zealand. As you read, think about this question:
• Why might business travelers need this kind of information?

Business Etiquette in New Zealand

General Advice

- Tipping is not common, and people often refuse to take tips.

5
- Be prepared to be formal until others have created a more relaxed atmosphere.

Greetings

- Shake hands when you meet or leave someone. Wait for women to give you their hand first.

Appointments/Punctuality

10
- Make appointments in advance and try to arrive a little early.

New Zealand and surrounding areas

Hospitality/Gift Giving

- Visitors usually invite customers to lunch at a hotel or restaurant. Otherwise, business meetings will be at the host's office.

15
- If you are invited to a New Zealander's home for a meal, you can take a modest gift of chocolates or wine, although it is not necessary.

Conversation

20
- New Zealanders like to talk about national and international politics, the weather, and sports. They appreciate visitors who understand their culture.

25
- Do not talk about racial issues.
- Do not include New Zealand as part of Australia or "AustralAsia and the South Pacific."

Source: *Do's and Taboos Around the World* (Axtell)

C. COMPREHENSION CHECK Read the statements. Circle *T* if the sentence is true or *F* if the sentence is false.

1. When you meet a New Zealander for the first time, it's a good idea to be informal.　　　　T　(F)

2. If you have an appointment in New Zealand, try to be on time.　　　　T　F

3. New Zealanders kiss when they greet each other.　　　　T　F

4. It's not a good idea to bring wine to a dinner at a New Zealander's home.　　　　T　F

5. It's O.K. to discuss politics in New Zealand.　　　　T　F

Critical Thinking Strategy

Exploring Implications and Consequences

Exploring implications and consequences is thinking about "What might happen if . . ." It can help you to expand your understanding of both new and familiar ideas. For example, when you read or hear advice on how to behave, think about what might happen if you *didn't* follow the advice.

D. EXPLORING IMPLICATIONS AND CONSEQUENCES With a partner, discuss what might happen if you did the following things while visiting New Zealand:

• gave a tip to a hotel clerk
• arrived ten minutes late to a business appointment
• had dinner at someone's house but did not bring a gift
• had dinner at someone's house and brought a gift of expensive jewelry
• said that you always thought New Zealand was a part of Australia

E. DISCUSSION In small groups, discuss these questions.

1. Why do you think that businesspeople might need advice on behavior in different countries?

2. Do you think that advice like this is useful? Do you think that it may cause more problems? Explain your answer.

3. Have you had a misunderstanding because of behavior differences in two cultures? If so, describe what happened.

4. Have you worked in a foreign country or with people from a different culture? If so, describe any problems that you had.

5. Have you done any personal business in a foreign country (for example, at a bank, a post office, or a store)? If so, describe any problems that you had.

F. RESPONSE WRITING In this book, you are going to keep a journal. In your journal, you are going to do *response writing* activities. In response writing, you write quickly about what you are thinking or feeling. Grammar and form are not very important in response writing. Your ideas and thoughts are important. You will have 10 minutes to write your responses. You can buy a special notebook for your journal, or you can write your ideas on separate pieces of paper and keep them in a binder or folder.

Choose *one* of these topics below. Write about it for 10 minutes. Don't worry about grammar and don't use a dictionary. Just write as many ideas as you can.

• Compare how a person from your culture might act in certain business situations with someone from New Zealand. If there are no differences, discuss similarities. Discuss one or more of the areas from the reading: tipping, greetings, appointments/punctuality, hospitality/gift giving, and appropriate conversation topics.

• Have you had a misunderstanding because of behavior differences in two cultures? If so, describe it.

• Have you worked with people from a different culture? What kind of conversation topics did you discuss?

PART ② SOCIAL LANGUAGE Doing Business Overseas

BEFORE LISTENING

A. THINKING AHEAD You are going to listen to Victor, Tanya, and Jennifer talk about **negotiation** (discussing something in order to come to an agreement). People negotiate in business situations, for example, when an employee wants a higher salary. People sometimes negotiate in their daily lives, for example, when they buy a house or a car.

Before you listen, ask a partner these questions.

1. What kind of negotiation have you done? Whom did you do it with? In what situations did you negotiate?

2. How do you feel about negotiating? Is it easy for you? Difficult?

3. Are you good at negotiating? If yes, what strategies do you use?

4. Have you had to negotiate something in a foreign country or in a foreign language? If yes, what difficulties did you have?

B. VOCABULARY PREPARATION Read the sentences below. The words and phrases in green are from the conversation. Match the definitions in the box with the words and phrases in green. Write the correct letters on the lines.

> a. experience a symbolic activity, usually on special occasions
> b. the first price that the seller asks for
> c. inexpensive items
> d. a market where people sell used items
> e. negotiate for
> f. speaks a language almost as well as a native speaker
> g. suggested

_____ b _____ 1. Don't pay the **asking price**. See if you can pay less.

_____ 2. Did you know that you can **bargain for** a house in the United States?

_____ 3. Jennifer **proposed** one price for the car and then the salesperson suggested another one.

_____ 4. Emma **is fluent in** Spanish, so she won't have any problems communicating in Spain.

_____ 5. Kevin likes to **go through a ritual** every time he negotiates a new contract: He puts a lucky coin in his pocket before he goes to the meeting.

_____ 6. Whenever I go on vacation, I often bring home a lot of souvenirs and **trinkets** for my friends.

_____ 7. I found a cheap lamp at a **flea market** last Saturday.

C. GUESSING THE MEANING FROM CONTEXT Read the sentences below. The phrases in green are idioms from the conversation. Guess their meanings from the context. Write your guesses on the lines. Then compare your guesses with a partner.

1. Brandon wanted to see a science fiction movie, and I wanted to see a romantic comedy. We kept **going back and forth** until we finally decided to see both.

   Guess: _negotiating_ _____

2. It's late and I'm tired. I'm going to **turn in**. See you in the morning.

   Guess: _____

3. Tanya is getting a new car. She wants to **get rid of** her old one because it uses too much gas.

   Guess: _____

4. Every time Evan and I try to make a date, we **go through** the same thing: He's not free at lunchtime, and I'm not free in the evenings.

   Guess: _____

LISTENING

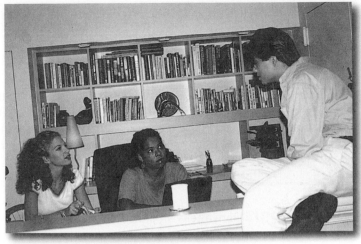

🎧 **A. LISTENING FOR THE MAIN IDEA** Listen to the conversation. As you listen, think about this question:
• What do Victor, Tanya, and Jennifer say about negotiating?

🎧 **B. LISTENING FOR EXAMPLES** Listen again. This time you are going to listen to only part of the conversation. Listen for Tanya's and Victor's examples of the difficulties of doing personal business in a foreign country. Take notes in the chart.

	What Country Did She or He Visit?	**Where Did the Problem Happen?**	**What Was the Difficulty?**
Tanya		at a bank	
Victor			

🎧 **C. LISTENING FOR DETAILS** Listen to part of the conversation again. Listen for information that answers these questions. Write your answers on the lines.

1. What *can't* you bargain for in a store in the United States?

   _____

   _____

2. What *can* you bargain for in the United States?

   _____

   _____

Listening Strategy

Listening for an Anecdote

An anecdote is a short story. It's one way to support an idea in a discussion. When you hear an anecdote, listen for how it explains, supports, or proves the speaker's point. Anecdotes often begin with phrases like *Once, I remember,* or *One time.*

Example: It's easy to miss opportunities to bargain if you don't know the local culture. **Once** I went to a flea market. Someone was selling wonderful old advertising signs. I had to have one! I paid the asking price without bargaining, but then I noticed the woman next to me. She and the seller were discussing the price. Finally, the woman and the seller agreed on a price. That woman got her sign for half the price that I paid!

 D. LISTENING FOR AN ANECDOTE Tanya tells an anecdote to show one way that people bargain in the United States. Listen to her anecdote. Then answer this question:

• Why did Tanya's dad probably get the car for the price that he wanted?

_____

_____

AFTER LISTENING

 A. TAKING A SURVEY Interview three classmates who have been to a foreign country. First, think of your answers to the questions in the chart. Add your own question to Part 4. Then ask three classmates the questions. Write their answers in the chart.

Example: **A:** What have you bargained for?
            B: Once I bargained for a car.

	Classmate 1	Classmate 2	Classmate 3
Part 1 Bargaining			
1. What have you bargained for?			
2. Were you successful? If so, what was your strategy? If not, what problems did you have?			
Part 2 Bargaining in a Foreign Country			
3. What have you bargained for in a foreign country? In which country?			

	Classmate 1	Classmate 2	Classmate 3
4. Were you successful? If so, what was your strategy? If not, what problems did you have?			
5. Have you gone to a bank in a foreign country?			
6. Was it the same as going to a bank in your own country?			
7. If it was different, please give me an example of how it was different.			
Part 3 Working in a Foreign Country			
8. Have you had a job in a foreign country?			
9. Was it the same as or different from working in your own country?			
10. If it was different, please give me an example of how it was different.			
Part 4 Your Question			
Write your own question here:			

👥 **B. DISCUSSING SURVEY RESULTS** In small groups, discuss the results of your survey. Answer these questions.

1. Do most people that you interviewed have experience with bargaining in a foreign country?

2. Do most people feel successful at bargaining?

3. What kinds of problems do people have with bargaining in their own country?

4. What kinds of problems do people have with bargaining in a foreign country?

5. What differences have people noticed in banking in different countries?

6. What differences have people noticed in working in a foreign country?

LANGUAGE FUNCTION

Asking for Confirmation

Sometimes you *think* you are right about something that you are discussing with another person. However, you want that person to *tell* you that you are right. This is asking for confirmation.

Examples: A: I had trouble negotiating for stuff at the market.
        B: Oh yeah, you're not supposed to pay the asking price, **right?**
           Oh yeah, you're not supposed to pay the asking price, **Isn't that right?**
           Oh yeah, you're not supposed to pay the asking price. **Isn't that true?**

Note: The structure of these sentences is a statement of what you think is right + a question.

A. ASKING FOR CONFIRMATION Read the confirmation responses below. Then listen to the speaker's statements. Listen a second time and choose the correct confirmation response for each statement. Write the letters of the correct responses on the lines.

_____ **1.**   **a.** Oh yeah, Americans like to make small talk, right?

_____ **2.**   **b.** Oh yeah, you're majoring in business. Isn't that right?

_____ **3.**   **c.** Oh yeah, people don't line up in some cultures. Isn't that true?

_____ **4.**   **d.** Oh yeah, you speak Spanish, right?

_____ **5.**   **e.** Oh yeah, it's impolite to discuss politics in some cultures, right?

INTONATION

⌒ Asking for Confirmation

If you really need information, your voice goes up when you ask for confirmation. In other words, it's a real question.

Example: You're not supposed to pay the asking price, **right**? ↗

If you know the answer, or if you are asking for confirmation of something that you *think* is right, your voice goes down.

Example: You're not supposed to pay the asking price, **right**? ↘

⌒ **B. ASKING FOR CONFIRMATION** Listen to the sentences. Is the speaker asking a "real" question or a confirmation question? Circle *Real* or *Confirmation*.

1. Real   Confirmation   **4.** Real   Confirmation

2. Real   Confirmation   **5.** Real   Confirmation

3. Real   Confirmation   **6.** Real   Confirmation

Now listen again. Repeat each sentence after the speaker.

C. ASKING FOR CONFIRMATION Read the sentences to a partner. Practice asking real questions and confirmation questions. If the cue is *Not sure*, make your voice go up. If the cue is *Sure*, make your voice go down. Draw an arrow above *right* to show the intonation you use.

1. Gary doesn't like it here, right? (Sure) ↘

2. You speak Spanish, right? (Sure)

3. They're working overseas, right? (Not sure)

4. Casey hasn't found a job yet, right? (Not sure)

5. Joe has been working hard, right? (Sure)

6. You're majoring in business, right? (Sure)

7. You speak Japanese, right? (Not sure)

8. Americans can bargain for cars, right? (Not sure)

9. Tanya's majoring in business, right? (Not sure)

10. Jennifer doesn't speak Spanish, right? (Sure)

LANGUAGE FUNCTION

Confirming Understanding

There are many ways to confirm understanding—in other words, to tell people that you agree with them or that what they said was correct.

Examples: **A:** I had trouble negotiating for stuff at the market.
B: Oh yeah, you're not supposed to pay the asking price, right?
A: Right.

B: Oh yeah, you're not supposed to pay the asking price. Isn't that right?
A: That's right.

B: Oh yeah, you're not supposed to pay the asking price. Isn't that true?
A: Yeah, that's true.

Notice that the answer often matches the form of the question at the end:

Questions		Answers
Right?	→	Right.
Isn't that right?	→	Yeah, that's right.
Isn't that true?	→	Yeah, that's true.

Note: "Uh-huh" is another way to confirm understanding. It's a very informal way to say "Yes."

🎧 **D. CONFIRMING UNDERSTANDING** Listen to the speaker ask you for confirmation. Check (✓) the best answer. Tell the truth.

Example: **A:** You like bargaining. Isn't that right?
 ✓   Right. (Because you *do* like it.)
 _____ No, I don't.

1. _____ Right.
 _____ No, I don't.

2. _____ Right.
 _____ No, I haven't.

3. _____ Yeah, that's true.
 _____ No, I'm not.

4. _____ Uh-huh.
 _____ No, I don't.

5. _____ Yeah, that's right.
 _____ No, I don't.

6. _____ Right.
 _____ No, I'm not.

PRONUNCIATION

🎧 Reduced Forms of Words: Verbs Followed by *to*

Listening is sometimes difficult because when people speak quickly, two or three words are often pushed together. This can make them sound like one word.

Examples:

Long Form		Reduced Form
You're not **supposed to** pay the asking price.	→	You're not **supposta** pay the asking price.
They were probably **going to** sell it anyway.	→	They were probably **gonna** sell it anyway.
Do you **want to** work overseas?	→	Do you **wanna** work overseas?
You **have to** know the rules of the culture.	→	You **hafta** know the rules of the culture.

Note: *Supposta, gonna,* and *hafta* are always followed by verbs.

🎧 **E. REDUCED FORMS OF WORDS** People say reduced forms, but write the long forms. Listen to the conversation and write the long forms of the reduced forms that you hear.

A: Do you _____ want to _____ try bargaining in the market?

   1

B: You mean you're not _____ pay the asking price?

   2

A: No way! You _____ know the rules of the culture. C'mon . . . let's try it!

   3

B: Uh, I'm not sure.

A: Are you afraid? Well, I'm not! I'm _____ give it a try.

   4

WORDS IN PHRASES

Expectations: *got to, have to, supposed to* + Verb

When you talk about behavior in different cultures and situations, you often talk about what people expect you to do. *Got to* + verb, *have to* + verb, and *supposed to* + verb are all ways to express expectations.

Examples: You've **got to learn** the language.
              You **have to know** the rules of the culture.
              You're not **supposed to pay** the asking price.

👥 **F. WORDS IN PHRASES** In small groups, explain what people in your culture expect a person to do in the following situations. Use the phrases in the box above.

• at the bank

• when you bargain for something

• at a market

• when you buy a car

PUT IT TOGETHER

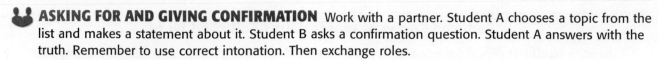 **ASKING FOR AND GIVING CONFIRMATION** Work with a partner. Student A chooses a topic from the list and makes a statement about it. Student B asks a confirmation question. Student A answers with the truth. Remember to use correct intonation. Then exchange roles.

Topics

• a favorite restaurant
• a movie you saw recently
• a favorite place to visit
• a food for a holiday or celebration
• something interesting you recently learned about how to behave in a foreign country or culture
• a bargaining experience

Example: **A:** My favorite restaurant is Tandoori House.
B: You really like Indian food, right?
A: Yes, I do.

A: I saw a Clint Eastwood movie last night.
B: Oh, you like Eastwood, isn't that right?
A: No, not really.

PART ④ BROADCAST ENGLISH Global Business Ethics

BEFORE LISTENING

A. THINKING AHEAD You are going to hear a radio program about global business ethics. **Ethics** are rules of behavior that people agree are good or right. Before you listen, find out more about your own business ethics. Read the situations below and circle *Agree* if you agree or *Disagree* if you disagree.

1. You want a government agency to hire your company to do a big project. It's O.K. for you to bribe someone who works for the agency (in other words, give him or her money or a gift) in order to get the project.

   Agree   **Disagree**

2. You hire people for a big corporation. An important job is available in the company. Your brother needs work, but he isn't the most qualified candidate for the job. It's O.K. to hire him anyway because he is your brother.

   Agree   **Disagree**

3. Your company is competing with another company for an important project. (In other words, both companies are trying to get it at the same time.) It's O.K. to send someone into the other company to learn information that will help you win the job instead of the other company.

   Agree   **Disagree**

4. You are a manager. Your company has sent you to work in an office in another country. You work with a local manager who has the same title and job as you. The local manager gets more money than you do. This is fair.

   Agree   **Disagree**

5. It's O.K. to tell a lie on a job application in order to get a job that you really want.

   Agree   **Disagree**

Now in small groups, share your answers. Explain why you agree or disagree with each situation.

Critical Thinking Strategy

Predicting

When you make a prediction about what you are going to hear *before* you hear it, it helps you to focus better while you listen. This helps you to understand more. When you know the topic before you listen, try to predict what you think the speakers might say.

Example: **You read:** The topic of a radio program is etiquette in New Zealand.
            You predict: The program will probably discuss the correct way to behave in New Zealand.
            When I listen to the program, I'll probably hear information about things to do and things *not* to do.

B. PREDICTING The radio program is about an international business ethics conference. Before you listen, make a prediction about what the speakers might say. Discuss these questions with a partner:

• Do you think that the program will say that different countries have different business ethics?
• What differences will they discuss?

C. VOCABULARY PREPARATION Read the sentences below. The words and phrases in green are from the radio program. Match the definitions in the box with the words and phrases in green. Write the correct letters on the lines.

a. chief executive officers
b. developing
c. get; earn
d. bravery to do the ethically correct thing
e. make easier; help to happen
f. narrow-minded; close-minded
g. people who represent the interests of a company or an industry
h. someone who has private information about a company
i. stop employing
j. the same everywhere in the world

_____ 1. How can companies help their employees have the moral courage to do the right thing in business?

_____ 2. Many large companies use lobbyists to influence the government. They try to do this to improve business.

_____ 3. A foreign businessperson tried to bribe Sue because she's an insider at Abex. Since Sue works for the company, he thought that Sue might have some information that would help him get a project with her company.

_____ 4. Some Xenrovian businesspeople have a very parochial idea of what is right and what is wrong, but doing business globally is making them more open-minded.

_____ 5. CEOs often earn very high salaries because they have much more responsibility than other employees do.

_____ 6. The Xenrovian businessman paid a government official to help facilitate a large construction project; however, in Xenrovia, bribing someone to help you get a project is unethical.

_____ 7. Professor Jackson teaches global business ethics. Part of his job is cultivating cross-cultural understanding among his students.

_____ 8. Is it possible to have universal business ethics, or do cultural beliefs and values vary too much?

_____ 9. Company presidents often rake in a lot more money than lower-level workers.

_____ 10. Abex is going to lay off some workers because there isn't enough work for them.

Finding a Cultural Informant

Some expressions that you hear in North American English refer to cultural things such as food, sports, and religion. For example, "The ball's in your court" refers to tennis, but it means "It's your turn to take action." People in the United States and Canada use many of these expressions in business discussions.

These expressions are difficult to understand unless you have lived in the country for a long time. Therefore, it's a good idea to find a cultural informant–a person (for example, a teacher or someone else in your school, or a neighbor) who knows the culture well. Ask your cultural informant to explain expressions that you can't figure out.

D. FINDING A CULTURAL INFORMANT The radio program is about ethics. Therefore, some expressions refer to religion and **morals** (rules of behavior). These might be difficult to understand. Read the sentences below. The expressions in green are from the radio program. In small groups, discuss what the expressions may mean. Write definitions on the lines. If possible, talk to a cultural informant to see if you were correct.

1. We wouldn't have misunderstandings in international business if everyone followed **the Golden Rule**: Do unto others as you would have them do unto you.

   _____

2. Some of the talks at the business ethics conference sounded like **Sunday sermons**, like lessons you might hear in church.

   _____

3. One of the speakers was a **Jesuit priest** who taught business courses at a Catholic university.

   _____

LISTENING

A. LISTENING FOR THE MAIN IDEA Listen to the radio program. As you listen, think about this question:
• Do different countries have different business ethics?

B. LISTENING FOR SUPPORTING IDEAS: SECTION 1 Listen to part of Section 1 of the radio program. As you listen, think about the question below. Write your answer on the line.
• What is one kind of cultural difference in business ethics?

_____

Listening Strategy

Listening for Examples

Speakers sometimes support their ideas by giving examples that explain their ideas or give more information about them. Examples are cases or situations that illustrate an idea. Sometimes (but not always), a speaker will introduce an example with an expression. Some of these expressions include the following:

for example . . .	an example (of this) is . . .	such as . . .
for instance . . .	take (for example) . . .	one is . . .

Example: Many of the speakers were businesspeople with international experience. **For example,** Marta Richards has worked as a manager in both Colombia and Korea.

For example and *for instance* can also be used after the example.

Example: Marta Richards has worked as a manager in both Colombia and Korea, **for example.**

C. LISTENING FOR EXAMPLES: SECTION 1   Listen to part of Section 1 again. Listen for an example of bribery. Write the example on the line. Then answer the question.

1. Example of bribery: _____

2. Is bribery the same in all countries? Give an example that supports your answer.

_____

_____

_____

D. LISTENING FOR SUPPORTING IDEAS: SECTION 2   Listen to Section 2. As you listen, think about this question:

• What is another kind of cultural difference in business ethics?

_____

E. LISTENING FOR EXAMPLES: SECTION 2   Listen to Section 2 again. Listen for an example that explains another important concept. Write the example on the line. Then answer the question.

1. Example about fairness: _____

2. Is fairness the same in all countries? Give an example that supports your answer.

_____

_____

_____

F. LISTENING FOR THE MAIN IDEA: SECTION 3 Listen to Section 3. As you listen, think about this question:

• Why is it becoming more important to identify common values in business?

Listening Strategy

Using Graphic Organizers

Graphic organizers can help you **visualize** (see in your mind) the main ideas and the details—supporting ideas and examples. They can also help you visualize connections among ideas. An example of one type of graphic organizer—a tree diagram—is shown below.

G. USING GRAPHIC ORGANIZERS Listen to the whole radio program. As you listen, complete the tree diagram to show the main idea, the supporting ideas, and examples.

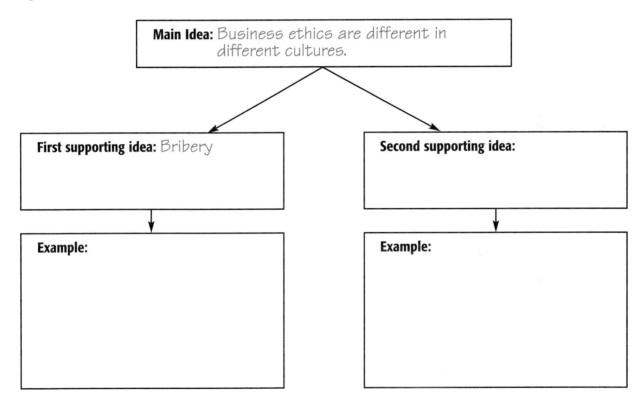

Main Idea: Business ethics are different in different cultures.

First supporting idea: Bribery

Example:

Second supporting idea:

Example:

AFTER LISTENING

👥 **DISCUSSION** In small groups, discuss these questions. Then report one of your group's answers to the class.

1. What was the purpose of the Code of Ethics conference?

2. Is bribery the same in all countries? Give an example that supports your answer.

3. Is fairness the same in all countries? Give an example that supports your answer.

4. Have you ever had an experience with bribery? If so, tell your group members about it.

5. Give an example from your personal experience of an act that was unfair.

PART ⑤ ACADEMIC ENGLISH
Ethics and Doing Business Internationally

BEFORE LISTENING

👥 **A. THINKING AHEAD** You are going to listen to a lecture about doing global business. In small groups, discuss these questions.

1. If someone said "no" right away when you were negotiating with him or her, would that seem polite or impolite to you?

2. How far apart do people stand in your culture when they discuss business? Stand up and demonstrate this to your group members.

3. How important are business cards in your culture? What do people do with them when they receive them? Take some small rectangular pieces of paper and pretend that they are business cards. Observe each other as you exchange them in a normal way for your culture. Are there any differences?

Listening Strategy ▸▸▸▸

Previewing: Having Questions in Mind

Before you listen to a lecture, it's a good idea to ask yourself questions about it. Asking questions before listening helps you to focus on the lecture because you are listening to see if the professor will answer your questions.

Example: **You read:** The lecture is "Doing Business in New Zealand."
You ask yourself: What do I already know about New Zealand?
How is New Zealand different from my culture?
Are business ethics different in New Zealand?

B. HAVING QUESTIONS IN MIND Look at the outline for the lecture on pages 26–27 and think about your discussion in Activity A (page 22). What *don't* you know about doing business globally and the ethics of international business? Write three questions about the subject on the lines. In small groups, share your questions.

Question 1: _____

Question 2: _____

Question 3: _____

C. GUESSING THE MEANING FROM CONTEXT Read the sentences below. The words in green are from the lecture. Guess their meanings from the context. Write your guesses on the lines.

1. Doing business in a **homogeneous** culture is less complicated for people who live in that culture. Doing business within the United States, however, is more difficult because people from so many different cultures work together.

   Guess: _____

2. The two companies had **prolonged** negotiations; they started in January and didn't end until June.

   Guess: _____

3. I was **suspicious** because he wouldn't look me in the eye while we were talking. I didn't think that he was telling me the truth.

   Guess: _____

4. You will be charged with **theft**; the police will officially blame you for taking documents from the company.

   Guess: _____

5. You can **deduct** business expenses from your income so your tax bill will be lower.

   Guess: _____

6. Some employees cannot **cope** with cultural differences. In fact, they have such a difficult time with them that they need to take training courses.

   Guess: _____

7. Tim was the company's **whistle-blower**—he told his manager every time he saw an employee behave unethically.

   Guess: _____

Now compare your answers with a partner's answers.

LISTENING

Test-Taking Strategy

Listening for the Meaning of Terms

Standardized tests often ask you to answer questions on the meaning of new terms (words and phrases). For example, you may hear a short lecture and then be asked to define terms from the lecture. Speakers have different ways of defining the terms that they use. One way that speakers present a definition is after the word *is*.

Example: A **code of conduct** is a set of rules that the company establishes for all its employees.

Speakers sometimes also insert a definition after the new term. These kinds of definitions are easy to see when you read because they use punctuation. It's more difficult when you are listening, but if you listen carefully, you sometimes hear pauses where the punctuation would be.

Example: A **whistle-blower**—a person who reports unethical behavior—has to be very careful about his or her own behavior.

A. LISTENING FOR THE MEANING OF NEW WORDS AND PHRASES Listen to these words and phrases in sentences from the lecture. You'll hear the sentences twice. Write the definitions that you hear on the lines.

1. **culture:** _____

2. **personal distance:** _____

Listening Strategy

Taking Lecture Notes

Questions on most course exams are based on material from both the textbook and in-class lectures. Therefore, it's important to take good notes when you listen to a lecture. You'll practice lecture note taking in every chapter of this book. Here are a few suggestions for taking good notes:

• Don't "just listen." Taking notes makes you an active listener, which helps you to remember information later.
• Don't try to write everything that you hear. Note taking is not dictation.
• Don't write complete sentences. Instead write key (important) words and abbreviations.

Example: **The professor says:** "In Japan, exchanging business cards is an important ritual."
You write: Japan: exchanging bus. cards important

Listening Strategy

Organizing Your Notes

It's a good idea to take notes in an organized way. This helps you to group related information. There are many ways to organize lecture notes, depending on the subject of the lecture. One of the most common ways is a formal outline. A formal outline distinguishes general ideas from specific ideas. In a formal outline, you write general ideas to the left, and indent specific ideas.

Example:
Types of Businesses in South Bay Island
I. Manufacturing
   A. Clothing
      1. Women's
         a. Bodega Fashions
         b. Sausalito Sweaters
      2. Children's
         a. BabyBoots, Inc.
         b. Tot Togs
   B. Furniture
      1. Natural Woods, Inc.
      2. Chairs R Us
II. Media
   A. Video Production
      1. Garnet Media, Inc.
      2. AllSports Videos
   B. Publishing
      1. Newspapers
         a. *South Bay Island Times*
         b. *South Bay Advertiser*
      2. Magazines
         a. *What's New?*
         b. *Marine Quarterly*

 Look at the outline above. How many *kinds* of numbers are there? How many *kinds* of letters are there? What are the two most general groups of ideas? What kind of number indicates the most general ideas? What kind of letter indicates the most specific ideas?

Ethics and Doing Business Internationally

Section 1

I. Introduction

    A definition of culture: <u>a set of beliefs and values that the members of a particular society commonly share</u>

II. One Area of Difference: Saying "No"

    A. Japanese example: _____

    _____

    _____

    B. American example: _____

    _____

    _____

Section 2

III. Another Area of Difference: Personal Distance

    A. Definition: _____

    _____

    _____

    B. Japanese and Latin American example: _____

    _____

    _____

    C. American example: _____

    _____

    _____

Doing business in Latin America

Section 3

The McGraw-Hill Companies

Mc Graw Hill Education

Hajime Shishido
Sales Manager
ELT/Higher Ed.

McGraw-Hill Education
1-12-3 Kandasuda-cho
Chiyoda-ku, Tokyo 101-0041
Tel(03)5298-7221
Fax(03)5298-7224
hajime.shishido@mcgraw-hill.co.jp

The McGraw-Hill Companies

Mc Graw Hill Education

宋戸 一
マネージャー
ELT/Higher Ed.

マグロウヒル･エデュケーション
〒101-0041
東京都千代田区神田須田町1-12-3
アルカディアビル　9階
電話 (03) 5298-7221
FAX (03) 5298-7224
hajime.shishido@mcgraw-hill.co.jp

A business card with English on one side and Japanese on the other side

IV. Another Area of Difference: Business Cards

   A. Japanese example: _____

      _____

   B. American example: _____

      _____

V. Differences in Ethical Behavior: Bribery

   A. In the United States, bribery is _____

   B. Examples in Europe:

      1. Spain: _____

      2. Germany: _____

      3. Russia: _____

Section 4

VI. How Companies Handle Ethical Issues

   A. Have a "code of ethics." This is (definition) _____

      _____

   B. Have "whistle-blower" laws. They are _____

      _____

      _____

   C. Train employees in: _____

      _____

   D. Think _____ , act _____

Source: Adapted from a lecture by Jeff Strieter, Ph.D.

Listening Strategy

Listening for Differences

Speakers use certain expressions to tell you that a different example is coming. These expressions introduce a contrast between two ideas or examples. To do this, speakers often use the phrases *however* and *on the other hand*.

Example: The Japanese take business cards very seriously and spend a lot of time examining them. However, Americans just put them into their pockets as soon as they receive them.

C. LISTENING FOR DIFFERENCES Listen to the lecture again. Fill in any missing information. This time, pay particular attention to the differences in the examples from different countries. Focus on the examples of bribery in Europe. Make sure that you complete Part VB with examples.

AFTER LISTENING

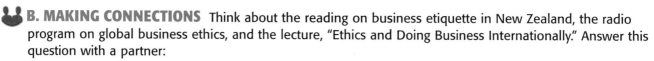

A. USING YOUR NOTES Use your notes to discuss these questions with a partner.

1. What are some cultural differences in doing business internationally?

2. Can you think of additional differences in doing business internationally?

3. How does the idea of bribery differ from one culture to another?

4. How do some companies in the United States help employees to cope with cultural difference in doing business? Do you think these actions really work? Do you have any other (or better) ideas?

Critical Thinking Strategy

Making Connections

Connecting the topic of a lecture to something that you already know increases your understanding of the topic. You can connect topics to:

• something that you read, discussed, or did recently
• a class that you took
• a program that you saw on TV or heard on the radio

Example: In the lecture, you learned about bribery in Europe. In the radio program from Part 4, you learned about bribery in Indonesia. You can connect the two by comparing the ethics of bribery in Europe and Indonesia.

B. MAKING CONNECTIONS Think about the reading on business etiquette in New Zealand, the radio program on global business ethics, and the lecture, "Ethics and Doing Business Internationally." Answer this question with a partner:

• Do you want to work overseas (or with people from different cultures)? Why or why not?

PUT IT ALL TOGETHER

GIVING A PRESENTATION You are going to collaborate (work together) in a small group to give a presentation. The presentation is on "How Our Company Copes with Cultural Differences in Business Ethics."

Step 1

Get into groups of three or four. Try to have both men and women and/or people from different cultures in your group, if possible. Your group has a business. You have employees from different countries and cultures, and you send employees to other countries to do business. First, decide the following and take notes on your decisions:

• the type of business you do
• the name of your business
• the country your business is located in
• the countries you do business with
• the number of employees you have and where they come from

Speaking Strategy

Taking Turns

When you collaborate in a group, it's important to take turns talking. If you like to talk, make sure to give quieter group members a chance to speak. You can help them by asking them for their opinions. If you don't like to talk, force yourself to make at least one comment. If you are shy, sometimes it helps to write down your ideas first and then say them.

Example:
A: I want to call our business *Fashion Explosion*!
B: Good idea. What do you think, Carla?
C: Well, I . . .
A: Or maybe *Fashion on Fire* . . . oh, I'm sorry. It's not my turn.
C: Thank you. What about *Fashion with Flair*?

Step 2

Decide what you will do about cultural differences. Decide which of the policies below your company will have. Also, decide how you will put them into action. Again, take notes on your ideas.

- A code of ethics. If you have this, what is your code? Write a list of at least five rules for employees. Identify which employees must follow it. (All or just the lower-level employees?)
- A way for employees to report unethical behavior, such as a toll-free telephone number. If you choose this, explain what will happen when an employee reports on someone.
- Cultural training classes. If you decide to give classes, describe them: What will you teach? Who will take the classes?
- Think of your own ways to solve problems.

Step 3

To help you make these decisions, go to company websites. Find information on their codes of ethics and what they do (if anything) about cultural training. Also, look for information on whistle-blower laws in different countries.

When you go to company websites, look for links that say "About Us" or "Company Information." If there is a search function on the company website, try the following key words:

ethics	training
business ethics	cultural training
code of ethics	cross-cultural training
core values	

Step 4

Now present your company to the rest of the class. Describe your company and explain how you plan to help your employees cope with cultural differences. Use your notes.

CHAPTER 2

Social Services
Around the World

Discuss these questions:
- What kind of place is in the photo?
- Who do you think paid for the food that the people are serving?
- Who should be responsible for taking care of poor people?

PART ① INTRODUCTION Education and Poverty

A. THINKING AHEAD You are going to read a story about how education changed the life of a young person in a **developing nation**, a country where a large part of the population lives in poverty. Before you read, share your ideas on the relationship between **poverty**—not having enough money and possessions—and education. Discuss these questions in small groups.

1. In your opinion, is there a connection between education and poverty? Explain your answer.

2. Do you think it's harder for girls to get an education in some parts of the world? Explain your answer.

3. Is it possible to educate all children, even those who live in very poor countries? Why or why not? Should developing nations spend money on educating all children? Why or why not?

4. Who should pay for educating children in developing countries?

B. READING Read about the role of education in the life of Lalita, a girl who lives in a developing nation. As you read, think about this question:
• How has Lalita's life changed?

Education and Poverty

According to UNICEF (The United Nations Children's Fund), one of the keys to reducing poverty in developing nations is improving educational opportunities for children, especially girls. It is often difficult for girls to receive an education in poor countries. Girls often do not attend school or
5 have to drop out (quit) because they must work or take care of their families. A great deal of research shows an important connection between increasing educational opportunities and improving the economies of poor countries.
10 Educating more children, especially girls, can keep children healthier. As a result, girls can grow into women with good jobs, and this strengthens the economy in the long term.

Here is the story of how one girl's life has
15 changed through education:

The Education of Lalita

The Sitamarhi District of India's poorest state of Bihar seems like the most unlikely place to encounter "girl power." However, one determined girl—Lalita Kumari—has overcome
20 many difficulties to become an educated young woman.

Bihar

In Sitamarhi District, where Lalita lives, almost two-thirds of the population is living in poverty. Female **literacy** (the ability to read) and girls'
25 education have never been the main concern in the district. About 26 percent of female residents are literate. This is only about half of the percentage for males in the district and far below the state and national level.

30 Like many other parents in the village, Lalita's parents wanted her to get married at the age of 10, and they didn't expect her to learn to read. However, Lalita didn't want to get married. She was excited about learning, and she secretly
35 attended a local day school for girls from poor communities. She finally learned to read at the age of 12.

Then, in 1997, the Education for Women's Equality (EWE) program started a **residential**
40 **school** (a school where the children live while they study) to provide basic education to girls. Lalita defied her parents by attending the school's **innovative** (using new ideas) eight-month course, along with 24 other illiterate to semi-literate girls.

A girl in Bihar

45 "In my village, I was doing nothing but cutting grass, getting firewood, and cleaning and cooking. In between, I used to attend the local day school, but this was without my parents' knowledge," says Lalita. At the EWE's residential school, Lalita and the other girls learned to read and write, and received life skills training. They also studied sports (including karate), health care, and public
50 speaking.

After attending the EWE residential school, Lalita returned home with the skills that helped her to set up a sewing shop. Later, Lalita asked the EWE for further education, and the school sponsored her in acquiring teaching skills in karate. Now Lalita teaches karate to girls in four EWE schools in the district.

55 The EWE program has become very popular. Many girls are asking to attend. Because of this, there is now a need for more schools and additional teachers.

Today, Lalita is an independent young woman who supports herself and her family. "I want to keep studying and become an accomplished teacher. I want to teach girls about the world, and I dream of a school in every village!"

Source: "Transformation through Education: The Story of Lalita" (UNICEF)

C. COMPREHENSION CHECK Discuss these questions about "Education and Poverty" with a partner.

1. Look back at the reading (pages 32–33). Find words to match these definitions. Write the correct words on the lines.

   firm; strong-minded (Lines 15–20)   _____

   disobeyed (Lines 40–45)   _____

   paid for (Lines 50–55)   _____

   getting (Lines 50–55)   _____

2. What two job skills does Lalita have now?

3. Explain in your own words the connection between educating girls and improving the economies of poor countries.

Critical Thinking Strategy

Making Inferences

Sometimes writers and speakers don't state something directly. You have to **infer** (guess or figure out) the meaning. One way to make an inference is to ask "Why."

Example: **You read:** In some cultures, the literacy rate for girls is much lower than the literacy rate for boys.
             You ask: Why is the rate for girls lower?
             You infer: In some cultures, teaching boys to read is more important than teaching girls.

D. MAKING INFERENCES With a partner, answer this question by making an inference about Lalita:
• Why do you think Lalita had to attend her first school secretly and then defy her parents to attend the residential school?

E. DISCUSSION In small groups, discuss these questions.

1. What are some other countries where girls' lives might improve if they went to school?

2. What are some of the challenges that a girl like Lalita may face?

3. How do you think Lalita feels about herself now?

F. RESPONSE WRITING Choose *one* of these topics. Write about it for 10 minutes. Don't worry about grammar and don't use a dictionary. Just put as many ideas as you can on paper.
• What is the connection between education and poverty?
• Should every child receive an education? Why? To what age?
• Whose responsibility is it to make sure that all children around the world receive an education?

PART ② SOCIAL LANGUAGE Help for the Poor

BEFORE LISTENING

👥 **A. THINKING AHEAD** You are going to listen to Evan interview people on the street. He's going to ask them for opinions on how to solve the problem of poverty. In small groups, discuss these questions.

1. What is the best way to help the poor?

2. Who should be responsible for helping the poor? The government? Religious groups? Private organizations? Individual people?

Share your groups' answers with the class. Did anyone have the same ideas?

Speaking Strategy

Predicting

When you make a guess about something that you haven't seen or heard yet, you are making a prediction. To show that you are not completely sure about an idea, you can introduce it with a predicting expression such as *I predict (that), I think (that),* or *I imagine (that).*

Examples: I think that most people will say that the government should improve education.
I imagine most people will say that the government should improve education.

Note: *That* is optional. You don't have to use it, but it makes the statement more formal.

👥 **B. PREDICTING** You are going to listen to seven people give their opinions on what the government should do to help the poor. Make predictions with a partner. What do you think that most people will say? Use predicting expressions from the box above.

C. VOCABULARY PREPARATION

Read the sentences below. The words and phrases in green are from the interviews. Match the definitions in the box with the words and phrases in green. Write the correct letters on the lines.

a. help make people strong, independent, and able to care for themselves
b. local government, usually city government
c. money someone gives without expecting to get it back
d. money that governments give to help the poor
e. provide; offer
f. stop receiving
g. without help

_____ 1. The government gave poor people jobs to **get** them **back on their feet**. Now, they can take care of themselves.

_____ 2. Some people would rather take **a do-it-yourself** approach to improving their lives instead of letting the government help them.

_____ 3. Education can help people learn how to take care of themselves so they don't need government **welfare**.

_____ 4. In some countries, the national government helps poor citizens. In others, there are programs for the poor at the **local level**.

_____ 5. Jack said that he didn't want a **handout**; instead he wanted a job that paid him enough money to feed his family.

_____ 6. Government programs have to **make provisions for** childcare for working mothers because childcare is very expensive.

_____ 7. For a short while, Jane was in a government program for the poor, but she was very happy to **get off** it when she got a job.

LISTENING

A. LISTENING FOR THE MAIN IDEA Listen to the interviews. Listen for the answer to the question below. Circle the letter of the correct answer.

• What solution do most people have to the problem?
   a. The government should help poor people help themselves.
   b. The poor should help themselves without government help.

B. LISTENING FOR DETAILS Listen again. Which speakers think that the government should create programs (for example, education and job training) to help the poor? Which speakers think that the government is not the solution? Which speakers have a different answer? Check (✓) the correct boxes.

Speakers	The Government Should Help	The Government Is Not the Solution	Different Solution
1	✓		
2			
3			
4			
5			
6			
7			

C. LISTENING FOR SPECIFIC IDEAS Listen to some of the speakers again. Listen for the answers to these questions. Write your answers on the lines.

1. **Speaker 2:** What does she think is wrong with giving people handouts?

_____

_____

2. **Speaker 4:** What does he say we need instead of government programs?

_____

_____

3. **Speaker 6:** Where does she think we need to improve schools?

_____

_____

4. **Speaker 7:** What concern does this woman have about working mothers?

_____

_____

AFTER LISTENING

A. CONDUCTING AN INTERVIEW Interview three classmates. Ask them for their opinions on how to solve the problem of poverty. Write their answers in the chart.

Questions	Classmate 1	Classmate 2	Classmate 3
1. What is the best way to help the poor?			
2. Why do you think this is the best way?			
3. If possible, give an example of an organization or government program that helps the poor in this way.			

B. DISCUSSING THE INTERVIEW RESULTS Form small groups. Try not to be in a group with someone that you interviewed. Discuss your interview results by answering these questions.

1. Did students suggest any one solution more often than another?

2. Do most students think that the government should help the poor?

3. What other solutions did students have?

4. What examples of successful organizations or government programs did students give?

PART ③ THE MECHANICS OF LISTENING AND SPEAKING

LANGUAGE FUNCTIONS

Asking for Permission

In English, there are different degrees of politeness. For example, when you ask a stranger or a person of authority for permission to do something, you usually use very polite, formal language.

Example: **Excuse me, may** I ask you a question?

You can use slightly less formal language if the situation is less formal, and/or the strangers are your **peers** (people just like you). Less formal situations might include being in class or at a party.

Examples: **Can** I ask you a question?
Could I borrow your pen?

Giving and Refusing Permission

When people ask you for permission, you can either give permission (say that they can do something) or refuse permission (say that they can't do something). Your answer can be formal or informal. It depends on the situation. Below are formal and informal ways of giving and refusing permission.

Formal examples: May I ask you a question?

Yes	No
Certainly.	No, I'm sorry. I'm late.
Of course.	I'm sorry. I'd rather you didn't.
	No, I don't have the time.

Less formal examples: Can I ask you a question?

Yes	No
Sure.	No.
Go right ahead.	Not now.
Shoot.	No way!

Note: Most North Americans will add an excuse in a formal situation. Also, most North Americans will use less formal language when giving permission, and more formal language when refusing permission.

A. GIVING AND REFUSING PERMISSION Work with a partner. Student A requests permission using the following questions. Student B reads each cue in parentheses and gives Student A an appropriate answer. Then exchange roles.

Examples: **A:** Can I ask you a question?
Cue: (Yes)
B: Sure.

A: Can I ask you a question?
Cue: (No)
B: No, I'm sorry. I have to meet my friend.

1. **Question:** Could I sit here?
   Cue: (Yes)

2. **Question:** Can I ask you a question?
   Cue: (No)

3. **Question:** Can I sit here?
   Cue: (No)

4. **Question:** May I borrow your pen?
   Cue: (Yes)

5. **Question:** Could I ask you a question?
   Cue: (No)

INTONATION

🎧 *Yes/No* **Questions**

When you ask a question that has *yes* or *no* as an answer, your voice goes up at the end. This is rising intonation.

Examples: Can I ask you a question?   May I open the window?

When you make a statement, your voice goes down at the end. This is falling intonation.

Examples: Go right ahead.   Sure.

B. *Yes/No* **QUESTIONS** Work with a partner. Student A reads the following statements and questions to Student B. Student B draws an arrow to show the intonation that he or she hears. Student A checks Student B's answers. Then exchange roles.

Remember: Your voice goes up for *yes/no* questions and down for statements.

Example: **A:** Can I ask you a question?

B draws: Can I ask you a question?

A: That's right. My voice went up.

1. Go right ahead.

2. I'm allergic to smoke.

3. May I sit here?

4. Can I borrow your pen?

5. Can I sit here?

6. Have a seat.

7. Please don't.

PRONUNCIATION

🎧 Reduced Forms of Words: Questions with *-d + you*

When people speak naturally, some words (and combinations of sounds) become *reduced*, or shortened. Here are some examples of reduced forms in questions with *you*.

Examples:

Long Form		Reduced Form
Would you mind if I sat here?	→	**Wouldja** mind if I sat here?
Could you help me?	→	**Couldja** help me?
Did you know her very well?	→	**Didja** know her very well?

Note: People usually *say* the reduced form but *write* the long form. (The reduced form is not correct in formal writing.)

🎧 **C. REDUCED FORMS OF WORDS** Listen to the sentences and write the long forms of the reduced forms that you hear.

1. _____ _____ help me with this problem?

2. _____ read the last chapter?

3. _____ mind if I asked you a question?

4. _____ hear what I just said?

5. _____ put out that cigarette, please?

WORDS IN PHRASES

Answering *Do/Would you mind if . . .?*

People often use *Do/Would you mind if . . . ?* when they want permission to ask you a question.

Examples: **Do you mind if** I ask you a question?
Would you mind if I asked you a question?

In the examples above, what is the form of *ask* after *do you mind if*? What is the form of *ask* after *would you mind if*?

These expressions mean *Is it a problem?* You can answer these questions honestly. If it's O.K. for the person to ask you a question, you answer, "No, not at all." This means, "No, I don't mind. You can ask the question." If you *do* mind, you might answer, "Sorry, I don't have time."

Examples: **A: Do you mind if** I open the door?
B: No, I don't mind.
No, go right ahead.
Yes, I do. I'm a little cold.
Please don't. The wind will blow my papers around.

D. WORDS IN PHRASES Work with a partner. Student A asks permission with *Do/Would you mind if.* Student B reads the cue and answers. Student B adds an excuse if the answer is "Yes" (that is, if you *do* mind). Then exchange roles.

Examples: **A:** Do you mind if I use your phone?
Cue: (No)
B: No, go right ahead. (Because you *don't* mind.)

A: Do you mind if I use your phone?
Cue: (Yes)
B: Yes, I do. I'm waiting for a call. (Because you *do* mind.)

1. **Question:** Would you mind if I sit here?
   Cue: (Yes)

2. **Question:** Do you mind if I borrow your pen?
   Cue: (No)

3. **Question:** Do you mind if I smoke?
   Cue: (No)

4. **Question:** Would you mind if I asked you a question?
   Cue: (Yes)

5. **Question:** Would you mind if I smoked?
   Cue: (Yes)

6. **Question:** Do you mind if I copy your notes?
   Cue: (No)

7. **Question:** Would you mind if I called you tonight?
   Cue: (Yes)

PUT IT TOGETHER

 **MAKING AND RESPONDING TO REQUESTS** Work with a partner. Make and answer requests for permission. Take turns playing the roles of Student A and Student B. Follow the cues in the boxes. Remember to use rising intonation for *yes/no* questions.

Example: **A:** May I ask you a question?
B: Sorry. I'm in a hurry.

Student A

1. You are sitting next to Student B. Ask if you can open the window.
2. The cafeteria is crowded. You see one empty seat at Student B's table. Ask if you can sit there.
3. You have to do an interview for a class assignment. Ask Student B if you can ask a question.
4. You need to get to Room 320, but you don't know where it is. Ask Student B if you can ask a question. Then ask where the room is.
5. Class is starting. You forgot to bring a pen. Ask Student B if you can borrow a pen.

Student B

When Student A asks you a question:
1. Refuse permission and give an excuse.
2. Give permission.
3. Refuse permission and give an excuse.
4. First refuse permission. Then change your mind.
5. Refuse permission and give an excuse.

PART ④ BROADCAST ENGLISH
Social Services in the United States: Health Care

BEFORE LISTENING

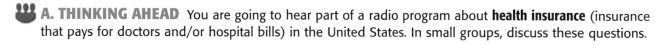 **A. THINKING AHEAD** You are going to hear part of a radio program about **health insurance** (insurance that pays for doctors and/or hospital bills) in the United States. In small groups, discuss these questions.

1. Who pays for basic health care in countries that you are familiar with?

2. Should governments pay for their citizens' health care?

B. PREDICTING Before you listen, make a prediction about what you are going to hear. Discuss this question with a partner:

• How do most U.S. citizens get health insurance? If you don't know, guess.

C. VOCABULARY PREPARATION Read the sentences below. The words and phrases in green are from the radio program. Match the definitions in the box with the words and phrases in green. Write the correct letters on the lines.

a. attitude	f. a lucky thing; a miracle
b. a belief in hard work	g. made a decision as a group; agreed
c. members of some Christian groups	h. organizations that provide free services to help people
d. gave for free	i. weaknesses
e. independence; ability to take care of oneself	j. sympathetic; caring

_____ **1.** A large corporation **donated** all the equipment—we didn't have to pay for a thing.

_____ **2.** The donated equipment was a **godsend**; we feel very lucky to have it.

_____ **3.** Some people think poverty is due to personal **deficits**, not bad luck.

_____ **4.** The government provided job training to help people get back on their feet. This encouraged **self-sustainability**.

_____ **5.** In some countries, **charitable** and **non-profit organizations** often provide the kinds of services—such as health care—that governments provide in other countries.

_____ **6.** Many of the original settlers in America were **Protestants**. They were mistreated in Europe because of their religious beliefs.

_____ **7.** Brittany has a strong **work ethic**, so she should have no trouble finding a job.

_____ **8.** We talked for a long time about how to solve the problem and finally **reached a consensus**.

_____ **9.** Aaron is a very **compassionate** person. He likes to help people.

_____ **10.** The organization has a very sympathetic **stance** towards poor people, so it has provided them with free health care.

LISTENING

The dining room at SOME, So Others Might Eat, a charitable organization in Washington D.C.

A free health clinic

A single, unemployed mother in Washington D.C.

🎧 **A. LISTENING FOR THE MAIN IDEA: SECTION 1** Listen to Section 1 of the radio program. As you listen, think about this question:
• How do most U.S. citizens get health insurance?

🎧 **B. LISTENING FOR DETAILS: SECTION 1** Listen to Section 1 again. This time, listen for the answers to these questions. Write your answers on the lines.

1. What type of clinic is John Adams describing? _____

2. Where did the clinic get its equipment? _____

3. Does the clinic have to pay all of the doctors that work there? Why or why not?

_____

_____

Listening Strategy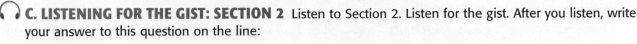

Listening for the Gist

Most of the time, it's difficult to understand every word that a speaker says. However, usually all you need to understand is the **gist**, or the main idea. To listen for the gist, don't worry about every word. Try instead to listen for the key words or expressions that are repeated. These usually give the main idea.

C. LISTENING FOR THE GIST: SECTION 2 Listen to Section 2. Listen for the gist. After you listen, write your answer to this question on the line:

• What American belief has influenced the American attitude toward the poor?

_____

_____

_____

Test-Taking Strategy

Listening for Numerical Information

In the listening sections of some standardized tests, you listen to a radio program or short lecture and then answer questions. Often the questions will focus on numerical information. Speakers often give important information as numbers. These numbers can show quantities, ranking (order), or amounts of time. Speakers use numerical information to support their ideas.

When listening for numerical information, listen for:

• clue words such as *estimated, approximately,* or *about* when amounts aren't exact.
• ordinal numbers (*first, second, third, fourth, fifth*) and words such as *ranked* and *ranking* when the speaker is indicating rank.
• time expressions such as *since* and *for* and words that indicate time periods such as *decade* (10 years) when listening for dates.

Examples: Every year, SOME provides **an estimated 300,000** meals for hungry children, women, and men in Washington, D.C.
John **ranked fifth** in a class of 100 students.
Dion has lived in Washington, D.C. **for three decades**.

D. LISTENING FOR NUMERICAL INFORMATION: SECTION 3 Listen to Section 3. You will hear it twice. Write the numbers that you hear on the lines. The numbers may include quantities, rankings, or amounts of time.

Rageh Omar: An estimated _____ 1 Americans are uninsured and the number is growing. Recently the World Health Organization rated the USA _____ 2 in terms of quality of health care. Those countries with universal health care systems generally had better results and the USA was ranked _____ 3 in terms of the fairness of financial contributions towards health care. But, says Gail Shearer, the director of health policy at the Consumers' Union in Washington, health coverage for all Americans is still a long way off.

Gail Shearer: There have been efforts to get national health insurance in the United States ever since the _____ 4 s, but there have been _____ 5 and _____ 6 of fights over this, and we haven't been able to reach a consensus of how you pay for a national health insurance program. Over the last _____ 7 or _____ 8 years the insurance companies, the doctors, the health maintenance organizations, and the pharmaceutical companies have been able to use their power and their money to resist major progressive changes in health policy in the United States.

E. LISTENING FOR NUMERICAL INFORMATION Listen to Section 3 again. As you listen, answer these questions. Circle the letters of the correct answers.

1. Approximately how many Americans are uninsured?
   A. 40 million   **B.** 44 million   **C.** 4 million

2. Where does the U.S. rank in terms of the quality of health care?
   A. thirty-seventh   **B.** fifty-fourth   **C.** fifty-seventh

3. Where does the U.S. rank in terms of fairness of financial contributions towards health care?
   A. forty-fifth   **B.** sixty-fourth   **C.** fifty-fourth

4. When did people first start trying to get national health care in the United States?
   A. the 1950s   **B.** the 1930s   **C.** the 1920s

5. Over what time period have insurance companies, doctors, pharmaceutical companies, and others been fighting against changes in health policy in the United States?
   A. over the last two or three decades   **B.** over the last three or four decades   **C.** over the last four or five decades

AFTER LISTENING

DISCUSSION Discuss these questions with a partner.

1. Why do you think the United States doesn't have national health insurance? Do you agree or disagree with Linda Donaldson's explanation?

2. Compare health insurance in the United States with health insurance in another country that you are familiar with.

3. Do you think health care is a basic human right?

PART **5** ACADEMIC ENGLISH Social Welfare in Sweden

BEFORE LISTENING

A. DISCUSSION You are going to listen to a lecture about the welfare system in Sweden. In small groups, discuss these questions.

1. Which countries have the best welfare systems? What makes them the best?

2. Which countries have the worst welfare systems? What makes them the worst?

B. HAVING QUESTIONS IN MIND Look at the outline for the lecture on pages 51–52. What *don't* you know about the economy of Sweden and its welfare system? With a partner, write two questions about the subject.

Question 1: _____

Question 2: _____

C. GUESSING THE MEANING FROM CONTEXT Read the sentences below. The words and phrases in green are from the lecture. Guess their meanings from the context. Write your guesses on the lines.

1. **Socialism** works well in Xenrovia. The government controls many of the industries and, as a result, the country has never experienced poverty.

   Guess: _____

2. The government of Xenrovia has policies that **redistribute** everyone's income. As a result, there are no very rich or very poor people; everyone earns about the same amount of money.

   Guess: _____

3. Xenrovia has **nurtured** small businesses by giving them money and special advantages to help them grow and become successful.

   Guess: _____

4. Equalizing people's incomes in Xenrovia resulted in a better quality of life for all citizens because no one was rich and no one was poor.

   Guess: _____

5. Xenrovians aren't interested in reforming their economy because it works so well as it is.

   Guess: _____

6. Because orange juice producers lowered the prices of their products to encourage consumption, they sold more juice this year than last year.

   Guess: _____

7. Some people are not able to prepare for professional jobs, so they attend vocational training programs instead.

   Guess: _____

Now compare your answers with a partner's answers.

D. VOCABULARY PREPARATION Match the economic terms on the left with the definitions on the right. Write the correct letters on the lines. If necessary, use a dictionary.

_____ **1.** free enterprise   **a.** laws about how much money people can earn

_____ **2.** industrial base   **b.** government money that helps people to work harder or to produce more

_____ **3.** inflation   **c.** doing business without much government control

_____ **4.** the private sector   **d.** businesses that are not controlled by the government

_____ **5.** subsidies   **e.** the presence of factories and large businesses in a country

_____ **6.** a wage policy   **f.** increasing prices

LISTENING

Listening Strategy

Listening for the Meaning of New Words and Phrases

Speakers have different ways of giving definitions of new terms. One way that speakers give a definition is after the expression *that is*.

Example: Xenrovia gives **subsidies** to new industries—that is, money to help make it cheaper to produce goods.

A. LISTENING FOR THE MEANING OF NEW WORDS AND PHRASES Listen to these words and phrases in sentences from the lecture. You'll hear each sentence twice. Write the definitions that you hear on the lines.

1. mobility of labor: _____

_____

2. incentives: _____

_____

Critical Thinking Strategy

Taking Notes: Abbreviations and Symbols

When you are listening to a lecture, you can't write down everything that the professor says. One way to write down information quickly is to use abbreviations and symbols.

Examples:
ex.	→	example
4	→	four (or any number)
+	→	and
=	→	is, equals, results in

When taking notes, you can make up abbreviations and symbols as long as *you* understand what they mean.

What other symbol in the outline on page 52 also means "and"?

B. TAKING NOTES: ABBREVIATIONS AND SYMBOLS Think of abbreviations for these words and expressions. Then in small groups, share your abbreviations.

1. twentieth century _____

2. government _____

3. economy _____

4. international _____

5. fifth _____

6. World War I _____

C. TAKING NOTES: USING AN OUTLINE Listen to the lecture. It's in four sections. You will listen to each section twice. Fill in as much of the outline as you can. Don't worry if you can't fill in everything. (You'll listen to the whole lecture again later.)

Social Welfare in Sweden

Section 1

I. The Swedish Economy

    A. Type of economy: <u>welfare state</u>

        or _____

    B. History:

        1. Swed. combined _____ and

           _____ to redistribute income

        2. Therefore, no _____ in

           Swed. After WWI, Swed. _____

           _____

    C. Swedes believe in _____

    _____

Sweden

Section 2

II. The First Component for Equalizing Income in Sweden:
protects people from ups and downs of
business cycles and unemployment

    A. Govt. offers _____ to promote _____

    B. Ensures both wages for _____ and tax revenue for _____

Section 3

III. The 2nd Component: Allows private ownership and control over production

    A. No govt. involvement in _____

        or _____

    B. Swed. dependent on _____

    _____

    C. Swed. markets unregulated = _____

    _____

IV. The 3rd Component: wage policy–reduces difference
between highest and lowest paid workers

    A. Unions negotiate: _____

    _____

    B. Unions also negotiate: _____

    _____

A Swedish family

Swedish union members negotiating a contract

Section 4

V. The 4th Component: policies ensure full employment and increase mobility of labor

  A. Swed. work ethic & employment =

  _____

  _____

  B. Vocational training for

  _____

  _____

  C. Subsidies for _____

  _____

VI. The 5th Component

  A. Ex: _____

  B. Ex: _____

VII. Swedes Happy with System

  A. Swed. has achieved more _____

  _____ than many other economies

  B. Result: _____

  _____

  C. However, Swed. must ___ _____

  _____ because

  _____

Source: Adapted from a lecture by Jeff Strieter, Ph.D.

D. CHECKING YOUR NOTES Listen to the lecture again. Fill in any missing information. As you listen, try to answer this question:

• What do Swedes believe that all individuals have a right to?

Listening Strategy

Listening for Causes and Effects

When speakers discuss economics, they often talk about the effects of actions, plans, and policies. It's important to know the difference between the cause of something and its effect or result. Some expressions that introduce causes and effects are *because of, due to, as a result, result in,* and *the result is (that).*

Examples: We have to pay more for goods and services **because of** inflation.
                                         Effect   Cause

   We have to pay more for goods and services **due to** inflation.
                                         Effect   Cause

   We are experiencing inflation. **As a result,** we have to pay more for goods.
                    Cause   Effect

   Inflation has **resulted in** higher prices.
   Cause   Effect

   We are experiencing inflation. **The result is that** now we have higher prices.
                    Cause   Effect

E. LISTENING FOR CAUSES AND EFFECTS Listen to some information from the lecture. Listen for expressions that introduce causes and effects. Complete the graphic organizer on page 54 to answer these questions.

1. Why do many countries in the world envy Sweden?

2. Why can Swedish businesses be competitive in the international economy?

3. The Swedes are happy with their system. What is the result of this?

Causes		Effects
	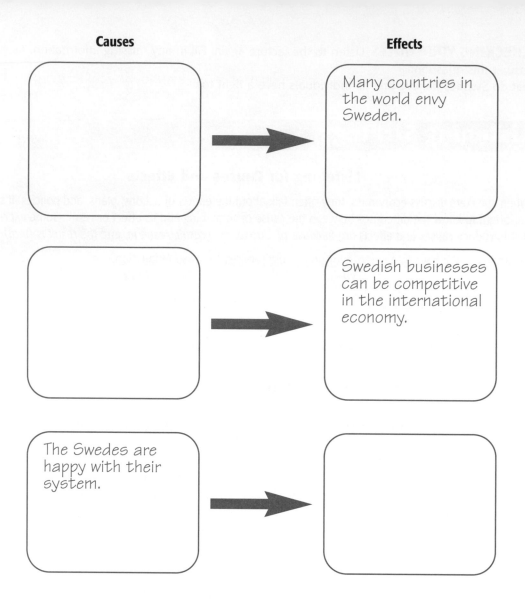	Many countries in the world envy Sweden.
		Swedish businesses can be competitive in the international economy.
The Swedes are happy with their system.		

AFTER LISTENING

A. USING YOUR NOTES Work with a partner. Use your notes to discuss these questions about the lecture.

1. What kind of economy does Sweden have?

2. What are some policies that help Sweden to equalize salaries for its citizens?

3. How do the people of Sweden feel about their welfare system?

4. Would you like to live in a country with a welfare system like Sweden's? Which kind of welfare system would you prefer?

B. MAKING CONNECTIONS In small groups, think about the reading in Part 1, the radio program in Part 4, and the lecture in Part 5. Answer the following question:
• What can different nations learn from each other about how to provide the best possible life for their citizens?

PUT IT ALL TOGETHER

GIVING A PRESENTATION In small groups, prepare and give a presentation on welfare. The presentation is entitled "What a Government Should Provide for Its Citizens."

Step 1

A. Your group will give a presentation on the programs that a government should provide for its citizens. Try to agree on three programs that a government should provide, such as the following:

- education
- childcare
- employment
- health care
- housing
- job training

Add items of your own.

B. Talk about any conditions that the government should place on each program. To do this, you may want to answer these questions:
- How long can people use the program?
- Who is allowed to use the program?
- Is the program completely free or subsidized (not free, but the government helps to pay for it)?

Add conditions of your own.

Speaking Strategy

Compromising

You might have a very different opinion about a subject than your group members do. However, when you work in a group, you must agree on things in order to accomplish the task. Therefore, it is often necessary to **compromise**. In other words, two or more people with different ideas might have to combine those ideas to make a new one that is less extreme.

Example: You think the government should pay for all health care. Most of your group thinks that people should buy their own health insurance. You compromise by having the government subsidize all the health care costs for some people.

C. Explain *why* a government should provide your three programs. One member of your group should write the reasons down.

D. Use the chart below and the chart on page 56 to plan your presentation. Your teacher will give you a time limit in which to finish the chart. Practice compromising to save time.

Should a Government Provide . . . ?	Yes	No	Reasons
Education			
Health Care			
Childcare			

Should a Government Provide . . . ?	Yes	No	Reasons
Housing			
Employment			
Job Training			

 Step 2

To prepare for your presentation, do Internet research to find information on how different countries provide such things as childcare, health care, and job training for its citizens. Try doing searches by combining key words such as the following:

childcare in _____
(country)

health care in _____
(country)

job training in _____
(country)

Speaking Strategy

Making Eye Contact

When you give a presentation, make eye contact with your audience. Look at the faces of the people you are speaking to. If you are speaking to a big group, move your eyes around the room to look at everyone. Don't keep your eyes on just one member of the audience.

Step 3

Now present your ideas to the class. Describe what the ideal government should provide its citizens and explain why you think these items are important. If possible, divide your presentation into parts so that each member of your group can present one part. Remember to make eye contact with the audience.

As you listen to each other's presentations, take notes. Ask questions about each other's ideas.

UNIT (1) VOCABULARY WORKSHOP

Review vocabulary items that you learned in Chapters 1 and 2.

A. MATCHING Match the words and phrases on the left to the definitions on the right. Write the correct letters on the lines.

Words and Phrases	Definitions
_____ **1.** bargain	**a.** chief executive officers
_____ **2.** charitable organizations	**b.** a person who represents the interests of an organization
_____ **3.** CEOs	**c.** negotiate
_____ **4.** lobbyist	**d.** a person who tells others when he or she sees employees behaving unethically
_____ **5.** nurtured	
_____ **6.** reforming	**e.** organizations that provide free services to help people
_____ **7.** self-sustainability	**f.** attitude
_____ **8.** stance	**g.** the ability to take care of oneself
_____ **9.** subsidies	**h.** helped to grow
_____ **10.** whistle-blower	**i.** changing
	j. government money that helps people to work harder or produce more

B. TRUE OR FALSE? Read the statements below. Circle *T* if the sentence is true. Circle *F* if the sentence is false.

1. If you pay **the asking price**, you pay the first price that the seller gives you.   T   F

2. In a **homogeneous** culture, people from many different cultures live together.   T   F

3. If you **defied** your parents when you were young, you did what they wanted you to do.   T   F

4. **Vocational training** helps people to prepare for nonprofessional jobs.   T   F

5. People who have **a strong work ethic** believe in hard work.   T   F

6. If you **lay** a person **off**, you are giving him or her a job.   T   F

7. If you are **fluent in** Spanish, it means that you cannot speak it at all.   T   F

8. If you are a **determined** person, you are strong-willed.   T   F

9. If you **donated** something, you expected people to pay you for it.   T   F

10. In a **free enterprise** system, there are a lot of government controls on businesses.   T   F

C. THE ACADEMIC WORD LIST
In the boxes below are some of the most common *academic* words in English. Fill in the blanks with words from these boxes. When you finish, check your answers in the readings on page 5 (for Items 1–5) and pages 32–33 (for Items 6–14).

appreciate	created	culture	issues	relaxed

Business Etiquette in New Zealand

General Advice: Tipping is not common, and people often refuse to take tips. Be prepared to be formal until others have _____ 1 a more _____ 2 atmosphere.

Conversation: New Zealanders like to talk about national and international politics, the weather, and sports. They _____ 3 visitors who understand their _____ 4 . Do not talk about racial _____ 5 . Do not include New Zealand as part of Australia or "AustralAsia and the South Pacific."

communities	economy	innovative	knowledge	residential
connection	economies	jobs	research	

Education and Poverty

According to UNICEF (The United Nations Children's Fund), one of the keys to reducing poverty in developing nations is improving educational opportunities for children, especially girls. It is often difficult for girls to receive an education in poor countries. Girls often do not attend school or have to drop out (quit) because they must work or take care of their families. A great deal of _____ 6 shows an important _____ 7 between increasing educational opportunities and improving the _____ 8 of poor countries. Educating more children, especially girls, can keep children healthier. As a result, girls can grow into women with good _____ 9 and this strengthens the _____ 10 in the long term.

The Education of Lalita

Like many other parents in the village, Lalita's parents wanted her to get married at the age of 10, and they didn't expect her to learn to read. However, Lalita didn't want to get married. She was excited about learning, and she secretly attended a local day school for girls from poor

_____. She finally learned to read at the age of 12.
                11

Then, in 1997, the Education for Women's Equality (EWE) program started a

_____ school (a school where the children live while they study) to provide
                12

basic education to girls. Lalita defied her parents by attending the school's _____
                                                                                                    13

(using new ideas) eight-month course, along with 24 other illiterate to semi-literate girls.

"In my village, I was doing nothing but cutting grass, getting firewood, and cleaning and cooking. In between, I used to attend the local day school, but this was without my parents

_____," says Lalita. At the EWE's residential school, Lalita and the other girls
                14

learned to read and write, and received life skills training. They also studied sports (including karate), health care, and public speaking.

ART

Chapter 3
Art Themes and Purposes

Chapter 4
Ancient Greek Art

CHAPTER 3

Art Themes and Purposes

Discuss these questions:
- Where are the people in the photo?
- What type of art are they looking at?
- What is your favorite type of art?

A. THINKING AHEAD In small groups, discuss the questions below.

1. Do you like fine art (painting, sculpture, photography, graphic art, etc.)? If yes, which types of fine art do you like?

2. What do you know about the following art periods: ancient art, renaissance art (1400s to 1500s), art nouveau (1890–1914), art deco (1930s), and modern art (late 1900s to 1970s)? Which periods do you like?

3. What do you know about art styles; for example, impressionism, surrealism, and realism? Which styles do you like?

B. PREDICTING You are going to read about an artist, Michael Cassidy. He created the poster *Waikiki Surf Festival*. Before you read, look carefully at the poster. With a partner, use the questions to make predictions about the artist.

1. What kind of life do you think Michael Cassidy has?

2. What kind of hobbies do you think he has?

3. How do you think he gets ideas for his posters?

4. How do you think he became an artist? Do you think he studied art in college?

5. How might he make his posters?

Waikiki Surf Festival by Michael Cassidy

C. READING Read about Michael Cassidy and his art. As you read, think about this question:
• What are some similarities between being a surfer and being a good poster artist?

Michael Cassidy

Michael Cassidy believes that making **posters** (art used for advertising) is the art of **reduction**—taking things away so that the image is simple and easy to understand. It must give its message clearly, quickly, and memorably. Cassidy has used this art of reduction in his own life: he's been a surfer since high school and
5   spends his time painting, being with his family, and surfing. He loves to travel and has visited some of the most beautiful places in the world: Tahiti, Hawaii, Mexico, Costa Rica, and Panama. "Most people work their whole lives, dreaming about where they'd go if they won the lottery," he says. "I've had the good fortune to go to those places, and I still dream about them."

10   Cassidy studied art at Palomar College in San Marcos, California, and at California State University in Long Beach. But he says he learned the most about his art by working in a sign shop. He has also learned a great deal by studying the masters of poster art: French poster artists from the beginning of the 20th century and American artists from the art deco period (the 1930s).

15   Cassidy's posters begin as paintings. He works on a **large scale**—his canvases can be seven feet (2.1 meters) high. He starts with a charcoal **sketch** (drawing) and then fills it in with oil paints. When he finishes, he photographs the painting, scans it into a computer, and then prints it using an inkjet printer.

It's not a coincidence that Cassidy has been a surfer all of his life. Surfing is a sport
20   of balance and **proportion**. In other words, the surfer must consider the size and shape of the board, the wave, and him- or herself in order to be successful. Cassidy uses these concepts in his art. In the poster *Waikiki Surf Festival*, for example, Cassidy uses only a few simple **elements** (things or parts) to send a message: the waves, the sky, Diamond Head in the background and, in the front, the single figure, balanced and
25   confident.

Source: "Michael Cassidy" (Moore)

D. DISCUSSION In small groups, discuss these questions.

1. Check the predictions you made in Activity B (page 64). Were you correct?

2. According to the reading, how is being a surfer like being a good poster artist?

3. Do you like the poster *Waikiki Surf Festival*? Why or why not?

4. Do you like poster art? Why or why not?

5. Are posters "real art," in your opinion?

E. RESPONSE WRITING Choose *one* of these topics. Write about it for 10 minutes. Don't worry about grammar and don't use a dictionary. Just put as many ideas as you can on paper.

• Describe your favorite kind of art. Choose one of the types you discussed in Activity A or another one.
• Describe one of your favorite works of art: a painting, a sculpture, a photograph, or any other kind of work. Give the title and the artist if you know them. Write why you like it.

BEFORE LISTENING

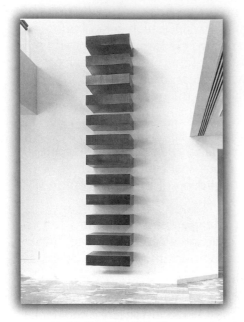

Untitled by Donald Judd, 1967
An example of minimalist art

Linda by Chuck Close, 1975-76
An example of photorealism

100 Campbell's Soup Cans by Andy Warhol, 1962
An example of pop art

A. THINKING AHEAD You are going to listen to Mike, Ashley, and Rachel talk about art that was popular in the 1960s and 1970s. Before you listen, look at the examples of art from the sixties and seventies on page 66. In small groups, discuss these questions.

1. What do you see in each picture?

2. How does each work of art make you feel?

3. Do you think any of these works of art has a message?

4. What do you think the artists were trying to say?

5. Do you know anything about the style of each work or artist?

B. GUESSING THE MEANING FROM CONTEXT Read the sentences below. The words and phrases in green are from the conversation. Guess their meanings from the context. Write your guesses on the lines.

1. Tony Smith's steel cube is an example of **minimalist art** because it has a simple shape and it is made of only one material: steel.

   Guess: _____

2. Some people like minimalist art because its purpose is to simplify objects, to **reduce** them to simple parts.

   Guess: _____

3. Minimalist art often uses **geometric shapes** such as cubes, circles, and triangles.

   Guess: _____

4. There are several artistic **elements** in a painting; for example, color, size, and shape. The part I always find the most interesting is color.

   Guess: _____

Die, Tony Smith, 1962

5. The only artistic style I understand is **realism** because I can understand a picture that shows things as they really are.

   Guess: _____

6. The example of **photorealism** was so realistic that I thought it was a photograph, not a painting.

   Guess: _____

Now compare your answers with a partner's answers.

C. VOCABULARY PREPARATION Read the sentences below. The words and phrases in green are from the conversation. Match the definitions in the box with the words and phrases in green. Write the correct letters on the lines.

a. and many things like that	e. popular
b. confused	f. That's disgusting!
c. I was certain	g. understand
d. let's go to	

_____ 1. Do you mean that it *wasn't* a photograph? It was so real looking that **I could have sworn** that it was a photograph!

_____ 2. Disco music was **big** in the 1970s—they played it on the radio and in all the dance clubs.

_____ 3. I don't know what's going on in our art history class. In fact, I'm totally **lost**!

_____ 4. Did you see the woman's face in the picture *Linda*? You can see every line and spot **and all**!

_____ 5. **Yuck**! I hate realistic art! I'd rather look at a piece of steel.

_____ 6. I don't understand the assignment. I just don't **get** it.

_____ 7. We've finished the second question. **On to** the third question!

LISTENING

A. LISTENING FOR THE MAIN IDEA Listen to the conversation. As you listen, think about this question:
• Why are the students discussing types of art?

Listen to the conversation again. Listen for the types of art that the students discuss and the examples that they give of each type. Complete the graphic organizer.

Types of Art:

Minimalist Art		Photorealism

Examples:

		a picture by Chuck Close

🎧 **C. LISTENING FOR DETAILS** Listen to part of the conversation again. Listen for the answers to these questions.

1. What does Mike think about the art history class?

_____

2. What is the students' assignment?

_____

3. What doesn't Ashley understand?

_____

AFTER LISTENING

Speaking Strategy

Describing Art

When people talk about art, they describe what they see and feel. They try to explain what they think the artist is saying.

When you talk about a work of art, you usually describe:

• the type, period, or style of the art
• the objects or people in the work
• other things you see, such as shapes and colors in the work
• the art process and materials: how the artist created the work and the materials that he or she used
• how the work makes you feel

A. DESCRIBING ART
Work in small groups and brainstorm words and phrases that you can use to talk about art. Go back to the poster on page 64 and the pictures on pages 66–67. Complete the chart below with words that you use to describe them.

Styles	Shapes	Processes/ Materials	Feelings
pop art	geometric		happy

Speaking Strategy

Trusting Your Instincts

When you talk about art, you don't just describe it. It's also important to interpret it—describe what isn't actually in the picture, but what the picture or the objects in it suggest to you. Don't be afraid to interpret art. Rita Gilbert, a professional writer who specializes in art, tells students: "Trust your instincts. You know more than you think you know." She says that because we have lived with art all of our lives, we already have a lot of information about it.

Example: When I look at the sculpture *Self-Portrait with Model* (page 71), I feel a little homesick. I think of my grandmother, but I don't know why. Why is the man looking at the woman? Why isn't she looking at him? I think the sculpture is about love, but also about loneliness. That's how it makes me feel.

B. TRUSTING YOUR INSTINCTS With a partner, take turns describing one of the works of art below. Use the vocabulary from the chart on page 70. As you are describing the works, answer these questions:

• What do you see? What shapes, art style, and art process does each artist use?
• How does it make you feel?
• What do you think the artist was trying to communicate with this piece?

Pergusa by Frank Stella, 1981

Three Flags by Jasper Johns, 1958

Blue Girl on Park Bench by George Segal, 1980

Self-Portrait with Model by Duane Hanson, 1979

LANGUAGE FUNCTIONS

Asking for Clarification: General

Sometimes in a conversation, you don't understand a word or phrase that someone says. If it's new to you, you may not even be able to repeat it. When this happens, you can ask for clarification with a general question or comment.

Examples: **A:** That's an example of minimalist art.

                    B: What?   **Less Formal**

                                   I didn't get that.

                                   What did you say?

                                   Sorry, I didn't get that.

                                   I didn't understand that.

                                   Would you mind repeating that?

                                   I'm sorry, what did you say?

                                   Excuse me, I didn't understand that.   **More Formal**

A. ASKING FOR CLARIFICATION Work with a partner. Student A makes statements about the works of art in this chapter. Student B asks for clarification using expressions in the box below. Then exchange roles.

Excuse me, I didn't understand that.	**What?**
I didn't get that.	**What did you say?**
I didn't understand that.	**Would you mind repeating that?**
I'm sorry, what did you say?	**Sorry, I didn't get that.**

Examples: **A:** *Self-Portrait with Model* is an example of photorealism.
   B: What did you say?

   A: *Linda* was painted by Chuck Close.
   B: Sorry, I didn't get that.

Asking for Clarification: Specific

If you know *what* you didn't understand, you need to ask for more specific clarification.

Example: **A:** That's an example of minimalist art.
   B: **What did you say?**
   A: Minimalist art.

Once you hear the word or phrase that you don't know, you can ask for more specific clarification.

Example: **A:** That's an example of minimalist art.
   B: What did you say?
   A: Minimalist art.
   B: **What's that?**
   What is minimalist art?
   Can you give me an example of minimalist art?
   What does that mean?
   I'm sorry. I don't know what that is.

B. ASKING FOR CLARIFICATION With a partner, practice asking for general and specific clarification. Student A makes statements about works of art in this chapter. Student B asks first for general and then for specific information. Then exchange roles.

Examples: **A:** My favorite kind of art is pop art.
   B: What did you say? (General)
   A: My favorite kind of art is pop art.
   B: Can you give me an example of that? (Specific)

Giving Clarification

When people ask you for general clarification, you don't always know exactly what they didn't understand. Sometimes you have to guess. To guess, you can repeat part of what you said.

Example: **A:** That's an example of minimalist art.
   B: What?
   A: Minimalist.

Then when they ask for more specific information, you give it.

Example: **A:** That's an example of minimalist art.
   B: What?
   A: Minimalist.
   B: What does that mean?
   A: Well, the purpose of minimalist art is to reduce things to simple elements.

Sometimes you know right away what the other person didn't understand. In that case, offer clarification immediately.

Example: **A:** That's an example of minimalist art.
   B: What kind of art?
   A: Minimalist. It means reducing things to simple elements.

Notice that Speaker A gives clarification by defining a term. Speaker A can also clarify by giving an example.

Example: **A:** I think minimalist art is going to be on the test.
   B: What? Minimalist art? Have we studied that?
   A: Yeah, minimalist art–like that steel cube on page 67.

C. GIVING CLARIFICATION Listen to the following short conversations. For each conversation, decide if Speaker B is asking for *general* clarification or for *specific* clarification. Circle the type of clarification question that you hear.

1. General   Specific   **4.** General   Specific

2. General   Specific   **5.** General   Specific

3. General   Specific   **6.** General   Specific

INTONATION

Wh- Questions

In Chapter 2 (page 40), you learned that your voice goes up at the end of a *yes/no* question. When you ask a question with a *wh-* word (*who, what, when, where, why,* and *how*), your voice goes down at the end of the sentence.

Examples: What kind of art is that? Where did you see that?

Compare the intonation of *yes/no* questions to that of *wh-* questions.

Examples: Is that an example of minimalist art? What is minimalist art?

D. Wh- QUESTIONS Listen to each question. Is it a *yes/no* question or a *wh-* question? Circle the type of question that you hear.

1. *Yes/No*   *Wh-*   4. *Yes/No*   *Wh-*
2. *Yes/No*   *Wh-*   5. *Yes/No*   *Wh-*
3. *Yes/No*   *Wh-*   6. *Yes/No*   *Wh-*

E. ASKING Wh- QUESTIONS With a partner, discuss your favorite pieces of art in this chapter. Ask *wh-* questions. Discuss the art, artists, and art movements. Pay attention to question intonation as you speak.

Example: **A:** What is your favorite painting?
                B: I like the painting on page 66.
                A: Who's it by?
                B: Andy Warhol.

PRONUNCIATION

/ɪ/ vs. /i/

Some learners of English have problems with the sounds /ɪ/ and /i/. They may not hear the difference between the two sounds, or they may not be able to pronounce the two sounds correctly.

/ɪ/	/i/
it	eat
ship	sheep
his	he's
Is that still for sale?	Is that steel for sale?

In the list above, what are the different spellings for the /i/ sound? (These are the most common spellings for this sound.)

F. HEARING THE DIFFERENCE BETWEEN /ɪ/ AND /i/ Listen to the sentences. Circle the word that you hear.

1. It's a little **bit / beet**.

2. The **bins / beans** are over there.

3. Don't **pick / peek** at it.

4. Mary's still **living / leaving**.

5. The **mitt / meat** is here.

6. I see the **ship / sheep** in the picture.

G. PRONOUNCING /I/ AND /i/ Say five of the words in the box. (Don't say the words in order.) Your partner will circle the words that you say. Check the circled words to see if they are correct. If any word is not correct, say the word again. Then exchange roles.

sit	mitt	deep	meat
seat	bit	bean	beet
pick	his	he's	peek
bin	it	eat	live
leave	dip	sick	seek

H. PRONOUNCING /I/ AND /i/ IN SENTENCES Now use words with these sounds in conversations. Interview your classmates. Use the questions in the chart below. If a classmate answers *yes*, write his or her name in the right column.

Example: **A:** May I ask you a question?
B: Yes.
A: Do you like minimalist art?
B: Yes, it's O.K.
A: Great. What's your name?
B: Alex. A-L-E-X.
A: (Writes *Alex* in the chart.)

Questions	Classmates
Do you like minimalist art?	
Have you ever seen Warhol's soup cans?	
Do you live near a museum?	
Would you like to meet a famous artist?	
Do you like the painting *Three Flags* on page 71?	
Do you know what was big in the seventies? (Notice another spelling for the /i/ sound.)	
Do you know what was popular in the sixties? (Be careful! *Sixties* has both sounds.)	

WORDS IN PHRASES

🎧 Noun Phrases for Types of Art

Noun phrases are combinations of adjectives and a noun or two nouns. In this chapter, there are many of these noun phrases for types of art. When learning noun phrases, it's important to remember these two words *together*. Listen to the examples. Notice that, in the noun phrases, the first word is stressed.

Examples: That's an example of **minimalist art**.
                              adj.   noun

                 Sculpture was the Greeks' greatest **art form**.
                                                    noun noun

🎧 **I. WORDS IN PHRASES** Find and underline the noun phrase in each sentence below. Then listen and repeat each sentence that you hear. Listen again and circle the stressed word in each noun phrase.

1. That's an example of pop art.

2. Chris is studying jewelry design.

3. That painting is an example of surrealist art.

4. There's some information about minimalist art on page 233.

5. My favorite art style is realism.

PUT IT TOGETHER

👥 **ASKING FOR AND GIVING CLARIFICATION** Work with a partner. Student A chooses a topic from the box below and makes a statement about it.

my favorite artist	something interesting I've learned so far in this chapter
my favorite kind of art	a famous artist that I know about
my favorite work of art	the strangest, ugliest, or worst art I've ever seen
an art exhibit I saw recently	

Student B asks for clarification. It can be general or specific, depending on how much Speaker B already knows. Student A offers clarification. If Student B asks a specific question, Student A offers a definition or an example.

Take turns playing the roles of Student A and Student B. Remember to use correct question intonation. Pay attention to the /I/ and /i/ sounds. Try to use the noun phrases for types of art.

Example: **A:** My favorite artist is Andy Warhol.
              B: I'm sorry. I didn't get that.
              A: Andy Warhol.
              B: What did he do?
              A: He painted *100 Campbell's Soup Cans*.
              B: What kind of art is that?
              A: I think it's pop art.

BEFORE LISTENING

Gay Liberation by George Segal

City on the High Mountain by Louise Nevelson

Puppy by Jeff Koons

A. THINKING AHEAD You are going to hear a radio program about the artist George Segal, a modern sculptor. In small groups, discuss these questions.

1. What are some typical subjects of sculpture (the people or things that sculpture shows)?

2. In what kinds of places can you see sculptures?

3. How do sculptors make their works of art? What kinds of materials (steel, stone, clay, etc.) do they usually use?

4. What are the differences among the sculptures in the photos on page 78 and on page 81?

5. How is a sculpture different from a painting or a photograph?

6. What other famous sculptors or sculptures do you know?

B. PREDICTING Before you listen, make a prediction about what you are going to hear. Look at the photos of George Segal's sculptures on page 78 and page 82. With a partner, discuss this question.

• How do you think Segal made his sculptures? (What kind of material did he use?)

C. VOCABULARY PREPARATION Read the sentences below. The words and phrases in green are from the radio program. Match the definitions in the box with the words and phrases in green. Write the correct letters on the lines.

a. dull; boring	g. a scene showing a group of people
b. met with	h. a scene showing a place
c. not realistic; not representational	i. a show of an artist's lifetime work
d. ordinary	j. unplanned
e. pretending	k. using
f. sadness; emptiness	

_____ 1. Segal didn't think ordinary life is **banal**. He thought that the everyday moments of life can be very interesting and special.

_____ 2. The subjects of George Segal's work are very **mundane**—he showed normal people doing normal, everyday things.

_____ 3. The professor wasn't prepared to talk to the class, but she gave a very good **impromptu** lecture without any notes.

_____ 4. The American painter Edward Hopper shows the **bleakness** of city life in his paintings of cold, empty city streets.

_____ 5. The museum is having a **retrospective** exhibit of Andy Warhol's work. It includes examples of all of his work, from the beginning of his career until his death.

_____ 6. We wanted to interview the artist, so we **caught up with** him at his studio.

7. A **landscape** isn't always a country scene; you can also paint a city landscape, as long as it shows a wide view of the scene.

8. Segal's sculptures are the opposite of **abstract** art: He shows things how they really are.

9. Segal's sculpture *Three People on Four Benches* (page 82) is a lifelike **tableau**: It shows three people sitting on benches.

10. When I paint, I am **dealing with** my emotions. My pictures show how I feel.

11. Jon's not really happy—he's just **putting on an act**. He's actually a very unhappy person.

Listening Strategy

Review: Using a Cultural Informant

In Chapter 1 (page 19) you learned to use a cultural informant. There are some cultural references in the radio program.

Examples: In one of Segal's works, a white figure sits on a real stool at a real **Formica diner counter**.

In another work, a man stands in a bar, under a **neon Budweiser sign**.

If you don't know these terms, try to find a cultural informant who knows what they mean.

LISTENING

George Segal, 1924–2000

A bust on a pedestal

A plaster cast

🎧 **A. LISTENING FOR THE MAIN IDEA: SECTION 1** You are going to hear an interview with the sculptor George Segal. Segal died in 2000. Segal gave the interview a few years before he died.

Listen to Section 1 of the radio program. Don't worry about understanding everything. As you listen, think about this question:

• What are the subjects of Segal's sculptures?

🎧 **B. LISTENING FOR DETAILS: SECTION 1** Listen to Section 1 again. Write the answers to these questions on the lines.

1. How did Segal first get the idea to use plaster bandages in his work?

_____

_____

2. When did Segal first get the idea to use plaster bandages in his work?

_____

3. Why was Segal interested in using the plaster bandages in his work?

_____

_____

🎧 **C. LISTENING FOR THE MAIN IDEA: SECTION 2** Listen to Section 2. Think about the "feeling" words that you listed when you brainstormed for art language on page 70. As you listen, think about this question:

• What are some of the feelings about his work that Segal and the interviewer discuss?

Identifying Impressions or Opinions

When people express their opinions and **impressions of** (feelings and ideas about) something, they often use certain phrases to introduce them. When you hear these phrases, you know that an opinion or impression is coming.

Examples: **I think that** George Segal cares very much about his sculptures.
I feel that art should show only very beautiful things, not ordinary people.
From Edward Hopper's painting, **I get a sense of** the loneliness of the big city.

Note: *That* is not necessary in the first two sentences, but it makes them sound more formal.

Three People on Four Benches by George Segal

🎧 **D. IDENTIFYING IMPRESSIONS OR OPINIONS: SECTION 2** Listen to Section 2 again. As you listen, think about this question:

• How are the interviewer's impressions of Segal's work different from Segal's impressions?

👥 After you listen, work with a partner to complete the T-chart below. Compare the interviewer's and Segal's impressions.

Interviewer's Impressions	Segal's Impressions

AFTER LISTENING

👥 **A. DISCUSSION** In small groups, discuss these questions.

1. How did Segal make his sculptures? Explain the process in your own words.

2. How does Segal describe his own work? In other words, what does he say that he is showing us about life?

3. What is your opinion of Segal's work, based on the examples on pages 78 and 82?

4. Have you ever created any sculpture? If so, tell the group about the experience. If not, would you like to create a sculpture?

Thinking Creatively

Creative thinking helps you to solve problems and to expand your understanding of new information. One way to think creatively is to think of new ways to use familiar objects.

George Segal is an example of a creative thinker. His creative thinking led to a new type of sculpture.

B. THINKING CREATIVELY George Segal found an artistic use for something that was not intended for art: medical bandages. In small groups, brainstorm a list of at least 10 everyday objects. Then think of how you can use them in art. Describe the items and the process.

Example: **Item:** rubber bands
Artistic use: You could glue hundreds of rubber bands to a board and then spray paint them with different colors.

When you finish, report your ideas to the rest of the class.

Rubber bands

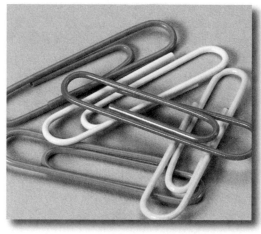

Paper clips

Forks and knives

Videos, CDs, and books

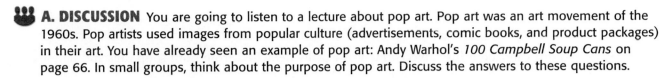

PART 5 ACADEMIC ENGLISH Pop Art

BEFORE LISTENING

A. DISCUSSION You are going to listen to a lecture about pop art. Pop art was an art movement of the 1960s. Pop artists used images from popular culture (advertisements, comic books, and product packages) in their art. You have already seen an example of pop art: Andy Warhol's *100 Campbell Soup Cans* on page 66. In small groups, think about the purpose of pop art. Discuss the answers to these questions.

1. Why do you think that pop artists used images from popular culture?

2. What do you think pop artists were trying to say in their art? For example, what does a picture of a soup can say?

B. THINKING AHEAD Look at the art on pages 88–93. The lecturer will discuss these works in the lecture. Before you listen, think about how the lecturer might use these works in the lecture. Look at each one and discuss the answers to these questions with a partner.

1. What is the style of each work?

2. What do you think each artist is trying to say?

3. What are the similarities among the works? What are the differences?

C. GUESSING THE MEANING FROM CONTEXT Read the sentences below. The words and phrases in green are from the lecture. Guess their meanings from the context. Write your guesses on the lines.

1. Jackson Pollock's art shows us his **internal struggles**—the painful and confused feelings that he had as he painted.

   Guess: _____

2. Like Pollock, some artists use art to express their **state of being;** you can see how they feel by looking at their work.

   Guess: _____

3. The **consumer culture** that we live in makes us want to spend money on new products, even if we don't need them.

   Guess: _____

4. That painting reflects a feeling of **randomness** because the objects in it are not organized in any particular way.

   Guess: _____

5. Pop art was **innovative** because it used images in a new way.

Guess: _____

6. Warhol liked the **streamlined** designs in advertising art, so he borrowed those simple styles to use in his own work.

Guess: _____

7. Warhol didn't care about his subjects: He was equally **detached** from both soup cans and famous people.

Guess: _____

8. Robert Rauschenberg is famous for using **found objects** in his paintings. He worked with old magazines, empty cigarette cartons, and other things he found while taking walks around New York City.

Guess: _____

Now compare your answers with a partner's answers.

LISTENING

Listening Strategy

Listening for the Meaning of New Words and Phrases

Professors often give examples of new words or phrases in their lectures. Listening for examples will help you to understand more. Some expressions used before examples are *such as, for example, one example is,* and *examples include.*

Examples: The artist's work reflects a range of sentiments, **such as** anger, confusion, and fear.
Pop art was very popular in the 1960s. **One example is** Warhol's *200 Campbell's Soup Cans.*

A. LISTENING FOR THE MEANING OF NEW WORDS AND PHRASES Listen to these words in sentences from the lecture. The lecturer helps you understand them by giving examples. Write the examples that you hear. You'll hear each sentence twice.

1. mass-produced visual media: _____

2. heroic: _____

Listening Strategy

Taking Notes: Images

Lecturers often use visual images such as slides or PowerPoint screens during their lectures. It's important to pay close attention to the images as you listen, but don't forget to continue taking notes. Write down the information about the image as the lecturer gives it to you. In some cases, it helps to sketch the image in your notes.

B. TAKING NOTES: IMAGES Listen to a part of the lecture. Look at the picture on page 88. As you listen, answer these questions.

1. Who is the artist? _____

2. What is the name of the painting? _____

3. Look for the "overlapping lines that swirl" that the lecturer describes. Draw a sketch of them in the box.

Listening Strategy

Taking Notes: Using Key Words

As with abbreviations, using key words can save you time as you take notes. Key words are important words—usually nouns and verbs. Use them instead of complete sentences, and leave out unimportant words such as *be*, *a*, and *the*. Combine key words with abbreviations to take notes even faster.

Example: You hear: Pop artists were inspired by mass-produced visual media and the design of common household objects.

You write: Pop artists inspired by mass-produced vis. med. & design of common household objs.

C. **TAKING NOTES: KEY WORDS** Listen to the lecture. It's in four sections. You will listen to each section twice. Fill in as much of the outline as you can. Don't worry if you can't fill in everything. (You'll listen to the whole lecture again later.)

As you listen, look at the art that accompanies each section. Notice in the outline the use of key words and abbreviations instead of complete sentences. Practice completing the outline in this way.

Pop Art

Section 1

I. Introduction

    A. Pop art _____

    B. Pop artists inspired by _____

    _____

II. The Difference between Pop Art and Abstract Expressionism

Autumn Rhythm by Jackson Pollock

    A. Abstract Expressionism: movement that _____

    _____

    B. *Autumn Rhythm* refers to _____

    _____

    C. Pollock believed _____

    _____

    D. Abstract expressionism reflected _____

    _____

III. American Culture in the 1960s

   A. Television: _____

   _____

   B. Pop artists different from 1940s and 1950s artists because _____

   _____

Section 2

IV. Robert Rauschenberg
   A. Background

      1. Born: _____

      2. Moved to New York: _____

   B. His goals: direct art away from _____ &

      toward _____

   C. Materials

      1. Exs.: _____

      2. His art reflected _____

Canyon by Robert Rauschenberg

   D. *Canyon*

      1. Description & date: _____

      2. Reflected: _____

E. In 1960s, was fascinated by _____

_____

Skyway by Robert Rauschenberg

F. *Skyway*

   1. Description and date:

   _____

   2. Gives viewer the sensation of

   _____

G. Rauschenberg's use of found objects was _____

   & _____

H. Pop artists were interested in _____

   because _____

Section 3

V. Andy Warhol

  A. Background

    1. Born: _____

    2. Education: _____

    3. First job: _____

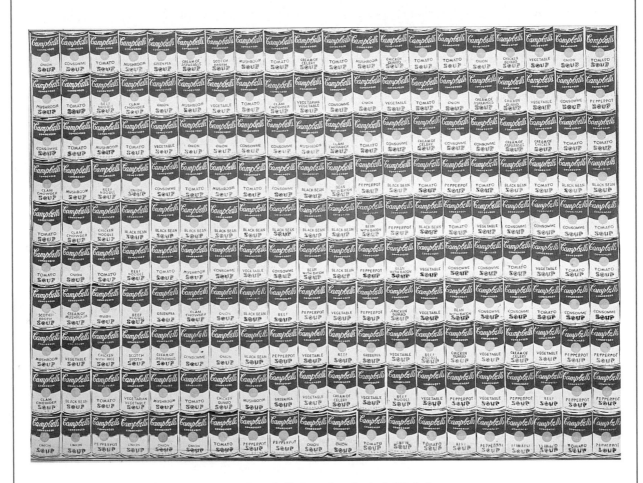

200 Campbell's Soup Cans by Andy Warhol

  B. Fine art painting: *200 Campbell's Soup Cans*

    1. Description and date: _____

    2. Showed his fascination for _____

    _____

    & _____

C. Quote (Remember to use key words here): _____

_____

D. Ideas about fame: _____

_____

E. Warhol's portraits

    1. Exs: _____

    2. Warhol wasn't interested in the people he painted; he was interested in _____

F. Warhol's work reflects _____

Section 4

Clothespin by Claes Oldenberg

VI. Other Pop Artists

    A. Other pop artists were Claes Oldenburg and Roy Lichtenstein

    B. Oldenburg

        1. Sculptures look like _____

        but are _____

        2. Ex.: _____

C. Lichtenstein

   1. Inspired by _____

   2. Ex.: _____

D. What pop artists saw: _____

Wham by Roy Lichtenstein

Source: Adapted from a lecture by Paul F. Fabozzi, M.F.A.

D. CHECKING YOUR NOTES Listen to the lecture again. As you listen, review your notes and fill in any missing information.

AFTER LISTENING

A. USING YOUR NOTES Use your notes to discuss these questions about the lecture with a partner.

1. What's the difference between abstract expressionism and pop art?

2. What was happening in American culture in the early 1960s? How did this influence pop art?

3. Who were two important pop artists? For each one, give one example of his or her work. Explain how it is an example of pop art.

4. Who were two other pop artists? Explain how their work is an example of pop art.

5. What other pop artists are you familiar with?

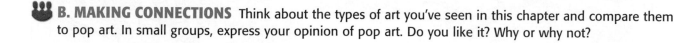
Forming and Expressing an Opinion

Many standardized tests include speaking sections. In these sections, you record an explanation, description, or short presentation. Often you are asked to express your opinion about certain topics. An opinion is more than a statement of like or dislike. You must also be prepared to support your opinion; in other words, say why you like or dislike something.

You can form your opinion while you listen to other people express theirs. Write notes while they express their opinions. Think about whether you agree or disagree, and how good their reasons are. You can also add or subtract ideas from what they say. Then use your notes when you have to speak.

B. MAKING CONNECTIONS Think about the types of art you've seen in this chapter and compare them to pop art. In small groups, express your opinion of pop art. Do you like it? Why or why not?

PUT IT ALL TOGETHER

GIVING A PRESENTATION You are going to give a short presentation on a work of art. In small groups, select a work of art from the 1960s or 1970s.

Step 1
Choose your work of art and do research. You can choose a painting, a sculpture, a photograph, or a poster. You can use one in this book, or find one in an art book at the library.

 You can also learn a lot about artists and their art at museums and galleries on the Internet. Here are some museums with useful websites:

• The Museum of Modern Art
• The Guggenheim Museum
• The Andy Warhol Museum

If possible, bring a picture of the work of art (from the book or from a website) that you are going to discuss to class.

Step 2

Use the outline below to organize your presentation. On a separate piece of paper, write an outline on the piece of art that you chose in Step 1.

I. Introduction

    A. Give the title of the work, the artist's name, and the date of the work.

    B. What movement does the work represent?

II. Discussion of the Artist

    A. His or her background

    B. Other important works

III. Description of the Artist's Work

    A. What do you see? (Who or what are the subjects?)

    B. How is it an example of the movement?

    C. What process(es) did the artist use to create this work?

    D. What is the purpose of the work? (What is the artist trying to express?)

Step 3

Give your presentations in small groups. Use your notes, but remember to make eye contact. Also, remember to trust your instincts. After you listen to each others' presentations, ask questions to clarify information.

CHAPTER 4

Ancient Greek Art

Discuss these questions:
• What do you see in the picture? Where is the building?
• When do you think it was built?
• What do you know about ancient Greece?

Greece and surrounding areas

👥 **A. THINKING AHEAD** Think about the answers to the questions below. Then ask as many classmates as you can the same questions.

1. What do you know about ancient Greek civilization?

2. What do you know about Greek myths and legends?

3. What do you know about ancient Greek art?

4. How has ancient Greek civilization influenced other cultures?

👥 **B. PREDICTING** You are going to read about ancient Greek civilization and art. Before you read, look carefully at the picture of the *Dipylon Vase* on the right. Discuss the answer to this question with a partner:
• What might this vase tell us about ancient Greek culture?

Dipylon Vase

Greek Civilization and Art

No doubt a major reason that we respect the ancient Greeks is that they excelled in many different fields. Their political ideas serve as a model for contemporary democracy. Their poetry and drama and philosophy survive as living classics. Their architecture and sculpture have influenced most later periods in the history of
5 Western art.

We assume that the Greeks' genius shone equally in painting, but we know very little about this because most painted works have been lost. We would know even less, except that a large number of painted clay vases were produced from about the eighth century B.C.E. These pots were made from terra cotta (baked clay), an
10 extremely strong material; it can break, but it won't disintegrate (in other words, it will last a long time), so the pieces can be reassembled. For this reason, a large quantity of Greek art has survived to our day.

Not many cultures can match the Greeks in the elaborate painting of vases. These terra cotta vessels served as grave monuments, storage urns for wine or oil, drinking
15 cups, and so forth. An early example is the so-called *Dipylon Vase*, named for the cemetery in Athens where it was found. Made in the eighth century B.C.E., the *Dipylon Vase* offers a superb example of the geometric style of vase painting. This is the first clearly defined style we know the Greeks followed. The reason for the term "geometric style" is obvious. Much of the vase's decoration consists of
20 geometric lines and patterns, including the "meander" pattern that runs around the top just under the rim. Images of people are simply stick figures, and they are integrated wonderfully into the overall geometric design.

The *Dipylon Vase* offers us information on the burial customs of the Greeks, especially as contrasted with the Egyptians. Objects found in the famous tomb of
25 Pharaoh Tutankhamun (King Tut) indicated he would enjoy a busy and prestigious afterlife, since that is what the Egyptians expected. The Greeks, on the other hand, were not so optimistic. To them, life after death was a gray and shadowy place, of little interest. A funerary urn like the *Dipylon Vase* was placed above the burial spot to receive liquid offerings and was intended to show the respect of the deceased's
30 relatives and friends. A funeral procession is painted on the vase. But there is no provision for enjoyment of the next world, only a recognition of the ones left behind.

Source: *Gilbert's Living with Art* (Getlein)

Note: B.C.E. means *before the common era*—that is, before Year 1 of the Western calendar.

D. COMPREHENSION CHECK Discuss the questions below with a partner.

1. Why are Greek vases so important?

2. What were Greek vases made from? Why did they last so long?

3. Describe the painting style of the *Dipylon Vase* on page 98.

4. What does the *Dipylon Vase* tell us about ancient Greek civilization?

5. How were the ancient Greeks different from the ancient Egyptians?

E. RESPONSE WRITING Choose *one* of these topics. Write about it for 10 minutes. Don't worry about grammar and don't use a dictionary. Just put as many ideas as you can on paper.

• Describe what you know or remember about ancient Greek civilization, Greek myths and legends, or ancient Greek art.
• Compare the *Dipylon Vase* to another work of art, from any time or civilization.
• Have you been to Greece? If so, describe your experience.

PART ② SOCIAL LANGUAGE Greek Art

BEFORE LISTENING

A. THINKING AHEAD You are going to listen to Tanya and a teaching assistant, Doug, talk about one type of Greek art: pottery. Before you listen, look at this photo of Greek pottery. In small groups, discuss the images on it.

As you did in Chapter 3, describe your impressions of the art. Interpret what you see. Remember to trust your instincts: You know more than you think you know. Who might the people be? Where do you think the idea for the picture came from?

Interior of a *kylix*, a drinking cup from around 490–480 B.C.E.

B. GUESSING THE MEANING FROM CONTEXT Read the sentences below. The words and phrases in green are from the conversation. Guess their meanings from the context. Write your guesses on the lines.

1. Greek art **illustrates** many aspects of Greek civilization; for example, a Greek vase now in the Boston Museum of Fine Art shows a scene from one of the Greek myths.

   Guess: _____

2. The ancient Greeks showed their **ideals** in their art; for example, people represented in statues were always perfectly formed, strong-looking, and beautiful.

    Guess: _____

3. Instead of choosing an easy topic to write about, Tanya took the more **challenging** one.

    Guess: _____

4. Tanya found **source information** for her paper in an art book in the library. Both the photos of the pots and the text of the book gave her enough information to write her paper on ancient Greek pottery.

    Guess: _____

5. Greek pots survived because they were **durable**; they were made of a material that could last for a long time.

    Guess: _____

6. Greek pots are very **detailed**. You can see many small things in the scenes such as the weapons and tools that people used, their clothes, and even the way that they wore their hair.

    Guess: _____

Now compare your answers with a partner's answers.

C. VOCABULARY PREPARATION Read the sentences below. The words and phrases in green are from the conversation. Match the definitions in the box with the words and phrases in green. Write the correct letters on the lines.

a. be leaving	d. to use as evidence
b. that existed in	e. You are doing a good thing.
c. that's convenient	

_____ **1.** You chose the most difficult assignment—**good for you**!

_____ **2.** We don't know much about that civilization because we don't have much **to go on**. The objects they created didn't survive.

_____ **3.** I'll **be out of here** by 5:00 P.M., so I can meet you there at 6:00 P.M.

_____ **4.** O.K., **that will work**—I'll see you at 6:00 P.M.

_____ **5.** We have many Greek pots at the museum **dating from** the 8th century, B.C.E.

LISTENING

A. LISTENING FOR THE MAIN IDEA Listen to the conversation. As you listen, think about this question:
• Why does Tanya come to Doug's office?

B. LISTENING FOR DETAILS Listen to part of the conversation again. Listen for information that answers these questions.

1. Why does Tanya need photos of pots? _____

_____

2. Why did Greek pottery survive? _____

_____

3. Where do we get information about ancient Greek civilization? _____

_____

C. LISTENING FOR THE MEANING OF NEW PHRASES Tanya and Doug use some phrases that describe academic life. Listen to parts of their conversation. Listen to each part twice. Guess the meanings of the phrases and write your guesses on the lines.

1. office hours: _____

_____

2. reading list: _____

_____

3. department secretary: _____

_____

AFTER LISTENING

Critical Thinking Strategy ⬭⬭⬭⬭

Acquiring and Applying Background Information

In academic situations, you often need to acquire (get) background information in order to understand new information. For example, it's a good idea to learn about or review Greek myths and legends when you study ancient Greek art. This is because ancient Greek art often depicts (shows) subjects from myths and legends. An important part of Greek mythology is the gods and goddesses. People who study art need to know their Greek and Roman names and the characteristics or activities that they represent.

👥 **A. INFORMATION GAP** With a partner, review the words in the box below. You both will ask and answer questions to complete a chart.

Words	Definitions
prophecy	knowledge of future events
crafts	the art of making everyday objects that people use or wear, such as furniture and jewelry
commerce	business activities
the underworld	according to ancient Greeks' beliefs, the place where people went after death
fertility	the ability to have many children or to produce many crops
blacksmith	a person who makes things from metal, such as horseshoes

Student A

Use the chart on page 249. Ask your partner for the missing information and write the answers in your chart. Take turns asking and answering questions. Refer to the vocabulary box above for help with difficult words.

Example: **A:** What is Aphrodite the goddess of?
B: Love and beauty. What is Aphrodite's Roman name?
A: Venus.

Student B

Turn to page 250. Ask your partner for the missing information and write the answers in your chart. Take turns asking and answering questions. Refer to the vocabulary box above for help with difficult words.

Example: **B:** What's Aphrodite's Roman name?
A: Venus. What is Aphrodite the goddess of?
B: Love and beauty.

B. APPLYING BACKGROUND INFORMATION In small groups, discuss these questions.

1. What myths and legends do you know about the Greek gods and goddesses? Share them with your group.

2. What myths and legends do you know from other ancient cultures or civilizations? Share them with your group.

3. Are there any similarities between the myths and legends of one culture and another? What are they?

4. Can you think of any works of art (from any time or place) that depict gods, goddesses, or stories from ancient myths and legends? If so, describe them to your group.

PART ③ THE MECHANICS OF LISTENING AND SPEAKING

LANGUAGE FUNCTION

Requesting an Explanation
Sometimes in a conversation you have difficulty understanding more than just a word or phrase; you don't understand an idea or a suggestion. When this happens, you need to ask for an explanation.

Examples: **A:** What you need are very good photos of the pottery.

        B: Why?   **Less Formal**
             Well, what's the reason for that?
             Can you tell me why?
             Excuse me, but why is that?
             Excuse me, but why do you say that?
             Excuse me, but would you mind explaining that?   **More Formal**

Note: Adding "excuse me" makes the request more polite.

A. REQUESTING AN EXPLANATION Practice asking for an explanation with a partner. Student A reads the statements below. Student B requests an explanation using one of the expressions in the box on page 104. Then exchange roles.

Example: **A:** You need good photos of Greek pottery.
B: Excuse me, but why is that?

1. Greek pottery is very durable.

2. Unfortunately, we do not have many examples of Greek jewelry.

3. Most of our information about ancient Greek culture comes from studying pots.

4. It's a good idea to review Greek myths and legends when you study ancient Greek art.

5. Ancient Greek statues usually showed men without clothes but women with clothes.

INTONATION

∩ Understanding Interjections

Several interjections in English are common in informal conversation. Interjections are sounds that have meaning. They are very informal. Listen to this one from the conversation:

Doug: Well, what can I do for you?
Tanya: Uh , you know that paper that's due on Friday?

Here are some more examples:

Interjections		Meanings
Uh-huh.	→	Yes. OR You're welcome.
Uh-uh.	→	No.
Huh?	→	What? (Excuse me?)
Uh . . . OR Um . . .	→	I'm thinking. OR I'm not sure what to say.
Uh-oh!	→	I made a mistake. OR There's a problem.

How can you tell *Uh-huh* (meaning "yes") and *Uh-uh* (meaning "no") apart?
Hint: Listen to the stress in each: *Uh-HUH* and *UH-uh.*

B. UNDERSTANDING INTERJECTIONS Listen to each conversation. What does the second speaker mean? Check (✓) the correct answer.

Conversation	Yes	No	You're welcome.	What?/Excuse me?	There's a problem!
1					
2					
3					
4					
5					

C. USING INTERJECTIONS With a partner, follow the directions in the boxes below.

Example: **A:** Have you ever been to Greece?
              B: Uh-huh. (Yes)

Student A

Say the following sentences to your partner. Wait for a response.

1. Have you ever been to Greece?
2. May I borrow your pencil?
3. Thanks a lot!
4. There's a large insect crawling on your shoe.
5. Are you from Egypt?

Then respond to your partner. Use one of the interjections on page 105 in your response.

Student B

Respond to your partner. Use one of the interjections on page 105 in your response.

Then say the following sentences to your partner. Wait for a response.

1. Do you speak Greek?
2. I think we're going to have a big test tomorrow!
3. Are you hungry yet?
4. Could I borrow some money from you?
5. Thank you.

PRONUNCIATION

🎧 /θ/ vs. /s/

The letters *th* have two sounds in English. One of them is /θ/, the sound in *th*anks. To pronounce /θ/, put the tip of your tongue *between* your teeth *just a little* and blow. *Don't stick your tongue between your lips!* If you don't put your tongue between your teeth, the /θ/ sound will sound like /s/. Listen to these contrasts. Can you hear the difference?

/θ/	/s/
thing	sing
think	sink
thank	sank
tenth	tense
eighth	eights

Many ordinal numbers (which we use to refer to time periods in history) contain the /θ/ sound at the end. Here are some examples:

fourth (4th)	seventh (7th)	tenth (10th)
fifth (5th)	eighth (8th)	eleventh (11th)
sixth (6th)	ninth (9th)	twelfth (12th)

Example: It's a Greek pot from the eighth century.

🎧 **D. HEARING THE DIFFERENCE BETWEEN /θ/ AND /s/** In each pair of words, circle the one that you hear.

1. sank	thank		**7.** sick	thick	
2. tense	tenth		**8.** seem	theme	
3. sing	thing		**9.** sigh	thigh	
4. sink	think		**10.** saw	thaw	
5. eights	eighth		**11.** force	fourth	
6. some	thumb		**12.** pass	path	

E. PRONOUNCING /θ/ AND /S/ Work with a partner. Say one of the words on the list. (Don't say the words in order.) Your partner will circle the word. Check each word to see if it matches. If your partner doesn't circle the correct word, try again. Then exchange roles.

sank	thumb	eights	sick	seem
tenth	saw	sing	thing	theme
some	thaw	thick	fourth	pass
sigh	tense	eighth	sink	path
force	thank	thigh	think	

F. PRONOUNCING /θ/ AND /S/ IN SENTENCES Now use words with the /θ/ and /s/ sounds in conversations. Interview your classmates. Use the questions in the box. If a classmate answers *yes*, write his or her name in the chart.

Example: **A:** Do you have something in your pocket?
B: Yes, I have my keys in my pocket.
A: What's your name?
B: Maria.
A: (Writes *Maria* in the chart.) Thanks.

Questions	Classmates
Do you have something in your pocket?	
Are you going to pass all your courses?	
Do you know what happened in the eighth century B.C.E. in Greece?	
Do you think Greek art is interesting?	
Do you like to sing?	
Have you been sick this year?	
Do you know what day the tenth of this month is/was?	

WORDS IN PHRASES

Time Phrases with Ordinal Numbers

Phrases for time periods often consist of an ordinal number (*first*, *second*, etc.), which acts like an adjective, and the noun *century*. You will hear and see many of these in this chapter. It's important to remember these two words *together* (plus the article *the*) to form a time phrase.

Example: It's a Greek pot from **the eighth century.**
                                    adj.   **noun**

PUT IT TOGETHER

REQUESTING AN EXPLANATION Work with a partner. Student A chooses a topic from the box below and makes a statement about it. Student B requests an explanation. Student A gives an explanation. Then exchange roles.

As you speak, use the interjections from the list on page 105 whenever appropriate. Pay attention to the /θ/ sound. Practice using time phrases with ordinal numbers, if possible.

Examples: **A:** I learned that most of the information that we have about ancient Greek civilization comes from pictures on pots.
            B: Excuse me, but why is that?
            A: Uh . . . because the pottery was durable.
            B: Thanks.
            A: Uh-huh.

            B: I like Greek art from the eighth century B.C.E.
            A: Can you tell me why?
            B: Uh . . . I'm interested in ancient Greek culture.
            A: Thanks.
            B: Sure.

---

something interesting I learned so far in this chapter

a famous myth or legend I remember from childhood

my favorite Greek god or goddess

a similarity between a Greek god, goddess, or myth and one from another culture

my favorite time period

what I like/dislike about art from ancient civilizations

why it is/is not important to know about ancient myths and legends

---

PART ④ BROADCAST ENGLISH Ancient Greek Statues

BEFORE LISTENING

A. THINKING AHEAD You are going to hear a radio program about the sculpture of ancient Greece. Before you listen, review with a partner what you learned about sculpture in Chapter 3. Discuss these questions:

• How do sculptors make their works of art?
• What kinds of materials do they use?
• How do you think ancient Greek statues were made?

Roman copy of a Greek original sculpture, about 450–440 B.C.E.

B. GUESSING THE MEANING FROM CONTEXT Read the sentences below. The words and phrases in green are from the radio program. Guess their meanings from the context. Write your guesses on the lines. Then compare your answers with a partner's answers.

1. Factories use **assembly lines**—many people working together—to put together all the pieces of an object.

   Guess: _____

2. I thought that there was only one copy of my vase, but I discovered that it was **mass-produced**.

   Guess: _____

3. Most furniture manufacturers take **custom orders**. For example, you can often choose your own color or pattern to cover a couch.

   Guess: _____

4. After the earthquake, the terra cotta statues broke into a million pieces. The **fragments** were all over the museum floor.

   Guess: _____

5. Some archaeologists thought that the ancient Greeks were **cannibals** because on one pot painting it looked as though people were eating human body parts.

Guess: _____

6. For some medical procedures, patients must be **sedated** so that they won't feel pain.

Guess: _____

C. VOCABULARY PREPARATION Read the sentences below. The words in green are from the radio program. Match the definitions in the box with the words in green. Write the correct letters on the lines.

a. ancient times	c. dug up	e. took apart
b. clay; terra cotta	d. naked	

_____ **1.** Archaeologists learn a lot from **earthenware** pots because the material that the pots are made from is very durable.

_____ **2.** You can learn a lot about history by studying the art of **antiquity**.

_____ **3.** Archaeologists have **unearthed** many ancient Greek statues of gods and goddesses.

_____ **4.** The chef carefully **dismembered** the entire chicken before putting the body parts into boiling water.

_____ **5.** Ancient Greek statues of men usually showed them **nude**.

D. VOCABULARY PREPARATION In the box are some technical terms that you'll need to know before you listen to the radio program. Read the terms and their meanings. Then in small groups, discuss the questions below.

Words	Definitions
smelt; smelted (verb)	Attaching metal pieces to each other to make statues. The sculptor sticks the pieces together using melted metal as a kind of glue.
lost-wax casting (noun)	A method for making metal sculpture. A sculptor builds a mold around a wax object. The wax object matches the shape of the desired sculpture. Then the sculptor heats the mold and the wax melts and is poured out of the mold. The sculptor then pours liquid metal into the mold. Once the metal cools, the mold is taken off the metal sculpture.
endoscope (noun)	A medical instrument. It's a small camera attached to a tube. The tube can go into small or hard-to-reach places (such as the human body or a statue) and take pictures.

1. What is melted metal used for in **smelted** statues?

2. What is similar about **smelting** and **lost-wax casting**? What is different?

3. What kind of person uses an **endoscope** to take pictures of the inside of a human body?

LISTENING

Mt. Olympus ▲
Legendary home
of the gods

THESSALY

Thermopylae

Delphi ▲ Mt. Parnassus
Thebes

ACHAEA

ATTICA • Marathon

Corinth • Athens
Mycenae Parthenon
Olympia • ARCADIA • Epidaurus

PELOPONNESUS

Sparta

LEMNOS

AEGEAN
SEA

LESBOS

AEOLIA

Troy
Story of the Trojan horse

SAMOS

IONIA

DELOS

CYCLADES

NAXOS

RHODES

Greece in the Age of Pericles
c. 440 B.C.

miles
0   100

CRETE • Knossos

MEDITERRANEAN
SEA

Ancient Greece, about 440 B.C.E.

🎧 **A. LISTENING FOR THE MAIN IDEA** Listen to the radio program about ancient Greek statues. As you listen, think about these questions:
• What do people now know about how ancient Greek statues were made? How do they know this?

🎧 **B. LISTENING FOR DETAILS: SECTION 1** Listen to Section 1 and write the answers to these questions on the lines.

1. Does the information about how Greek statues were made make them seem less valuable, in Carol Mattusch's opinion?

_____

_____

2. What did people in the 1800s think about the ancient Greeks when they first saw a pot painting showing the ancient statue workshops?

_____

_____

🎧 **C. LISTENING FOR DETAILS: SECTION 2** Listen to Section 2 and write the answers to these questions on the lines.

1. Why were there three different versions of a statue of Aphrodite, in Mattusch's opinion?

_____

2. What does a beard indicate on a statue of a man from classical times?

_____

Listening Strategy ⬤⬤⬤

Understanding Time Abbreviations

Archaeologists use certain time abbreviations to refer to the past. You might hear some or all of the following when people talk about the ancient world:

Abbreviations for time periods before Year 1 in the Western calendar include these:

B.C.	→	Before Christ
B.C.E.	→	Before the Common Era

Abbreviations for the time periods from Year 1 to the present include these:

A.D.	→	*Anno Domini* (Latin: Year of our Lord)
C.E.	→	Common Era

Note: The years before Year 1 go in reverse order. For example, 800 B.C.E. is earlier in time than 200 B.C.E.

👥 **D. UNDERSTANDING TIME ABBREVIATIONS** A timeline is a type of graphic organizer. With a partner, put the dates in order on the timeline.

440 B.C.E.	200 C.E.	500 A.D.	570 C.E.	400 B.C.	600 B.C.E.

_____ _____ _____ **Year 1** _____ _____ _____

Test-Taking Strategy ⬤⬤⬤

Listening for Time Periods

Standardized tests often ask you to answer questions about the time periods mentioned in short lectures. Therefore, it's important to hear the centuries that a speaker refers to in a history lecture. As you saw in Part 3, we refer to centuries using ordinal numbers. Most of these end in the *th* sound /θ/.

Example: I like Greek pottery from the four**th** century.

It's also important to listen for the abbreviation that means that a date is before or after the Year 1.

Examples: the fourth century B.C.E.   the eighth century C.E.

🎧 **E. LISTENING FOR TIME PERIODS** Listen to an excerpt from the radio program. Fill in the blanks with the correct time period information.

Well, in the _____ and the _____ centuries

_____ in what we would call high classical times, the most popular type of

statue was a naked male.

AFTER LISTENING

👥 **A. DISCUSSION** In small groups, discuss these questions.

1. How did people in the past think Greek statues were made?

2. What do people now know about how ancient Greek statues were made? How do they know this?

3. Do you think that the art historian Carol Mattusch was disappointed when she learned how Greek statues were actually made?

4. What mistaken belief did people in the 1800s have about ancient Greek civilization?

5. Can you think of any other misunderstandings that people have had about a foreign or ancient culture? How did they make the mistake? How did they correct it?

6. Have you ever seen a Greek statue? If so, explain where you saw it, what it looked like, and what you thought of it.

Speaking Strategy 🔵🔵🔵

Correcting a Misunderstanding

In academic discussions, you often have to tell someone that he or she is mistaken (wrong). It's important to do this in a polite way. Starting the correction with an apology ("I'm sorry, but . . .") is the best way to do this. You can correct a misunderstanding formally or informally, depending on the situation.

Example: **Sorry.** That's not right. It's a robe, not a dress.   **Less Formal**
I'm sorry, but you're mistaken. It's a robe, not a dress.   ↓
I'm sorry, but I think you're mistaken. It's a robe, not a dress.
I'm sorry, but I'm afraid you may be mistaken. It's a robe, not a dress.   **More Formal**

B. USING ART TO ANALYZE A CIVILIZATION Archaeologists often study art, for example, pots and statues, to learn about ancient civilizations. You are going to do the same thing. Follow these steps.

Step 1

1. Divide into two groups: Civilization X and Civilization Y. These imaginary civilizations will create art.

2. The two groups should meet at opposite ends of the classroom.

3. In each group, choose two kinds of art, for example, sculpture, pottery, or painting.

4. Choose an important idea, activity, or kind of person that represents your culture.
   Examples: **Idea:** In our culture, people believe that only women fight in wars.
   Activity: Sports and games are important in our culture.
   Person: In our culture, leaders always have long hair.

5. Have an artistic member of your group draw the two art objects. Each object should clearly show the idea, activity, or person that you chose to represent your culture.

Step 2

1. Now you are groups of modern archaeologists. Exchange drawings.

2. In your group, guess what the other civilization's art object says about its culture.

3. Report your guesses to the other group. Correct any misunderstandings. Use phrases from the Speaking Strategy box on page 114.

4. As a class, discuss the process of analyzing a civilization through its art. Is the process a good idea? Why or why not?

PART ⑤ ACADEMIC ENGLISH Ancient Greek Art

BEFORE LISTENING

A. THINKING AHEAD You are going to listen to a lecture about ancient Greek art. You have already seen and heard about two kinds of Greek art: pottery and statues. In the lecture, you will hear about these again, plus an additional type of art. In small groups, discuss what other kind of art may have survived since ancient times. (Hint: It's something that people wear.)

B. PREDICTING Look at the pictures on pages 120–123. The lecturer will discuss these works of art in the lecture. Before you listen, think about how the lecturer might use these visual images. Discuss each one with a partner.

1. **Figure 1 (page120):** Do you recognize this building? Where is it?

2. **Figure 2 (page 121):** Why do you think this statue is nude?

3. **Figure 3 (page 121):** How is this statue different from Figure 2?

4. Figure 4 (page 122): What can you see in the painting on this vase?

5. Figure 5 (page 122): What can you see in the painting on this vase?

6. Figure 6 (page 123): On what part of the body do you think ancient Greeks wore this object?

C. GUESSING THE MEANING FROM CONTEXT Read the sentences below. The words and phrases in green are from the lecture. Guess their meanings from the context. Write your guesses on the lines.

1. The goddess Athena Parthenos was very important to the ancient Greeks. That's why they built the Parthenon and **dedicated** it to her.

   Guess: _____

2. The ancient Greeks had a lot of **admiration** for the human body. We can see this in the perfectly formed statues that they created.

   Guess: _____

3. The subject of the statue was probably very strong: his **musculature** was very clearly carved by the sculptor.

   Guess: _____

4. Sorry, I can't think of an example of ancient Greek jewelry; nothing **comes to mind**.

   Guess: _____

5. A Greek vase called a *kylix*, or cup, is an example of a **utilitarian** art object. People used them every day in their homes.

   Guess: _____

6. We know that some people were buried with their jewelry because archaeologists have found it with them in their **tombs**.

   Guess: _____

7. They **excavated** an ancient burial site to find old jewelry. After they dug a big hole, they found beautiful objects made from gold.

   Guess: _____

Now compare your answers with a partner's answers.

👥 **D. VOCABULARY PREPARATION** In the box are some technical terms that you'll need to know before you listen to the lecture. Read the terms and their meanings. Then in small groups, discuss the questions below.

Words	Definitions
glazing (noun)	A coating painted onto ceramic pots. It becomes glassy (hard and shiny, like glass) when it is heated.
kiln (noun)	An oven in which ceramic pots are heated. The heat makes them permanently hard.

1. What are three objects that have **glazing**?

2. Is a **kiln** exactly the same as the oven in a normal kitchen? How is it different?

LISTENING

🎧 **A. LISTENING FOR THE MEANING OF NEW WORDS** Listen to these words in sentences from the lecture. You'll hear each sentence twice. Write the definitions that you hear on the lines.

1. kouros: _____

_____

2. kore: _____

_____

3. contrapposto: _____

_____

4. torques: _____

_____

5. diadems: _____

_____

Listening Strategy

🎧 Using Phonetic Symbols

You are going to hear several Greek names in the lecture. They may be foreign sounding and you may not know how to spell them when you hear them. You can write foreign-sounding names phonetically, that is, using letters or symbols that represent sounds. One system that you can use is the IPA (International Phonetic Alphabet). Here are some examples of words from this chapter transcribed using IPA symbols:

Parthenon	/'par θə nan/		Actaeon	/'æk te an/
Dipylon	/'di pə lan/		Olympia	/o 'lɪm pi ə/
Athena	/ə 'θi nə/		Pergamon	/'pɚ gə man/
kouros	/'ku ros/		Laocoon	/le 'o ko an/
Hephaestus	/hə 'fɛs təs/		Andokides	/æn 'do kə diz/
Delphi*	/'dɛl fi/		Artemis	/'ar tə mɪs/
kore	/'kɔr re/			

*Also (in English): /'dɛl fai/

🎧 **B. USING PHONETIC SYMBOLS** Listen to parts of the lecture. Use symbols to write the names you hear on the lines. Use any symbols that you want. You'll hear each part twice.

1. **Archaic:** _____

2. **Aphrodite:** _____

3. **Praxiteles:** _____

4. **Knidos:** _____

Listening Strategy

Getting the Main Idea from the Introduction

Speakers often introduce a lecture by explaining exactly what they are going to cover (discuss). Getting the main idea of the lecture from the introduction helps you focus on getting the details that support the main idea.

Examples: Today, I'm going to **cover** the art of the 1960s and 1970s.
Today, I'm going to **discuss** the art of the 1960s and 1970s.
Today, I'm going to **talk about** the art of the 1960s and 1970s.

C. GETTING THE MAIN IDEA FROM THE INTRODUCTION Listen to the introduction to the lecture and think about this question:

• What three kinds of Greek art will the speaker discuss in this lecture?

Listening Strategy

Taking Notes: Timelines

There are different ways to take lecture notes. Some ways depend on your thinking style. Some depend on the topic of the lecture. Sometimes it is a good idea to use a timeline to take notes when you are listening to a history or art history lecture.

A timeline is a vertical or horizontal line with dates on it in **chronological order** (time order). Next to (or below) the dates, you can write down names of the people, objects, or events associated with the dates. Look at this timeline of art movements in Europe from the 1700s to the present:

1750	1800	1875	1900	2000
Neoclassicism	Romanticism	Impressionism	Expressionism	Neo-Expressionism

D. TAKING NOTES: TIMELINES Listen to Section 1. Complete the chart below with the time periods that you hear. (The lecturer doesn't give the periods in chronological order, so building a timeline will help.)

Time Periods (in chronological order)		
Geometric	*900* –	*700*
Orientalizing	–	
Archaic	–	
Classical	–	
Hellenistic	–	

Now fill out the timeline below with the information from the box. Write the dates above the line and the time periods below the line.

E. TAKING NOTES: USING AN OUTLINE Listen to the lecture. It's in four sections. You will listen to each section twice. Fill in as much of the outline as you can. Don't worry if you can't fill in everything. (You'll listen to the whole lecture again later.)

As you listen, look at the art that accompanies each section. Notice the use of key words and abbreviations in the outline instead of complete sentences. Practice completing the notes in this way.

Ancient Greek Art

Section 1

I. Introduction

   A. Parthenon as an example of ancient Greek art

      1. Built between _____

      2. Dedicated to _____

      3. Located on _____

   B. 5 periods in Greek art

      1. Classical–dates: _____

      2. Geometric–dates: _____

      3. Orientalizing–dates _____

      4. Archaic–dates: _____

      5. Hellenistic–dates: _____

Figure 1: The Parthenon, Athens, Greece

Section 2

II. Greek Sculpture

  A. Basic characteristics

    1. 3 positions _____

    _____

    _____

    2. Difference btwn male & female figs: _____

    _____

    _____

    3. Earliest _____

    sculpted by Praxiteles for the city of Knidos, Asia Minor.

    4. Kouros = _____

    _____

    5. Kore = _____

    _____

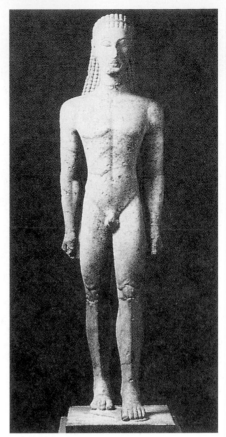

Figure 2: A *Kouros*

Figure 3: *The Spear Bearer*

  B. Classical Period vs. Hellenistic Period

    1. Classical period

      a. *The Spear Bearer:* musculature becomes _____

      _____

      _____

      b. Contrapposto = _____

      _____

      _____

      c. In Hellenistic period, _____

      _____

      _____

III. Vase Painting

    A. Description

        1. Subject matter: _____

        2. Made by: _____

        3. Uses: _____

    B. Techniques

        1. Artists perfected different techniques of: _____

        2. Purpose of glaze: _____

            _____

        3. Decorated with bands that: _____

            _____

    C. Styles in different periods

        1. Geometric period

          a. Vases have _____ designs

          b. Figs. appear: _____

        2. In Archaic period, painters use _____

          which is _____

        3. Later, Andokides developed _____

        _____ technique

Figure 4: A *Dipylon* Vase

Figure 5: *Artemis Slaying Actaeon* from the Bell Krater

Section 4

IV. Jewelry

    A. Who wore it: _____

    B. Type: _____

    C. Much didn't survive because:

        _____

        _____

Figure 6: A Diadem, late fourth century

    D. Some jewelry has survived. Exs.:

        1. _____

        2. _____

        3. _____

V. Conclusion

    A. Because of _____, Gk. art exported throughout the Mediterranean

    B. Gk. ideals carried to the _____ and everywhere else that

        _____ went.

Source: Adapted from a lecture by Dr. Jacqueline A. Frank, Ph.D

F. CHECKING YOUR NOTES Listen to the lecture again. As you listen, review your notes and fill in any missing information.

AFTER LISTENING

Speaking Strategy

Interpreting Time Periods

Sometimes a speaker will refer to a time period precisely, for example, "between 480 and 320 B.C.E." Sometimes, however, a speaker may refer to a time period more generally, for example, "the third century." Century numbers are one less than the hundred year period that they correspond to. For example, 430 B.C.E. is in the fifth century B.C.E., and 320 C.E. is the second century. It's a good idea to be able to go back and forth from specific to general time periods when you are listening to a history lecture.

A. INTERPRETING TIME PERIODS Work with a partner. Use the time periods in the chart on page 119 or make up your own. Say a specific time period to your partner. Your partner will say the corresponding century. Then exchange roles.

Example: **A says:** 950 B.C.E.
           B says: the tenth century

B. USING YOUR NOTES Work in small groups and use your notes to discuss these questions about the lecture.

1. What three kinds of Greek art does the speaker discuss in this lecture?

2. What does Greek sculpture tell us about the Greek feeling about the human body?

3. What were Greek vases used for?

4. What did the paintings on the earliest Greek pots look like?

5. What are the two main techniques of pot design?

6. What kind of jewelry did the ancient Greeks wear? Who wore it?

C. MAKING CONNECTIONS Think about the reading in Part 1, the radio program in Part 4, and the lecture in Part 5. In small groups, discuss this question:

• Are there any examples of the influence of ancient Greek ideals on art, architecture, or design at your school or in your community? If so, explain how they are examples of Greek artistic ideas.

PUT IT ALL TOGETHER

GIVING A PRESENTATION You are going to give a short presentation on an example of ancient Greek art.

Step 1
Select one of the pieces of art on this page or on page 125.

Agesander, Athenodorus, and Polydorus of Rhodes,
Laocoon Group, late second century B.C.E.

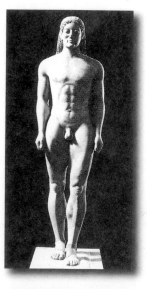

Kroisos, about 525 B.C.E.

The Three Goddesses, about 438–432 B.C.E.

You are going to present the work of art that you chose. When you present your piece of art, make sure you:
• describe it
• say what period it is from (Hellenistic, Classical, etc.)
• explain what it tells us about ancient Greek civilization

 Step 2

You can find out more about Greek art in an art book or at an online museum. If you do Internet research, the following museum websites might be helpful:
• Hellenic Ministry of Culture: National Archaeological Museum of Athens
• The Beazley Archive
• The Getty Museum

As you do research, use an outline like the one you saw on pages 120–123 to take notes and to plan your presentation.

Speaking Strategy

Giving a Presentation from Notes

When you give a presentation, it's better to speak from notes than to read your information word for word from a piece of paper.

One way to do this is to make a detailed outline of what you want to discuss. Although your outline should be detailed, don't write down complete sentences. Next, memorize your outline. Then make a less detailed outline, with just the main points (for example, the Roman numeral headings and the capital letter headings). See if you can remember the missing details. Finally, make an outline with only the Roman numeral headings. When you can give your presentation by just glancing at these headings, you're ready to speak in front of the class. This way, you can make eye contact and be a more interesting speaker.

Step 3

Form new small groups, give your presentations. Use your notes. Remember to make eye contact. After you listen to each presentation, ask questions to request further explanation.

UNIT ② VOCABULARY WORKSHOP

Review vocabulary items that you learned in Chapters 3 and 4.

A. MATCHING Match the definitions to the words and phrases. Write the correct letters on the lines.

Words and Phrases	Definitions
_____ **1.** antiquity	**a.** understand it
_____ **2.** excavated	**b.** pieces
_____ **3.** fragments	**c.** confused
_____ **4.** get it	**d.** ancient times
_____ **5.** illustrates	**e.** a female figure
_____ **6.** kore	**f.** ordinary
_____ **7.** lost	**g.** art that has a simple shape and is usually made of one material
_____ **8.** minimalist art	**h.** dug up
_____ **9.** mundane	**i.** shows
_____ **10.** realism	**j.** art that shows things as they really are

B. TRUE OR FALSE? Read the statements below. Circle *T* if the sentence is true. Circle *F* if the sentence is false.

1. A **challenging** assignment is an easy one.   T   F

2. If a type of art is **big**, not many people like it.   T   F

3. **Cannibals** are people who eat people.   T   F

4. A **kouros** is a statue of a female.   T   F

5. **Tombs** are places where people are buried.   T   F

6. A **landscape** is a painting of a person.   T   F

7. If something is **banal**, it isn't very exciting.   T   F

8. If you **dismembered** something, you put it together.   T   F

9. The god of **prophecy** has knowledge of future events.   T   F

10. If a work of art is an example of **photorealism**, it looks a lot like a photograph.   T   F

C. WHICH WORD DOESN'T BELONG? In each row, cross out the word without a connection to the other words.

1. kouros ~~diadem~~ kore

2. sketch sculpture realism

3. Aphrodite Apollo Archaic

4. mundane innovative banal

5. excavated dismembered unearthed

6. minimalism torque photorealism

7. reduces depicts illustrates

8. streamlined geometric nude

D. THE ACADEMIC WORD LIST In the boxes below are some of the most common *academic* words in English. Fill in the blanks with words from these boxes. When you finish, check your answers in the readings on page 65 (for Items 1–5) and page 99 (for Items 6–14).

coincidence	computer	concepts	elements	proportion

Michael Cassidy

Cassidy's posters begin as paintings. He works on a large scale—his canvases can be seven feet (2.1 meters) high. He starts with a charcoal sketch (drawing) and then fills it in with oil paints. When he finishes, he photographs the painting, scans it into a _____ , and then prints it using an inkjet printer.

1

It's not a _____ that Cassidy has been a surfer all of his life. Surfing is a

2

sport of balance and _____ . In other words, the surfer must consider the size

3

and shape of the board, the wave, and him- or herself in order to be successful. Cassidy uses these

_____ in his art. In the poster *Waikiki Surf Festival*, for example, Cassidy uses

4

only a few simple _____ (things or parts) to send a message: the waves, the

5

sky, Diamond Head in the background and, in the front, the single figure, balanced and confident.

assume	major	produced
classics	periods	survived
contemporary	philosophy	works

Greek Civilization and Art

No doubt a _____ (6) reason that we respect the ancient Greeks is that they excelled in many different fields. Their political ideas serve as a model for _____ (7) democracy. Their poetry and drama and _____ (8) survive as living _____ (9). Their architecture and sculpture have influenced most later _____ (10) in the history of Western art.

We _____ (11) that the Greeks' genius shone equally in painting, but we know very little about this because most painted _____ (12) have been lost. We would know even less, except that a large number of painted clay vases were _____ (13) from about the eighth century B.C.E. These pots were made from terra cotta (baked clay), an extremely strong material; it can break, but it won't disintegrate (in other words, it will last a long time), so the pieces can be reassembled. For this reason, a large quantity of Greek art has _____ (14) to our day.

UNIT 3

●●●●● PSYCHOLOGY

Chapter 5
States of Consciousness

Chapter 6
Abnormal Psychology

States of Consciousness

Discuss these questions:
- What happens while we sleep?
- What happens while we dream?
- What do dreams mean? Do you pay attention to your dreams?

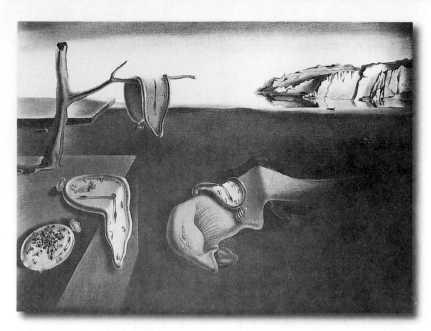

The Persistence of Memory by Salvador Dali

A. THINKING AHEAD Discuss these questions with a partner.

1. What do you think dreams mean? What do you know about dream **interpretation** (analysis)?

2. Have you ever dreamed that you were flying? What do you think this kind of dream means?

3. If people dream about flying and have difficulty staying **aloft** (up in the air), what do you think that means? What does it mean if people keep bumping into things in their flying dreams? What does it mean if they feel that they are flying to get away from danger?

B. READING Read a letter from the website: Ask the Dream Doctor. On this website, people describe dreams to the Dream Doctor, a psychologist. He interprets the dreams. As you read, think about this question:

• What's the Dream Doctor's interpretation of Jenny's dream?

Jenny's Dream

Dear Dream Doctor,

Ever since I was about seven years old, I have had the same dream. I am flying in the air, but I always have trouble staying up. I never touch the ground, but it is difficult for me to keep my arms flapping to stay up in the air. Sometimes I hit
5 electrical power lines or just barely miss them. Usually when I am flying, it is to get away from someone! I am 20 years old now, and I have had this dream maybe once or twice a week since the age of seven. Please help me understand this dream!

—Jenny, Age 20

San Francisco

10 Hi Jenny,

Many people enjoy flying dreams. However, not all flying dreams are the same. Some are exhilarating and are accompanied by a sense of power and freedom—we fly easily and are thrilled by the view below us. In others, however, like yours, we have difficulty staying aloft and seem to be flying in order to escape danger.

15 Power lines are a recurring (repeating) symbol in flying dreams. Dreamers frequently write of "trying to fly above the power lines" or of bumping into them. I believe that *how* we are flying in our dreams—whether we are soaring easily or struggling to stay aloft—is an indication of our personal sense of power.

Because flying dreams recur so frequently for you, I suggest that you try to create
20 the association in your mind that, whenever you are flying, you must be dreaming. The activity of flying can serve as a reminder that you must be dreaming, which will then allow you to explore your dream consciously—this is also known as lucid dreaming.

Your dream suggests that your life right now may be something of a "struggle to stay aloft." Once you recognize that you are dreaming, why don't you ask yourself in
25 the dream what the power lines that you keep bumping into represent? I would be interested to know your response in the dream to your question. In the meantime, what, or who, do you think the power lines symbolize? Whatever it is, I think it is a situation you want to get on top of (get control of).

Source: "Ask the Dream Doctor" (McPhee)

C. DISCUSSION In small groups, discuss these questions.

1. Do you agree with the Dream Doctor's interpretation of Jenny's dream? Why or why not?

2. Do you have recurring dreams? If so, describe one. What do you think the dream means? Why do you think it recurs?

3. The Dream Doctor refers to lucid dreaming. Describe what you think this means in your own words. Have you had a lucid dream?

D. RESPONSE WRITING Choose *one* of these topics. Write about it for 10 minutes. Don't worry about grammar and don't use a dictionary. Just put as many ideas as you can on paper.

• Do you think that dreams have meaning? What is the purpose of dreaming? Explain your answer.
• Describe an unusual or recurring dream that you have had. Explain what you think it means.
• What are the advantages and disadvantages of having a psychologist interpret a person's dreams?

PART ② SOCIAL LANGUAGE Do You Remember Your Dreams?

BEFORE LISTENING

A. THINKING AHEAD You are going to listen to Chrissy interview people on the street. She's going to ask them if they remember their dreams. In small groups, discuss these questions.
• Do you remember your dreams? If you don't, do you know why not?

B. PREDICTING You are going to listen to six people answer the question: "Do you remember your dreams?" What do you think most people will say? Do most people remember their dreams? In small groups, make predictions about the interviews.

C. VOCABULARY PREPARATION Read the sentences below. The words and phrases in green are from the interviews. Match the definitions in the box with the words and phrases in green. Write the correct letters on the lines.

a. a 26.4 mile (42.9 km) foot race	d. was able to
b. became	e. without any advance notice, unexpectedly
c. situation comedy: a type of TV program where people resolve difficult situations in funny ways	

_____ **1.** Last night I dreamed that I ran in a **marathon** and won! That's pretty strange, considering that, in the dream, I had a broken leg.

_____ **2.** Even though I had a broken leg, I **managed to** win the race because I flapped my arms and flew over all the other runners.

_____ **3.** I had a very funny dream last night. I think I had it because I went to sleep right after watching my favorite **sitcom**.

_____ **4.** I haven't seen my friend Jim in years, but I had a dream about him last night. Then, **from out of the blue**, he called me today.

_____ **5.** I dreamed that I found a hundred dollar bill on the street. When I reached down to pick it up, it **turned into** a snake and bit me.

LISTENING

🎧 **A. LISTENING FOR THE MAIN IDEA** Listen to the interviews. As you listen, think about this question:
• Are most of the people able to remember their dreams?

🎧 **B. LISTENING FOR DETAILS** Listen again. Which speakers remember their dreams? Circle *Yes* or *No* in
the chart below.

Speakers	Remember?	Answers	Frequencies
1	(Yes) / No	Yeah.	(All the time) / Most of the time / Some of the time
2	Yes / No		All the time / Most of the time / Some of the time
3	Yes / No		All the time / Most of the time / Some of the time
4	Yes / No		All the time / Most of the time / Some of the time
5	Yes / No		All the time / Most of the time / Some of the time

Listen again. This time, listen for how often people remember their dreams. In other words, do they remember them *All the time*, *Most of the time*, or *Some of the time*? Write down their exact answer in the chart on page 135 and then circle one of the options in the *Frequencies* column.

C. LISTENING FOR DETAILS Listen to some of the speakers describing their dreams. As you listen, answer these questions. Write your answers on the lines.

1. **Speaker 1:** What did she do in Japan?

_____

_____

2. **Speaker 3:** What kind of dreams does she usually remember?

_____

_____

3. **Speaker 4:** What happened to the papers on her desk?

_____

_____

4. **Speaker 5:** What did he dream about?

_____

_____

5. **Speaker 6:** How does she respond?

_____

_____

AFTER LISTENING

Critical Thinking Strategy

Interpreting Symbols

Interpreting is giving meaning to something. Students are often asked to interpret symbols in academic subjects such as literature and anthropology.

When you interpret something, say what you think it means. Remember that one person may interpret something one way and another person may interpret it another way. There are no right or wrong interpretations. Here are some expressions for making interpretations.

Examples: **I think** a dream about birds **means** that you'll have good luck.
                    A black bird **might represent** death.
                    For me, birds **symbolize** freedom.
                    A bird **could be a symbol of** your soul or spirit.

A. INTERPRETING SYMBOLS In small groups, use the chart below to discuss this question:
• In Part 1, you read about a common dream theme, flying. In the interviews, Speaker 4 describes a dream about snakes, a common dream symbol. What are some more common dream themes and symbols?

Write some common dream themes and symbols in the chart below. Then discuss possible interpretations for each. Think about psychological, cultural, and common sense interpretations. Write your ideas in the *Possible Interpretations* column.

Dream Themes/Symbols	Possible Interpretations
Flying	Desire for freedom, desire to travel
Snakes	

 B. INTERPRETING DREAMS In the same small group, create a dream scenario (description). Use typical dream themes and symbols from your discussion in Activity A. Make your group's dream as fantastic, strange, or scary as you want. Use your imagination. Write it down or write enough details so that you can describe it later.

Then choose one group member to describe the dream to the class. As you listen to each group's dream, take notes.

Next, in your small group, use your notes to interpret each group's dream. Refer to the chart you made in Activity A for interpretation ideas.

LANGUAGE FUNCTION

Avoiding Answering Questions

Sometimes you don't want to answer a question that someone asks you. There are many reasons not to answer a question: It seems impolite to you; it makes you uncomfortable; you're not sure how to answer it; or you simply don't have time to answer it. There are many ways to avoid answering questions in polite ways.

Example: **A:** May I ask you a question? Do you remember your dreams?
                B: I'd rather not answer that.
                      I'd prefer not to answer.
                      I'm not interested in discussing that.
                      Sorry, that's personal.
                      Sorry, I don't have time.

A. AVOIDING ANSWERING QUESTIONS Below are some questions that many people in North America find impolite and don't want to answer. Work with a partner. Student A asks each question. Student B gives one of the answers in the box above to avoid answering the question. Then exchange roles.

Example: **A:** How much do you weigh?
                B: I'd rather not say.

1. How much do you weigh?

2. How much money do you earn?

3. What score did you get on the exam?

4. What is your religion?

5. How old are you?

PRONUNCIATION

> ⌒) *Can* vs. *Can't*
>
> It's sometimes difficult to hear the difference between *can* and *can't*, especially when people speak quickly. However, in statements, most people shorten the vowel sound in *can* and lengthen it in *can't*.
>
> **Examples:** You **can** come with us if you want.
> Sure, you **can** say that.
> Sorry, I **can't** go. I've got homework.
> No, you **can't** say that.

⌒) **B. HEARING THE DIFFERENCE BETWEEN *Can* AND *Can't*** Check (✓) the statement that you hear.

1. _____ You can ask me that.

_____ You can't ask me that.

2. _____ I can see over your head.

_____ I can't see over your head.

3. _____ She can come with us.

_____ She can't come with us.

4. _____ Mike can sing very well.

_____ Mike can't sing very well.

5. _____ I can understand French.

_____ I can't understand French.

6. _____ They can hear you.

_____ They can't hear you.

👥 **C. PRONOUNCING *Can* AND *Can't*** Practice saying *can* and *can't* with a partner. Say either statement *a* or *b* below. Your partner will circle the letter of the statement that he or she hears. Check to be sure the correct letter is circled. Then exchange roles.

1. a. You can ask me that.

b. You can't ask me that.

2. a. I can see over your head.

b. I can't see over your head.

3. a. She can come with us.

b. She can't come with us.

4. a. Mike can sing very well.

b. Mike can't sing very well.

5. a. I can understand French.

b. I can't understand French.

6. a. They can hear you.

b. They can't hear you.

🎧 Verbs Ending in -ed

The -ed verb ending is pronounced three different ways. It is pronounced as an extra syllable /ɪd/ or as /t/ or as /d/. The pronunciation of -ed depends on the last *sound* of the simple form of the verb.

1. Pronounce -ed as an extra syllable /ɪd/ when the simple form of the verb ends in a /t/ or /d/ sound.

   Examples: wai**t** → wait**ed**   nee**d** → need**ed**

2. Pronounce -ed as /t/ when the simple form of the verb ends with a voiceless consonant sound (/f/, /k/, /p/, /s/, /ʃ/, /tʃ/, /ks/).

   Examples: lau**gh** → laugh**ed** (gh = /f/)   cra**sh**   → crash**ed** (sh = /ʃ/)
                wal**k** → walk**ed**   wat**ch**   → watch**ed** (ch = /tʃ/)
                wra**p** → wrapp**ed**   fa**x**   → fax**ed** (x = /ks/)
                mi**ss** → miss**ed**

3. Pronounce -ed as /d/ when the simple form of the verb ends with a voiced consonant sound (/b/, /g/, /dʒ/, /m/, /n/, /ŋ/, /l/, /r/, /ð/, /v/, /z/) or a vowel sound.

   Examples: descri**be** → describ**ed**   ca**ll**   → call**ed**
                bra**g**   → bragg**ed**   orde**r** → order**ed**
                ju**dge**   → judg**ed** (dg = /dʒ/) ba**the** → bath**ed** (th = /ð/)
                na**me**   → nam**ed**   wa**ve** → wav**ed**
                rai**n**   → rain**ed**   bu**zz** → buzz**ed**
                ba**ng**   → bang**ed** (ng = /ŋ/)   pl**ay** → play**ed**

Note: The pronunciation of -ed depends on the last *sound* of the simple form of the verb, not on the last letter.

🎧 **D. VERBS ENDING IN -ed** Listen to the following simple past tense verbs. Do you hear /ɪd/, /t/, or /d/? Check (✓) the sound that you hear.

	/ɪd/	/t/	/d/			/ɪd/	/t/	/d/
1. studied	____	____	____	**7.** called		____	____	____
2. ripped	____	____	____	**8.** molded		____	____	____
3. raided	____	____	____	**9.** looked		____	____	____
4. hitched	____	____	____	**10.** traded		____	____	____
5. aimed	____	____	____	**11.** sprayed		____	____	____
6. weaved	____	____	____	**12.** skated		____	____	____

E. SAYING VERBS ENDING IN –ed Work with a partner. Decide on the pronunciation of the words below. Practice saying them and write /ɪd/, /t/, or /d/ on the lines.

_____ 1. turned	_____ 7. interviewed	_____ 13. pressed
_____ 2. pointed	_____ 8. evaluated	_____ 14. dreamed
_____ 3. thanked	_____ 9. switched	_____ 15. heated
_____ 4. appreciated	_____ 10. sewed	_____ 16. clothed
_____ 5. valued	_____ 11. kissed	_____ 17. sailed
_____ 6. admired	_____ 12. analyzed	_____ 18. changed

F. SAYING VERBS ENDING IN –ed IN SENTENCES Now use words with the three sounds of the -ed ending (/ɪd/, /t/, and /d/) in conversations. Interview your classmates. Use the questions in the box. If a classmate answers *yes*, write his or her name in the chart.

Example: **A:** Have you ever ask**ed** someone an embarrassing question?
B: Yes.
A: Great. How do you spell your name?

Questions	Classmates
Have you ever interview**ed** a famous person?	
Have you ever ask**ed** someone an embarrassing question?	
Have you ever wait**ed** in line to see a movie?	
Have you ever analyz**ed** someone else's dreams?	
Have you ever collect**ed** stamps as a hobby?	
Have you ever sail**ed** across an ocean?	
Have you ever camp**ed** on a beach?	

WORDS IN PHRASES

Verb Phrases with Prepositions

Verbs phrases are often verbs and prepositions that go together. It's important to remember these two words *together*. Notice the prepositions in these verb phrases:

sailed across/to	I dreamed I **sailed across** the ocean.
turned over	Kelly **turned over** a rock and saw a snake.
dreamed about	Eric **dreamed about** a scary monster.
headed for	I **headed for** home after school.
asked about	I **asked about** the homework assignment.
bragged about	Have you ever **bragged about** your grades?
called up	Have you ever **called up** an old boyfriend or girlfriend?

G. VERB PHRASES WITH PREPOSITIONS Talk with a partner about a dream you had recently. If you can't think of a dream, talk about a trip that you went on. Use verb phrases with prepositions.

PUT IT TOGETHER

Speaking Strategy

Avoiding Impolite Questions

Some questions are polite if a close friend asks them, but not if a stranger asks them. For example, you might tell a friend how much you weigh but not someone you've just met.

Also, some questions are polite in one situation but not in another. For example, a friend can ask you in private what you did on your date last night, but he or she shouldn't ask about such things in front of the class.

Finally, questions that are polite in one culture may be considered impolite in another. For example, in some countries, it's O.K. to ask people how much money they make, but in North America, this is considered an impolite (rude) question.

A. IMPOLITE QUESTIONS In small groups, discuss these questions. Have one member of your group write down your answers.

1. What are three questions that can be polite or impolite, depending on who is asking them?

2. What are three questions that can be polite or impolite, depending on the situation?

3. What are three questions that may be polite in some countries, but are impolite in North America?

4. What are three questions that may be polite in North America, but are rude in other countries?

Now share your answers with the class.

B. ASKING AND AVOIDING IMPOLITE QUESTIONS Take turns asking questions and avoiding answering questions with a partner. Get ideas for questions from the lists that the class made in Activity A.

Use the statements for avoiding answering questions in the box on page 138. Pay attention to the pronunciation of *can* and *can't*, if applicable. Use verb phrases with prepositions, if possible.

BEFORE LISTENING

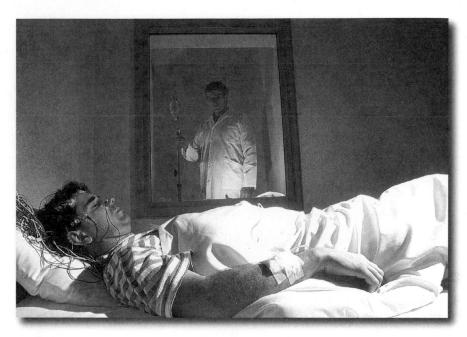

A sleep research lab

A. THINKING AHEAD You are going to listen to a radio program about one theory on why we sleep. In small groups, discuss these questions.

1. Why do we sleep, in your opinion?

2. About what percent of our lives do we spend asleep?

3. What do you think happens if a person doesn't get enough sleep?

B. PREDICTING Before you listen, make a prediction about what you are going to hear. Discuss this question with a partner:
• According to the latest theories, is dreaming a message from our unconscious minds or simply the result of brain activity while we sleep?

1. Most sleep researchers agree that sleep has a **restorative** purpose, but they disagree on whether sleep refreshes the mind or the body.

   Guess: _____

2. The basketball player's energy was completely **depleted** after the big game, so she drank a lot of juice to get her energy back.

   Guess: _____

3. "Don't **deprive** us of sleep," Joe told his noisy neighbors. "Turn that music down!"

   Guess: _____

4. My energy **reserves** are low, but I'll get my energy level back to normal if I eat something.

   Guess: _____

5. Julian's a good **mimic**; he can talk just like Mickey Mouse!

   Guess: _____

6. **Glucose** is a type of sugar in the blood that the body uses for energy.

   Guess: _____

7. Brian spends the **bulk** of his time—about 12 hours a day—working on his novel.

   Guess: _____

D. VOCABULARY PREPARATION Read the sentences below. The words and phrases in green are from the radio program. Match the definitions in the box with the words and phrases in green. Write the correct letters on the lines.

a. doing the correct thing	**d. using up (depleting) power or energy**
b. figured out; solved	**e. your imagination**
c. use up (deplete) supplies	

_____ **1.** It took them years to understand the code, but they finally **cracked** it.

_____ **2.** I was having trouble with that problem, but I'm **on the right track** now.

_____ **3.** Jenny isn't really angry with you—it's **all in your head**!

_____ **4.** Don't leave the car lights on! We're **running down** the battery.

_____ **5.** Whenever I have a big research paper to turn in, I **run out of** paper. Then I have to go to the office supply store.

LISTENING

Listening Strategy

Understanding Scientific Terms

In a radio or TV program about a technical or scientific subject, the speakers usually explain or define difficult terms for the audience. Often the explanations are general or simplified because the audience doesn't have to know the exact definitions in order to understand the main ideas of the program. It's important not to worry when you don't understand a scientific term exactly.

Example: **You hear:** "There's a chemical in the brain called adenosine that's released when energy stores are depleted."
You understand: That adenosine is a chemical in the brain.

In the example above, you might not know exactly what adenosine is, but you do know that it's a chemical in the brain. That's probably all you need to know to understand the program.

Note: In some academic settings, such as biology class, it's *very* important to understand new scientific terms you hear.

🎧 **A. UNDERSTANDING SCIENTIFIC TERMS** Listen to parts of the program. Listen for explanations of the scientific terms below. You'll hear each explanation twice. Write on the lines what you think the terms mean.

1. glycogen: _____

_____

2. glial cells: _____

_____

3. non-REM sleep: _____

_____

4. REM sleep: _____

_____

🎧 **B. LISTENING FOR THE MAIN IDEA** Listen to the radio program. As you listen, think about this question:
• According to sleep researcher Craig Heller, what is the purpose of sleep?

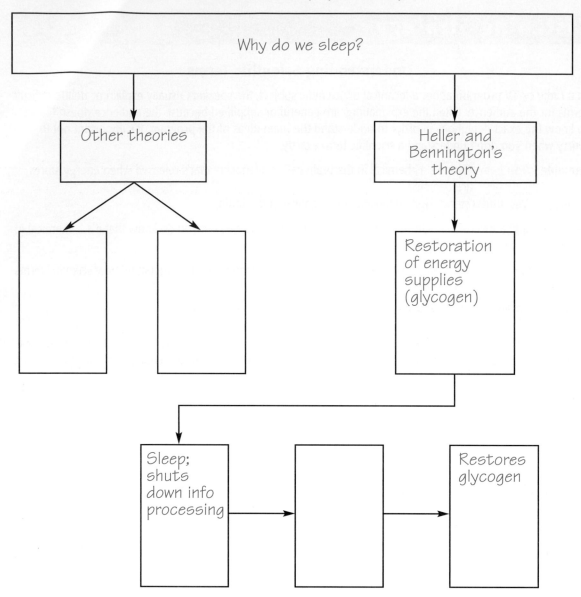

🎧 **C. LISTENING FOR DETAILS: SECTION 1** Listen to Section 1. As you listen, complete the tree diagram below to record information on theories about the purpose of sleep.

Why do we sleep?

Other theories

Heller and Bennington's theory

Restoration of energy supplies (glycogen)

Sleep; shuts down info processing

Restores glycogen

👥 Now use your tree diagram to answer these questions with a partner. Write your answers on the lines.

1. According to Heller and Bennington's theory, what part of the body needs to be restored during sleep?

_____

2. What does the brain use for fuel?

_____

3. Why can't the brain restore its energy sources while you're awake?

_____

146   **UNIT 3** Psychology

D. LISTENING FOR SUPPORTING INFORMATION: SECTION 2 Listen to Section 2. As you listen, complete the tree diagram with information on how the difference between two sleep stages supports Heller and Bennington's theory.

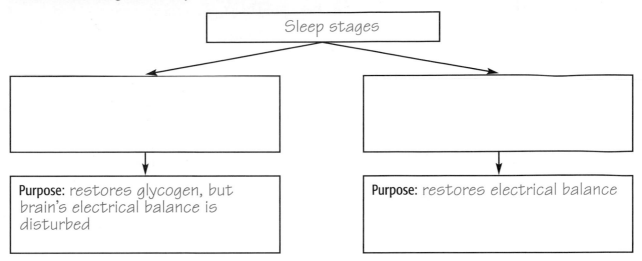

Now use your notes to answer these questions with a partner.

1. When we sleep, do we spend more time in REM sleep or non-REM sleep?

   _____

2. When does the brain restore its glycogen reserves, during REM sleep or non-REM sleep?

   _____

3. What is the purpose of dreaming?

   _____

Critical Thinking Strategy

Separating Fact from Theory

In the radio program you have listened to, you heard a theory about sleep. In these types of programs, it's important to separate facts from theories. The difference between facts and theories is whether or not they can be proven. In other words, facts are things that are true or have been proven to be true through *a number* of scientific experiments. On the other hand, theories are reasonable ideas based on fact, but have not been proven.

You can distinguish theories from facts by paying attention to some verbal cues. For example, people present (or should present) theories with verbs such as *propose, think,* and *believe.* They might also introduce a theory with *perhaps* or use modals such as *might* and *may* within the statement.

Examples: Some scientists **think** that fallout from an asteroid created a climate change that eventually extinguished the dinosaur population.

Dinosaurs **may** have become extinct because of an asteroid.

E. SEPARATING FACT FROM THEORY Listen to some statements from the radio program. Circle *Fact* if the speaker presents the information as a fact and *Theory* if the speaker presents it as a theory.

1. Fact   Theory   **3.** Fact   Theory

2. Fact   Theory   **4.** Fact   Theory

Now compare your answers with a partner's answers.

AFTER LISTENING

DISCUSSION In small groups, discuss these questions.

1. Why are scientists so interested in sleep?

2. Explain in your own words Heller and Bennington's theory on why we sleep.

3. Why do we dream, according to Heller and Bennington? Do you agree or disagree?

4. Do you agree with Heller and Bennington's theory? Why or why not?

PART ⑤ ACADEMIC ENGLISH Sleep and Dreaming

BEFORE LISTENING

A. DISCUSSION You are going to listen to a lecture about sleep and dreaming. In small groups, discuss these questions.

1. What happens to your body when you're asleep? What happens to your brain?

2. What happens if you don't get enough sleep?

3. What happens to your body when you're dreaming? What happens to your brain?

4. What are some scientific theories on why we dream?

B. THINKING AHEAD Look at the outline for the lecture on pages 151–155 and think about your discussion in Activity A. What would you like to know about sleep and dreaming? Write three questions about the subject on the lines.

Question 1: _____

Question 2: _____

Question 3: _____

C. GUESSING THE MEANING FROM CONTEXT Read the sentences below. The words in green are from the lecture. Guess their meanings from the context. Write your guesses on the lines.

1. Josh is very **moody** today: one minute he's happy and the next he's depressed.

   Guess: _____

2. This new exercise routine will **rejuvenate** you; you'll feel years younger in a few weeks.

   Guess: _____

3. When an animal is in **hibernation**, it's in a state that is like sleep and it needs very little food.

   Guess: _____

4. Heller and Bennington believe that the purpose of sleep is **cerebral** restoration; that is, they think the brain needs to shut down to restore itself.

   Guess: _____

5. The **cortex** covers the outside of the brain.

   Guess: _____

6. Researchers use an electroencephalograph (EEG) to measure waves that the brain **emits**, or sends out, during sleep.

   Guess: _____

7. I used to know the capitals of every state in the United States, but I can **recall** only a few of them now.

   Guess: _____

Now in small groups, compare your guesses.

LISTENING

A. LISTENING FOR THE MEANING OF NEW WORDS AND PHRASES Listen to these words and phrases in sentences from the lecture. You'll hear each sentence twice. Write the definitions on the lines.

1. **consciousness:** _____

2. **an altered state of consciousness:** _____

3. **incoherent:** _____

4. **circadian rhythms:** _____

5. **EEGs (electroencephalographs):** _____

Test-Taking Strategy

Listening for Topic Change Signals

In the listening sections of some standardized tests, you listen to a short lecture and then answer questions about its organization. Speakers often use signals in lectures. These are words and expressions that help you to understand the organization of the lecture. Some signals let you know when the speaker is going to change the topic. Here are three types of topic-change signals.

1. Speakers sometimes move away from the topic when giving a lecture. This is called a **digression.** They often give the audience a signal when they do this.

   Examples: **By the way,** we will have a test next Thursday.
   That reminds me, don't forget to read Chapters 3 and 4 by Monday.

2. Speakers also signal the audience when they return to the topic.

   Examples: **As I was saying,** the most important feature of . . .
   Getting back to what I was saying, this feature . . .
   Moving on, the feature we want to pay attention to is . . .

3. In addition, speakers sometimes signal the audience when they are going to introduce the next subtopic of the lecture.

   Examples: **Now let's take a look at** the reasons for . . .
   Let's turn our attention to the reasons why . . .
   This brings us to the topic of . . .

B. LISTENING FOR TOPIC CHANGE SIGNALS Listen for signals like the ones in the box above. Write the signals on the lines and indicate the purpose of each one: moving off the topic, returning to the topic, or introducing a new subtopic.

1. Signal: _____   Purpose: _____

2. Signal: _____   Purpose: _____

C. TAKING NOTES: USING AN OUTLINE Listen to the lecture. It's in four sections. You will listen to each section twice. Fill in as much of the outline as you can. Don't worry if you can't fill in everything. (You'll listen to the whole lecture again in Activity D.) Remember to use key words and abbreviations.

Sleep and Dreaming

Section 1

I. Consciousness

   A. Consciousness is _____the state of being aware_____

      1. Humans use senses to _____

      2. Hums. can use any or all senses—for ex.: _____

         _____

   B. Human consciousness is _____

      1. Hums. have the capacity _____

      2. Hums. can _____

II. Sleep

   A. Sleep is _____

      1. Experts know the longer someone goes w/out sleep, _____

         _____

         W/out sleep:

         a. People have difficulty _____

         b. They have _____

         c. They get _____

         d. W/ prolonged sleeplessness, people become _____

      2. Record for person staying awake: _____

         _____

Section 2

   B. The cycle of sleep: circadian rhythms

      1. Sleep is a _____

         a. Our bodies have biological need to _____

         b. Our bodies' natural bio. need for rest is _____

         c. This natural rhythm is known as _____

      2. Some researchers describe circadian rhythms as _____

         _____

      3. 1st internal clock controls _____

      4. 2nd internal clock controls _____

      5. Some researchers describe circ. rhythms as _____

6. Circ. rhythms have these features: _____

    a. _____

    b. _____

    c. _____

    d. _____

7. Our natural circ. rhythms may be disturbed by _____

_____

C. Sleep: A process of rest or recovery? 3 perspectives:

    1. _____

    2. _____

    3. _____

D. Why do some people need more sleep than others?

    1. Everybody requires some sleep.

    2. Most people require _____

    3. An individual's sleep needs vary from _____

    4. _____ sleep longer than _____, the

    _____ sleep less than young people.

    5. _____ do not influence the amount of sleep people need.

Section 3

E. Cycles & stages of sleep

    1. Our sleep cycles are _____

    2. A full sleep cycle lasts approx. _____

    3. Average sleep pattern (8 hrs.) has _____

    4. Using EEGs, researchers have _____

    5. 4 stages of sleep

        a. Stage 1: _____

        b. Stages 2 & 3: _____

        c. Stage 4: _____

F. Rapid eye movement

    1. REM & non-REM sleep

        a. REM sleep is _____

        _____

b. _____ identifies REM sleep

c. REM sleep occurs when _____

d. It begins after _____

e. It's necessary for _____

_____

f. Non-REM sleep is _____

_____

2. Alpha & delta waves

EEG readout showing alpha waves

a. The brain emits alpha waves _____

_____

b. The brain emits delta waves _____

_____

c. The brain emits intense wave activity during _____

_____

G. Sleep deprivation: Going w/out REM sleep

1. People who are denied REM sleep are _____

and become _____

2. People who are denied REM sleep for a considerable amount of time

_____

3. People who sleep, but are denied REM sleep _____

_____

Section 4

III. Dreams

    A. What is a dream?

        1. A dream is _____

        2. Dreams begin _____

        3. A dream includes _____

        4. A dream can include _____

        5. During dreams:

           a. _____ is increased

           b. _____ occur

           c. _____ can be identified

           d. _____ is minimal

        6. Non-REM sleep is _____

        7. Most people have _____ dreams per night

        8. Dreams last from _____ to _____

    B. Why do we remember some but not all our dreams?

        1. We have _____ ea. night, yet only remember

        _____

        2. Some people have _____

        3. Most dreams are about _____

        4. Most dreams include _____

        5. Most dreams have common themes incl. _____

        _____

        6. Sounds and other sensations that do not wake up a sleeper _____

        _____

        7. We remember a dream if _____

        8. We remember dreams by our pattern of awakening:

           a. People who _____ remember more dreams

           b. People who _____ remember fewer dreams

    C. Lucid dreaming

        1. Lucid dreaming is _____

        2. Lucid dreaming makes you feel _____

        _____ ; can be

        _____

D. The meaning of dreams

    1. Many cultures and traditions _____

    _____

    2. In Western culture, _____

    _____

    3. Other researchers believe _____

Sigmund Freud

Carl Jung

    a. During sleep _____

    _____

    b. The brain's _____

    _____

Source: Adapted from a lecture by Rafael Mendez, Ph.D.

 D. CHECKING YOUR NOTES Listen to the lecture again. As you listen, review your notes and fill in any missing information.

AFTER LISTENING

A. USING YOUR NOTES In small groups, use your notes to discuss these questions about the lecture.

1. What are some explanations for why we sleep?

2. What are the four sleep stages?

3. What happens if you don't get enough sleep?

4. What happens to our bodies when we are dreaming?

5. What are some cures for sleeplessness?

B. MAKING CONNECTIONS Think about the dream you read about in Part 1, the radio program you heard in Part 3, and the information in the lecture. Discuss this question with a partner:
• Why do we dream?

PUT IT ALL TOGETHER

GIVING A PRESENTATION You are going to give a short presentation (three to five minutes) to the class or a small group on an aspect of sleep or dreaming that interests you.

Step 1
Pick a subject related to sleep or dreaming that interests you. Some possibilities might include the following:
• a recent theory (or theories) on why we sleep
• a recent theory (or theories) on why we dream
• dream interpretation

   a. cultural or folk beliefs about the meanings of dreams

   b. psychological theories on what dreams mean

   c. a description of one of your (or someone else's) dreams and what you think the dreams mean
• remedies for sleeplessness
• a summary of a news article, website, or radio or TV program on sleep and dreaming and your opinion of it

 ### Step 2
Do library or Internet research on your topic. If you do Internet research, try doing searches by combining key words such as the following:
• dream interpretation
• folk beliefs + dreaming
• latest research + dreaming
• latest research + sleep

Make sure that you evaluate the source of the information that you find on the Internet. For example, URLs (website addresses) that include *.edu* may have better information than URLs that end in *.com*. This is because only *.edu* indicates that the website belongs to an educational institution such as a university. Therefore, the information may be more reliable.

Step 3
Take notes as you do your research. Make an outline like the example outline on page 157.

Topic: _____

Main Idea: _____

Supporting Ideas: (Facts, details, examples, or anecdotes that support your main idea. Try to have at least three.)

1: _____

2: _____

3: _____

Sources: (List the source(s) of your information and comment on how useful they were.)

_____

_____

Speaking Strategy

Asking Questions and Keeping the Audience in Mind

You saw how speakers use signals when they give a lecture. Another way speakers signal the audience is by asking questions. This not only signals the organization of the lecture, it also helps keep the audience interested. Some examples of questions from the lecture on sleep and dreaming that you heard include the following:

• What are the cycles and stages of sleep?
• So, why do we sleep?
• What is a dream?

A similar technique is to imagine what the audience might think about the topic. For example, in the lecture on sleep and dreaming, the speaker says:

• You might wonder why we remember some, but not all, of our dreams.
• We often wonder why some people need more sleep than others do.

Step 4

Prepare a presentation from your notes. Practice your presentation. Think about ways to use signals and questions to keep the audience's interests in mind, and to help your listeners pay attention. Write some of these down on your note cards so that you remember to use them when you speak.

Step 5

Give your presentation. Use your notes. Remember: Don't read your presentation. (See page 125.) Make eye contact as you speak and keep your audience in mind.

Step 6

Evaluate each others' presentations. For each presenter, answer the questions below:
• Did the speaker use notes to make the presentation (rather than reading)?
• Did the speaker make eye contact with the audience?
• Did the speaker use signals or questions to help the audience pay attention?

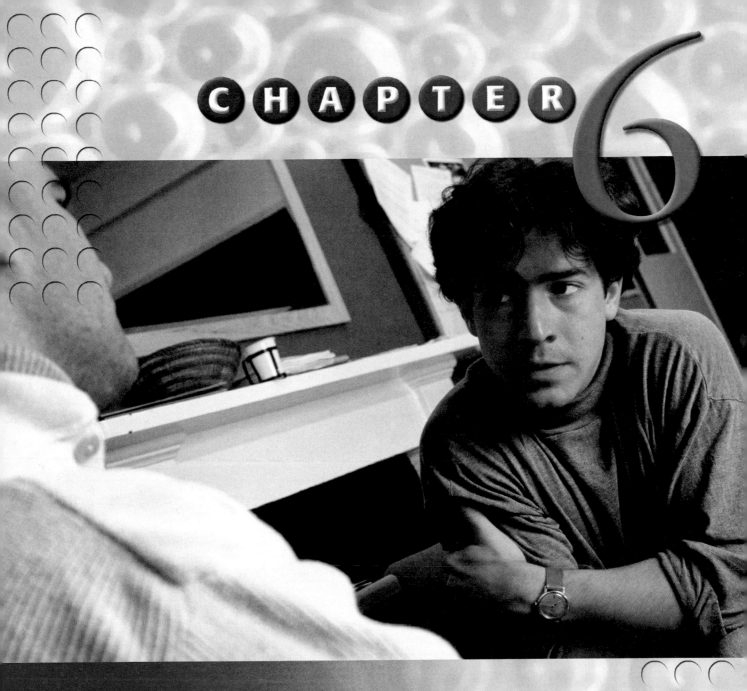

Abnormal Psychology

Discuss these questions:

• Whom do you talk with about your negative emotions?

• How often do normal people feel anxious, afraid, or angry?

• What are some ways of dealing with negative emotions?

PART ① INTRODUCTION What Is Abnormal Behavior?

A. DISCUSSION You are going to read some definitions of **abnormal** (not normal) behavior. Before you read, discuss with a partner the descriptions of different kinds of behavior in the chart below. Decide whether each behavior is normal or abnormal. Check (✓) the appropriate column.

Behaviors	Normal	Abnormal
1. A woman cheats on her income taxes.		
2. A man takes 10 showers a day.		
3. A woman refuses to eat in order to keep her weight down.		
4. A man cannot get or keep a job and lives on the streets.		
5. A woman lives alone and has no friends.		
6. A man wears rings in his ears and nose.		
7. A man is afraid of flying in an airplane.		
8. A woman claims that aliens from outer space communicate with her through her television.		
9. A man doesn't cry at his mother's funeral.		
10. A female corporate executive plans never to marry or have children.		

B. THINKING AHEAD In small groups, discuss these questions.

1. Have you seen anyone whose behavior seemed abnormal to you? Describe the behavior.

2. How do *you* define abnormal behavior?

What Is Abnormal Behavior?

For nine months, 54-year-old Richard Thompson lived happily and without any problems in a downtown storm drain (sewer) in San Diego,
5 California. Because the city does not allow people to live in sewers, they evicted Thompson (forced him to leave). Although Thompson later lived in several care centers and mental
10 hospitals, he preferred the privacy and the comfort of the sewer.

There are three ways to decide whether Thompson's behavior—living in the sewer—was abnormal.

Statistical Frequency

15 The statistical frequency approach says that a behavior may be considered abnormal if it occurs rarely or infrequently compared to the behaviors of most people.

20 By this definition, Thompson's living in a sewer would be considered very abnormal, since out of over 230 million people in the United States, only a very few prefer this kind of home. However,
25 so would getting a Ph.D., being president, living in a monastery, or selling a million records. As these last examples show, the statistical frequency definition of abnormality isn't too useful.

Deviation from Social Norms

30 The social norms approach says that a behavior is considered abnormal if it deviates (is very different) from social standards, values, or norms (what is O.K. in a particular society).
35 Thompson's decision to live by himself in a sewer greatly deviates (differs) from society's norms about where people should live. However, a definition of abnormality based only on being

40 different from social norms doesn't work when social norms change with time. For example, 60 years ago, no man would consider wearing an earring, while today, many males consider
45 earrings very fashionable. Similarly, at certain times in the past, a woman who was thin was considered to be ill. Today our society pressures women to be thin like the fashion models in the media.

50 So you can see that defining abnormality on the basis of social norms is difficult because these norms may and do change over time.

Richard Thompson lived happily in a San Diego sewer until he was evicted by the city.

Maladaptive Behavior

The maladaptive behavior approach
55 defines a behavior as abnormal if it interferes with an individual's ability to function in one's personal life or in society. For example, being afraid of flying, hearing voices that make you do
60 dangerous things, feeling compelled to

wash your hands for hours on end,
starving yourself to death, and committing
mass murder would all be considered
65 maladaptive and, in that sense, abnormal.

However, Thompson's seemingly
successful adaptation to living in a sewer
may not be maladaptive for him and
certainly has no adverse consequences
70 to society. Of the three definitions

discussed here, the most useful
definition of abnormal behavior is based
on the maladaptive definition—that is,
whether a particular behavior or
75 behavior pattern interferes with a
person's ability to function normally.

Source: "Definitions of Abnormal Behavior" (Plotnik)

D. COMPREHENSION CHECK In small groups, discuss these questions.

1. Why is there no single definition of abnormal behavior?

2. According to the article, what are the three definitions of abnormal behavior? Outline them by completing the graphic organizer below.

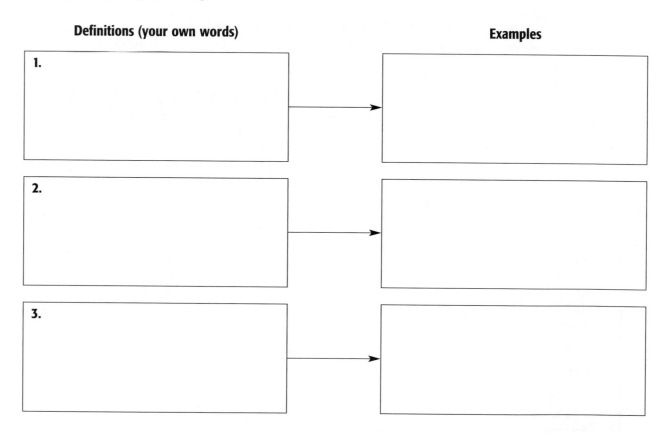

Definitions (your own words)   Examples

1.

2.

3.

3. According to the article, which definition of abnormal behavior would most people agree with?

4. Look again at the chart in Activity A, page 160. Using the definitions of abnormal behavior from the reading, would you change any of your answers? Why or why not?

5. Are there cultural differences in defining abnormal behavior? Give examples to support your answer.

E. RESPONSE WRITING Choose *one* of these topics. Write about it for 10 minutes. Don't worry about grammar and don't use a dictionary. Just put as many ideas as you can on paper.

• What is your definition of abnormal behavior? Has it changed at all after reading the article on pages 161–162?

• Describe someone's behavior that you think is abnormal.

• Describe some cultural differences in defining abnormal behavior. Give examples to support your answer.

PART ② SOCIAL LANGUAGE What Are You Afraid Of?

BEFORE LISTENING

A. THINKING AHEAD You are going to listen to Chrissy interview people on the street. She's going to ask them what they are afraid of. In small groups, discuss these questions.

1. In your opinion, what fears are "normal"? That is, what *should* a person be afraid of? What fears are abnormal, in your opinion?

2. Some fears are irrational—unreasonable and extreme. An irrational fear can **disrupt** (cause serious problems in) a person's daily life. Do you ever experience "irrational" fears?

B. PREDICTING You are going to listen to seven people answer the question: "What are you afraid of?" What do you think most people will say? With a partner, make predictions about their answers.

C. VOCABULARY PREPARATION Read the sentences below. The words and phrases in green are from the interview. Match the definitions in the box with the words and phrases in green. Write the correct letters on the lines.

| a. dying from breathing water | c. recovered from | e. slippery and disgusting |
| b. partly, but not completely | d. saved | f. strange; unusual |

_____ **1.** I hate the feel of seaweed when I swim in the ocean because it's so **slimy**.

_____ **2.** Cheryl used to be afraid of flying, but she's **gotten over** it with the help of a psychiatrist.

_____ **3.** I used to have **weird** dreams, but now they're not very exciting.

_____ **4.** I used to know the names of all the countries in Africa, but I've **sort of** forgotten them now.

_____ **5.** Even though she's a good swimmer, Jenny often dreams that she's **drowning** in the middle of the ocean.

_____ **6.** In one of Jenny's dreams, a lifeguard **rescued** her. He carried her out of the water to a safe place on the shore.

LISTENING

A. LISTENING FOR THE MAIN IDEA Listen to the interviews. As you listen, think about this question:
• Do all the speakers have some kind of fear?

B. LISTENING FOR DETAILS Listen again. This time, write information about each speaker in the chart below.

Speakers	What is the speaker afraid of?	Why is the speaker afraid?
1		
2		
3		
4		
5		
6		
7		

C. LISTENING FOR SPECIFIC INFORMATION Listen again to some of the speakers describe their fears. Listen for the answers to these questions.

1. **Speaker 1:** Is she still afraid of spiders? _____

2. **Speaker 3:** Did she almost drown as a child? _____

3. **Speaker 6:** How does she describe seaweed? _____

   _____

4. **Speaker 7:** How does she sound when she gives her answer? In other words, does she sound bored,

   confident, or uncertain? _____

   _____

AFTER LISTENING

A. TAKING A SURVEY As you heard in the interview, most people have mild fears that they don't mind talking about. You are going to interview three classmates about their fears.

Step 1
Make predictions about your classmates' fears. In small groups, discuss these questions.

1. Will most people discuss their fears? Does age or gender (male or female) have anything to do with this?

2. What do you think will be the most common fears?

3. Do you think that your classmates will say that their fears disrupt their lives? Explain your answer.

Now in your groups, create a list of at least six common fears. Write your ideas on the lines below.

1. _____

2. _____

3. _____

4. _____

5. _____

6. _____

Step 2

Think about your answers to the questions in the chart. Write your own question about fears in Part 3. Then ask three classmates the questions. If possible, talk to both men and women of different cultures and of different ages. Write their answers in the chart. If a person does *not* want to discuss his or her fears, that's O.K. Thank them and ask someone else.

Questions	Classmate 1 ☐ Male ☐ Female	Classmate 2 ☐ Male ☐ Female	Classmate 3 ☐ Male ☐ Female
Part 1			
1. Are you willing to discuss discuss your fears?	☐ Yes ☐ No	☐ Yes ☐ No	☐ Yes ☐ No
Part 2			
2. Do you have any fears?	☐ Yes ☐ No	☐ Yes ☐ No	☐ Yes ☐ No
3. What, if anything, are you afraid of?			
4. Does this fear cause you any problems? If yes, what are they?			
Part 3			
5. Your question:			

B. DISCUSSING SURVEY RESULTS In small groups, discuss the results of your survey. Now that you have your results, use them to answer again the questions you discussed in Step 1 (page 165).

PART ③ THE MECHANICS OF LISTENING AND SPEAKING

LANGUAGE FUNCTIONS

Asking for Information Over the Phone

People often try to get as much information as they can over the phone before they go somewhere—this saves them time, energy, and sometimes money. There are many ways to ask for information over the phone.

Examples: **A:** Bright Lights Video. What can I do for you?
B: Hi. **Can you tell me if you have** *Star Wars?*
Yes, hello. **Do you have** *Star Wars?*
Uh, yeah, hi. **Would you happen to have** a copy of *Star Wars?*
Uh, hi. **I was wondering if you have** *Star Wars.*

Note: Depending on the information you want, you might also ask **Do you sell . . . ?**

A. ASKING FOR INFORMATION OVER THE PHONE With a partner, practice asking for information over the phone. Student A answers the phone by saying, "Bright Lights Video. What can I do for you?" Student B asks for the following movie titles using the expressions in the box above. Use as many different expressions as you can. Then exchange roles.

Examples: **A:** Bright Lights Video. What can I do for you?
Cue: Ask for *The Incredibles.*
B: Yes, hello. Do you have *The Incredibles?*

1. Ask for *Casablanca.*

2. Ask for *Harry Potter and the Order of the Phoenix.*

3. Ask for *Monsters, Inc.*

4. Ask for *The Lord of the Rings: The Return of the King.*

5. Ask for *Shrek.*

6. Ask for *Psycho.*

Asking Someone to Hold

Sometimes you have to ask the person that you're speaking to on the phone to hold (stay on the line while you go away from the phone). Here are some ways to ask someone to hold.

Examples: **A:** Can you tell me if you have *Star Wars?*
B: **Hang on a minute.**   **Less Formal**
Hold on a minute. I'll check.
Can you hold?
Please hold.
Can you hold on for a minute?
Would you mind holding on for a minute?   **More Formal**

B. ASKING SOMEONE TO HOLD With a partner, practice asking someone to hold. Student A asks for a movie. You can ask for one of the movie titles in the box below or use your own ideas. Student B asks Student A to hold using one of the expressions in the box on page 167. Then exchange roles.

Forrest Gump	*Finding Nemo*	*Frankenstein*
Raiders of the Lost Ark	*King Kong*	*Spider-Man*

PRONUNCIATION

/ɛ/ vs. /æ/

It is important to hear the difference between these two sounds: /ɛ/ and /æ/. Do you hear the difference in the examples below?

/ɛ/	/æ/
bed	bad
send	sand
men	man
pen	pan
said	sad
Do you have a pen?	Do you have a pan?

In the list above, what are the different spellings for the /ɛ/ sound? (These are the most common spellings for this sound.)

C. HEARING THE DIFFERENCE BETWEEN /ɛ/ AND /æ/ Listen to the following words. Circle the word that you hear.

1. said   sad
2. lend   land
3. pen   pan
4. trek   track
5. bend   band

6. send   sand
7. ten   tan
8. left   laughed
9. guess   gas
10. gem   jam

D. HEARING /ɛ/ AND /æ/ IN SENTENCES Listen to the statements. Check (✓) the ones you hear.

1. _____ **a.** Can you send that for me?

   _____ **b.** Can you sand that for me?

2. _____ **a.** Can you see the gem?

   _____ **b.** Can you see the jam?

3. _____ **a.** Can I borrow your pen?

   _____ **b.** Can I borrow your pan?

4. _____ **a.** I bought ten shirts.

   _____ **b.** I bought tan shirts.

5. _____ **a.** Keith left when he heard the joke.

   _____ **b.** Keith laughed when he heard the joke.

E. PRONOUNCING /ɛ/ AND /æ/ Work with a partner. Say one of the statements from each item in Activity D. (Don't say them in order.) Your partner will say *a* or *b*. Check to make sure that your partner heard you correctly. If your partner didn't say the correct letter, try again. Then exchange roles.

F. PRONOUNCING /ɛ/ AND /æ/ IN SENTENCES Now use words with the sounds /ɛ/ and /æ/ in conversations. Interview your classmates. Use the questions in the box. If a classmate answers *yes*, write his or her name on the chart.

Example: **A:** Do you like to wear tan clothes?
              B: Yes, I often wear tan clothes.

Questions	Classmates
Do you like to wear tan clothes?	
Do you have a funny laugh?	
Do you play in a band?	
Do you have a favorite gem?	
Do you buy a lot of gas?	
Do you eat jam on toast?	
Are you left-handed?	
Do you guess answers on exams?	

WORDS IN PHRASES

Asking for Help: *I'd like* + Infinitive or Noun Phrase

When you're asking for help or information over the phone, you often use *I'd like* followed by an infinitive (*to* + verb) or a noun phrase.

Examples: I'd like **to order** some tickets.
                   infinitive

              I'd like **the phone number** for . . .
                       noun phrase

PUT IT TOGETHER

A. DECIDING WHO TO CALL Practice asking for information over the phone. First, in small groups, discuss the most common situations in which you have to ask for information over the phone. Think of seven places (services, businesses, and organizations) that you call and the things that you ask for (items, help, information). On a separate piece of paper, write your group's ideas.

Examples: bookstore—book title/find a book
restaurant—menu items/make a reservation

B. ASKING FOR INFORMATION OVER THE PHONE Work with a partner. Take turns asking for information and giving information. Find ideas for questions from the information that you thought of in Activity A above. If you are giving the information, ask the other person to hold, if applicable.

Use the expressions for asking for information and asking someone to hold on page 167. Pay attention to the /ɛ/ and /æ/ sounds. Use *I'd like*.

Example: **A:** Megabooks International. Can I help you?
B: Yes, I'd like a copy of *Foundation* by Isaac Asimov. Do you have it?
A: Hold on a minute. I'll check.
B: Thanks.

PART 4 BROADCAST ENGLISH What Is Paranoia?

BEFORE LISTENING

A. THINKING AHEAD You are going to listen to a radio program about paranoia, a kind of mental illness. A person who has paranoia irrationally fears things. Before you listen, talk about fear. In small groups, discuss these questions.

1. The program was recorded in the late 1990s. A frightening crime trend in the United States in the 1990s was drive-by shootings (people in cars shooting other cars or people on the street). What are some additional things that people fear in today's world? Think about natural disasters, new diseases, crime, etc.

2. Why are people afraid of certain things? What purpose does fear serve?

B. PREDICTING Before you listen, make a prediction about what you are going go hear. With a partner, discuss this question:

• Is there an effective treatment for paranoia?

C. GUESSING THE MEANING FROM CONTEXT Read the sentences below. The words in green are from the radio program. Guess their meanings from the context. Write your guesses on the lines. Then compare your answers with a partner's answers.

1. Edvard Munch's painting *The Scream* **evokes** a very definite feeling—it expresses feelings of fear and anxiety.

   Guess: _____

2. According to Ronald Siegel, the basis for paranoia is **lurking** deep inside everyone's brain; it only comes to the surface and becomes a problem when you have trouble dealing with the fears of the everyday world.

   Guess: _____

3. Very upsetting experiences can act as **triggers**, events that can cause people to change their behavior.

   Guess: _____

4. Vince takes a drug that **activates**—wakes up—a certain part of his brain. This stimulation helps him pay better attention in class.

The Scream by Edvard Munch

   Guess: _____

5. I used to get very **agitated** when I watched the evening news on TV; it made me so upset that I decided not to watch it any more.

   Guess: _____

6. Stacey has a **deep-seated** fear of flying: She's had it all her life, she doesn't understand the cause, and she can't get rid of it.

   Guess: _____

7. There has been a **resurgence** in the number of paranoia cases; there are more new cases now than at any time since the late 1980s.

   Guess: _____

8. If a person has a **neurological** problem, it means that he or she has a problem with brain function.

   Guess: _____

9. The **limbic system** is the part of the brain that controls basic functions such as emotion and motivation.

Guess: _____

10. Fears of natural disasters were **pervasive** in 2005; they affected many people around the world.

Guess: _____

Test-Taking Strategy

Interpreting Figurative Language

Standardized tests often ask you to answer questions on the meaning of new words. Many words and phrases in English have two meanings, a **literal** meaning and a **figurative** meaning. The literal meaning of a word is its main meaning. It is usually the first definition of the word in the dictionary. A figurative meaning of a word is a meaning other than its usual meaning. It often makes a word picture or a comparison. When you find a new word, if the literal meaning doesn't make sense to you, think about what the figurative meaning might be.

Look at the literal and figurative meanings of the word *sweet*.

Literal: I can't drink this coffee because it's too **sweet** (containing a lot of sugar)

Figurative: I like our new neighbor—she's very **sweet** (nice or kind)

D. VOCABULARY PREPARATION: INTERPRETING FIGURATIVE LANGUAGE Read the sentences below. The words and phrases in green are used figuratively in the radio program. First, guess their meaning from the context. Then match each word or phrase with the correct meaning in the box. Write the letters on the lines.

a. become extremely influenced by	d. take control of
b. powerful negative feeling	e. uncovered; exposed
c. slowly destroy	

_____ **1.** Sometimes irrational fears can **grip** you, and you can't do anything about them.

_____ **2.** Sometimes paranoia can **eat away at** your confidence until you have no self-esteem left.

_____ **3.** Even though I'm afraid of crime in the city, I'm not going to **get carried away** about it and become so paranoid that I don't leave my house!

_____ **4.** The **demon** of paranoia has brought pain to many famous people throughout history, such as the musician Kurt Cobain and the author Ernest Hemingway.

_____ **5.** Brianna's emotions have been very **raw** ever since she witnessed that terrible accident. She's very nervous and moody.

LISTENING

🎧 **A. LISTENING FOR THE MAIN IDEA** Listen to the radio program. As you listen, think about this question:
• According to Ronald Siegel, why is it "normal" to feel some paranoia?

🎧 **B. GUESSING THE MEANING FROM CONTEXT** Listen to parts of the program. This time, listen for explanations of the following terms. Then write in your own words what you think the terms mean.

1. streptococcus A infection: _____

_____

2. premonitions: _____

_____

🎧 **C. LISTENING FOR REASONS** Dr. Siegel says that many people called the 1990s the Age of Paranoia. Listen for the reasons for this and write them in the cluster diagram—a kind of graphic organizer—below.

```
   ⭕                          ⭕


              ⭕
           1990s
      The Age of Paranoia


   ⭕                          ⭕
```

👥 Now in small groups, use the cluster diagram to discuss this question:
• Why did some people call the 1990s "The Age of Paranoia"?

_____

_____

D. LISTENING FOR DETAILS Listen to the program again. This time, listen for details that answer the questions below. Write your answers on the lines.

1. Why can anyone become paranoid? _____

   _____

2. What percent of hospital admissions are for paranoia? _____

   _____

3. Is there a treatment for paranoia? _____

AFTER LISTENING

A. COMPREHENSION CHECK With a partner, answer these questions.

1. Why is it "normal" to feel some paranoia?

2. Why do you think there was an increase in the cases of paranoia in the 1990s?

3. Why is paranoia so difficult to treat?

B. MAKING CONNECTIONS You heard people describe their fears in Part 2, and you learned about paranoia, an extreme type of fear, in this section. In small groups, discuss these questions.

1. Many people enjoy experiencing fear in a safe way, such as by reading about or watching extremely frightening situations. Can you think of any popular TV shows or movies that provide this experience?

2. What other types of frightening situations do people like to experience?

3. Why do people like to be frightened? Do you like to be frightened? Why or why not?

PART ⑤ ACADEMIC ENGLISH Anxiety Disorders

BEFORE LISTENING

A. THINKING AHEAD You are going to listen to a lecture about anxiety disorders. An anxiety disorder is a mental illness that results when worry or fear becomes so extreme that a person cannot function normally. You've already learned about one type of anxiety disorder—paranoia. In small groups, discuss these questions.

1. Most people feel anxious (extremely nervous and uncomfortable) from time to time. What kinds of things make people feel anxious? Have you ever felt anxious?

2. What are some of the effects of feeling extremely anxious? In other words, can it affect your health? What other aspects of your life can it affect?

3. If you had a friend who felt anxious, what would you suggest that he or she do in order to feel less anxious?

B. PREDICTING In the lecture, you are going to hear about different types of anxiety disorders and about treatments for them. What do you think some treatments for anxiety might be? With a partner, try to think of at least three types of treatments.

1. _____

2. _____

3. _____

C. HAVING QUESTIONS IN MIND Look at the note-taking chart for the lecture on page 184 and the outline on pages 179–182 and think about your discussion in Activity A above. What would you like to know about anxiety disorders? Write three questions about the subject.

Question 1: _____

Question 2: _____

Question 3: _____

D. GUESSING THE MEANING FROM CONTEXT Read the sentences below. The words in green are from the lecture. Guess their meanings from the context. Write your guesses on the lines.

1. If you feel so much **apprehension** about flying, I suggest that you see a psychologist and try to find out why it frightens you.

Guess: _____

2. Tyler is so **preoccupied** by his mother's illness that he is having trouble paying attention in class.

Guess: _____

3. Some of the **physiological** problems that result from anxiety are muscle tenseness and skin irritations.

   Guess: _____

4. Some therapists say that you must **confront** your fears, because if you face them, you can get rid of them.

   Guess: _____

5. The therapist had Harrison climb slightly higher steps on each visit. Gradually his fear of heights **diminished** until his fear was completely gone.

   Guess: _____

6. Terry stopped taking the drug for her anxiety disorder because of the **side effects**. When she took the pills, she was sleepy all the time and got headaches.

   Guess: _____

7. The most disturbing symptom that Emily's anxiety disorder caused was **withdrawal**—she refused to go out or even speak to anyone for days.

   Guess: _____

Now compare your answers with a partner's answers.

E. VOCABULARY PREPARATION Read the sentences below. The phrases in green are idioms and verb phrases from the lecture. Match the definitions in the box with the phrases in green. Write the correct letters on the lines.

a. anything he thinks of	**c.** stop thinking about
b. handle; deal with	**d.** say something

_____ **1.** This problem has gotten so big that I can't **cope with** it any more—I need help.

_____ **2.** If you don't agree, you should **speak up**.

_____ **3.** I just can't **get** that song **out of my mind**; I keep hearing it over and over!

_____ **4.** Jason doesn't think about what he says; he just says **whatever comes to mind**.

LISTENING

Listening Strategy

Understanding The Meaning of New Words: Medical Roots

One way to understand the meaning of new words is by using your knowledge of word roots. For example, *agoraphobia* comes from the root *agora-*, meaning an open or crowded place, and *-phobia*, meaning fear. So *agoraphobia* is a fear of open places. Study this list of roots used in many medical terms and their meanings.

Roots	Meanings
acro-	a high place
agora-	the market place; an open, crowded place
arachno-	spider
claustro-	a closed place
hydro-	water
-phobia	fear, dislike
-phobic	afraid of
photo-	light
psycho-	the mind
-tropic	affecting; turning towards
xeno-	foreign (pronounced /'zi no/)

A. UNDERSTANDING MEDICAL ROOTS Practice using some roots to name psychological problems. Read the situations with a partner and use the roots in the box above to answer the questions.

1. Molly is afraid of spiders. What problem does she have? _____

2. Jack is uncomfortable in bright light. What's his problem? _____

3. June doesn't like foreigners. What's her problem? _____

4. Morgan is afraid of water. What problem does he have? _____

B. USING MEDICAL ROOTS TO GUESS THE MEANING OF NEW WORDS Listen to parts of the lecture. Use your knowledge of roots to guess the meaning of each of the following words. Then write in your own words what you think the words means.

1. **acrophobia:** _____

2. **claustrophobia:** _____

3. **psychotropic drugs:** _____

Listening Strategy

Listening to a Lecture Introduction

The introduction to a lecture often contains a lot of important information. It can do any or all of the following:
- explain or define the topic
- define important terms
- present the structure of the rest of the lecture

All of these help you to prepare for taking notes, so it's important to listen carefully to the introduction of a lecture.

Example: **Today we will discuss** the problem of agoraphobia—**that is,** the fear of crowds and public spaces. We will view the topic from two perspectives: **first,** we'll look at the possible causes of this phobia, and **second,** we'll look at the available forms of treatment.

C. LISTENING TO A LECTURE INTRODUCTION   Listen to the introduction to the lecture. Listen for information that answers these questions. Write your answers on the lines.

1. How is anxiety defined?

_____

_____

2. What are some examples of the kinds of anxiety that we all experience as part of our daily lives?

_____

_____

3. What are some ways we cope with anxiety?

_____

_____

4. What do we call anxiety that is frequent, persistent, painful, and unpleasant?

_____

_____

5. What are three common anxicty disorders?

_____

_____

D. TAKING NOTES: USING AN OUTLINE Listen to the lecture. It's in four sections. Listen to each section twice. Fill in as much of the outline as you can. Don't worry if you can't fill in everything. (You'll listen to the whole lecture again later.) Remember to use key words and abbreviations.

Anxiety Disorders: Types and Treatments

Section 1

I. Characteristics of Anxiety

  A. Definition: *an emotional state of fear, apprehension, or worry that affects many areas of functioning*

    1. Affects _____

    2. Anxious person might not know _____

  B. Anxiety part of daily life. Exs.:

    1. _____

    2. _____

    3. _____

  C. Ways to cope w/anxiety. Exs.:

    1. Test: _____

    2. Staying healthy: _____

  D. "Normal" anxiety becomes an anxiety disorder when

    _____

    _____

  E. Types of anxiety disorders:

    1. _____

    2. _____

    3. _____

A nervous student

II. Types of Anxiety Disorders

  A. Generalized anxiety disorder

    1. Person continually tense w/excessive worry about 2 or more life problems such as:

      a. _____

      b. _____

      c. _____

      d. _____

2. Develops physical symptoms such as:

    a. _____

    b. _____

    c. _____

    d. _____

    e. _____

Section 2

B. Phobic disorder

    1. Definition: _____

    _____

    2. Causes: _____

    _____

    3. 2 types of phobic disorder: _____

        a. _____

        Exs.:

        1) _____

        2) _____

        b. _____

        Exs.:

        1) _____

        2) _____

        3) _____

C. Obsessive-compulsive disorder

    1. Definition of obsessions: _____

    _____

    Exs.:

        a. _____

        b. _____

    2. Definition of compulsions: _____

    _____

    Exs.:

        a. _____

        b. _____

III. Treatments for Anxiety Disorders

    A. Psychodynamic therapy

        1. Definition: _____

           _____

        2. How it works: _____

           _____

        3. Two basic techniques:

           a. _____

           b. _____

A psychotherapy session

Section 3

    B. Behavioral therapy

        1. Definition: _____

           _____

        2. Used in treatment of _____

           _____

        3. 3 major behavioral techniques

           a. _____

              1) Phobic patient learns to _____

                _____

              2) 3 phases of systematic desensitization: _____

                a) _____

                b) _____

                c) _____

           b. _____

              1) Exposed to _____ many times

              2) Patients made to realize _____

             Exs.:

                a) Claustrophobic: _____

                  _____

                b) Obsessive-compulsive: _____

                  _____

           c. _____

1) Form of learning in which _____

_____

2) Confronts feared objects while _____

_____

Exs.:

a) _____

_____

b) _____

_____

Section 4

C. Drug therapies

  1. Psychotropic drugs

    a. Definition: _____

    b. Kinds of psychotropic drugs: _____

      1) Anti-anxiety drugs: minor tranquilizers that _____

_____

      2) Most popular group of anti-anxiety drugs are _____

_____

        a) _____

        b) _____

        c) _____

Xanax, an anti-anxiety drug

      3) Anti-psychotic; help relieve

        a) Confused thinking

        b) Withdrawal

        c) Generalized anxiety disorder

  2. Drugs, if overused, may cause _____

Source: Adapted from a lecture by Paulette V. Starling, Ph.D. and Grace G. Cukras, Ph.D.

Taking Notes: Using a Chart

One way to take lecture notes is to make a chart and fill it in as you listen. Sometimes you can use a chart alone to take notes; other times, you'll need a chart in addition to a traditional outline. This works especially well for lecture topics that naturally suggest some sort of grouping.

One example of this type is a lecture that presents information in categories. Another type is a lecture that compares things. It helps if you know the major categories of information or items that will be compared *before* you hear a lecture so you can draw the chart before the lecture begins. Sometimes the title of the lecture will give you the major categories covered in the lecture. Below are some examples of lecture topics and the charts that they suggest:

Examples:

Types of Phobias		
Names	**Definitions**	**Examples**
claustrophobia	fear of enclosed places	fear of riding in elevators

Types of Abnormal Behavior		
Names	**Definitions**	**Examples**
schizophrenia	loss of contact with reality	hearing voices that aren't there

Treatments for Abnormal Behavior		
Names	**Definitions**	**Examples**
psychotropic drugs	drugs that affect the brain	Benzodiazepines (tranquilizers)

A Comparison of Western and Non-Western Psychological Disorders			
Disorders	**Definitions**	**Western Examples**	**Non-Western Examples**
Anorexia nervosa	Obsession with weight; refusal to eat	United States and Europe	Not found in some developing nations

E. TAKING NOTES: USING A CHART Listen to the lecture again. This time take notes using the chart. Write down as much information as you can in each category.

Types of Anxiety Disorders		
Names	**Definitions**	**Examples**

Treatment for Anxiety Disorders		
Names	**Definitions**	**Examples**

AFTER LISTENING

A. DISCUSSION Discuss the answers to the questions with a partner.

1. Which note-taking method worked best for you, filling in a chart or using a traditional outline? Why?

2. Could you combine the two methods? How?

B. USING YOUR NOTES In small groups, use your notes to discuss these questions about the lecture.

1. When does normal anxiety become an anxiety disorder?

2. What are some types of anxiety disorders?

3. What are the ways of treating anxiety disorders? How does each one work?

4. Do you ever experience "normal" anxiety? What do you do to cope with it?

PUT IT ALL TOGETHER

 PARTICIPATING IN A PANEL DISCUSSION In small groups, you are going to do research on a topic related to anxiety disorders, paranoia, or another aspect of abnormal behavior that interests you. Then you'll present your topic to the class in a panel discussion. (In a panel discussion, three or more people present their ideas on different aspects of the same topic.)

Step 1
First, in small groups, discuss the questions below. Then pick a question from this list that interests your group, or think up your own question:
• What are the ways of treating anxiety disorders?
• Are there cultural differences in treating anxiety disorders?
• Who is more likely to have a phobia, a woman or a man?
• Who is more likely to have an anxiety disorder, a man or a woman?
• Are there phobias that exist in some cultures but not in others?
• Does paranoia exist in all cultures?
• Are there cultural differences in the way people define abnormal behavior?
• How successful are treatments for paranoia?

 Step 2
Now on your own, research the question that your group chose in Step 1. Do Internet or library research, or find an introductory psychology textbook. Answer your question, and find at least three examples that support your answer.

If you do Internet research, try combining key words on your topic and remember to check the URLs that you see in your search results. Websites that have *.org* (organization), *.gov* (government), or *.edu* (education) in the URL may be more reliable sources of information when you are doing research on psychology.

You may find useful information on the following websites:
• American Psychiatric Association
• National Institute of Mental Health
• Medical Research Council
• Wellcome Trust
• Canadian Institutes of Health Research

You are going to present your information from your notes (see Chapter 4, page 125), so as you do your research, take notes on index cards, or use a form like the example form below.

Your question: _____

Your answer: _____

Example 1: _____

Example 2: _____

Example 3: _____

More examples: _____

Additional notes: _____

Critical Thinking Strategy

Paraphrasing

In academic discussions, you sometimes need to paraphrase—explain in your own words—the ideas of experts. One way to do this is to use synonyms—words or phrases that have the same meaning—when you are taking your notes.

Example:

In an article on kinds of treatment for anxiety disorders, you read:

Modeling is a form of learning in which a patient acquires responses by observing and imitating others. In this treatment, the therapist is the one who confronts the feared object while the fearful patient watches.

In a class discussion, you say:

A patient can learn new responses by modeling—that is, watching and imitating another person. So, in this type of treatment, a patient can watch the therapist face the object that the patient is afraid of. Then the patient can learn to imitate the therapist who successfully copes with the feared object.

Notice that the paraphrase:
- can be longer than the original statement
- means exactly the same thing as the original statement
- contains a few words that have not been changed—it's O.K. *not* to paraphrase specialized words, such as *modeling*

C. PARAPHRASING With a partner, practice paraphrasing the following statements about anxiety disorders. Write your paraphrased sentences on the lines.

1. A generalized anxiety disorder develops when a person is continually tense with excessive or severe worry about two or more life problems.

_____

_____

2. Obsessions are unwanted, disturbing, and unreasonable thoughts or ideas that people cannot get out of their minds. An obsession can involve a disturbing concern with dirt and germs or a concern that something terrible might happen.

_____

_____

_____

3. If psychotropic drugs are overused or misused, they can cause physical dependency and mild to severe side effects. Also, these drugs do not provide a permanent solution for most cases of anxiety.

_____

_____

_____

Step 3

Now present your information in a panel discussion. To start, get together with the people who chose the same question as you. Go over your notes and organize your information. Your discussion will be more interesting if you each present a different answer to the question, or different examples that support the answer. Then decide as a class on the time limit for each panel, or each speaker on the panel.

Panel discussions usually have a moderator—a person who watches the time and makes transitions from one speaker to the next. The moderator can be your teacher or someone from your group.

Now have each panel present its information. Be sure to:
• paraphrase information from your research
• use your notes; don't read
• make eye contact with the audience
• stay within the time limit
• take and answer questions from the audience when you are finished

Speaking Strategy

Asking Questions after a Presentation

Professors and other speakers often want the audience to ask questions when their lecture or presentation is finished. Sometimes you'll have a question in mind before the presentation begins; other times, you'll think of one while you are listening. Keep a piece of paper nearby while you are listening to write down your question so you won't forget it when the time for questions comes. Asking questions after a presentation not only increases your knowledge on the subject, it also helps you to pay attention, and it shows the speaker that you are interested in the subject.

Example: **The professor says:** The rate of cigarette smoking among adults declined from 1993 to 2000.
You write a note: Rate of smoking after 2000?
After the lecture, you ask: After 2000, did the rate of smoking continue to decline?

Step 4

In small groups (different from your own panel group), evaluate the panel discussion. Use the following questions in your evaluation:
• Were the presentations easy to understand?
• Were the topics interesting?
• Did the speakers use notes and make good eye contact?
• Did the speakers present their points with appropriate examples?
• Did the speakers get interesting questions after their presentations? Did they give useful answers?

UNIT ③ VOCABULARY WORKSHOP

Review vocabulary items that you learned in Chapters 5 and 6.

A. MATCHING Match the definitions to the words and phrases. Write the correct letters on the lines.

Words and Phrases	Definitions
_____ **1.** cope with	**a.** became
_____ **2.** cracked	**b.** slowly destroy
_____ **3.** eat away at	**c.** doing the right thing
_____ **4.** marathon	**d.** handle; deal with
_____ **5.** on the right track	**e.** a 26.4 mile (42.5 km) foot race
_____ **6.** phobia	**f.** use up supplies
_____ **7.** run out of	**g.** fear
_____ **8.** slimy	**h.** strange
_____ **9.** turned into	**i.** slippery
_____ **10.** weird	**j.** figured out

B. TRUE OR FALSE? Read the statements below. Circle *T* if the sentence is true. Circle *F* if the sentence is false.

1. If you have **agoraphobia**, you are afraid of high places.   T   F

2. If you have **claustrophobia**, you are afraid of closed spaces.   T   F

3. **Physiological** problems are mental problems.   T   F

4. If you are **preoccupied**, you might have trouble paying attention. T   F

5. If a person has a **neurological** problem, it means that he or she has a problem has a problem with brain function.   T   F

6. A **moody** person usually feels the same every day.   T   F

7. When a person is **agitated**, he or she is feeling very calm and relaxed.   T   F

8. When an animal is in **hibernation**, it is active and eats a lot.   T   F

9. **Glucose** is a form of sugar.   T   F

10. You usually dream during **non-REM sleep**.   T   F

C. THE ACADEMIC WORD LIST
In the boxes below are some of the most common *academic* words in English. Fill in the blanks with words from the boxes. You will use some words more than once. When you finish, check your answers in the readings on page 133 (for Items 1–7) and page 161 (for Items 8–18).

accompanied	create	response	symbolize
consciously	indication	symbol	

Jenny's Dream

Hi Jenny,

Many people enjoy flying dreams. However, not all flying dreams are the same. Some are exhilarating and are _____ by a sense of power and freedom—we fly easily and

1

are thrilled by the view below us. In others, however, like yours, we have difficulty staying aloft and seem to be flying in order to escape danger.

Power lines are a recurring (repeating) _____ in flying dreams. Dreamers

2

frequently write of "trying to fly above the power lines" or of bumping into them. I believe that *how* we are flying in our dreams—whether we are soaring easily or struggling to stay aloft—is an

_____ of our personal sense of power.

3

Because flying dreams recur so frequently for you, I suggest that you try to

_____ the association in your mind that, whenever you are flying, you must

4

be dreaming. The activity of flying can serve as a reminder that you must be dreaming, which will then

allow you to explore your dream _____—this is also known as lucid dreaming.

5

Your dream suggests that your life right now may be something of a "struggle to stay aloft." Once you recognize that you are dreaming, why don't you ask yourself in the dream what the power lines that

you keep bumping into represent? I would be interested to know your _____ in

6

the dream to your question. In the meantime, what, or who, do you think the power lines

_____? Whatever it is, I think it is a situation you want to get on top of

7

(get control of).

abnormal	allow	definition	mental	over	statistical
abnormality	approach	evicted	occurs	privacy	

What Is Abnormal Behavior?

For nine months, 54-year-old Richard Thompson lived happily and without any problems in a downtown storm drain (sewer) in San Diego, California. Because the city does not

_____ people to live in sewers, they _____ Thompson
       8   9

(forced him to leave). Although Thompson later lived in several care centers and

_____ hospitals, he preferred the _____ and the
       10   11

comfort of the sewer.

There are three ways to decide whether Thompson's behavior—living in the sewer—was

_____ .
       12

Statistical Frequency

The statistical frequency _____ says that a behavior may be considered
       13

abnormal if it _____ rarely or infrequently compared to the behaviors of most
       14

people.

By this _____ , Thompson's living in a sewer would be considered very
       15

abnormal, since out of _____ 230 million people in the United States, only a
       16

very few prefer this kind of home. However, so would getting a Ph.D., being president, living in a

monastery, or selling a million records. As these last examples show, the _____
       17

frequency _____ of _____ isn't too useful.
       18   19

UNIT 4

HEALTH

Chapter 7
Addictive Substances

Chapter 8
Secrets of Good Health

CHAPTER 7

Addictive Substances

Discuss these questions:
• What might be the purpose of the advertisement in the picture?
• What are some negative effects of cigarette smoking?
• What are some other habits that have negative effects on health?

Caution: Cigarettes and alcohol are addictive substances

A. BRAINSTORMING You are going to read about the use of an addictive substance (something that causes a physical or psychological need, such as a drug) on college campuses in the United States. Before you read, in small groups, write five addictive substances in the chart below. Then check (✓) if they are legal or illegal—against the law. Finally, for the legal substances, write the legal age that you must be to use them.

Addictive Substances	Legal	Illegal	Age

Now compare your chart with other groups' charts.

B. THINKING AHEAD Before you read, discuss these questions in small groups.

1. Have you noticed students using addictive substances at your school? Which ones are the most common?

2. What are some ways that people become addicted to substances?

C. PREDICTING The reading is about smoking cigarettes, which contain the addictive substance nicotine. Before you read, make predictions with a partner. How will the reading answer these questions?
- In recent years, has the number of adult cigarette smokers in the United States declined, increased, or stayed the same?
- Has the number of smokers in the United States between the ages of 18 and 24 declined, increased, or stayed the same?

D. READING Read about the use of tobacco on college campuses. As you read, think about this question:
- How are tobacco companies selling their products to college students?

Smoking on Campus

College life has long provided young people with a variety of late-night activities. But now students have been gathering at bars, nightclubs, and campus parties for a new kind of social event: tobacco-industry-sponsored parties, complete with complimentary (free) cigarettes. A new study suggests these parties are a powerful
5 marketing tool that encourages some students to start smoking.

Nearly one in 10 college students have gone to an industry-sponsored party, according to an article in a recent edition of the *American Journal of Public Health*. Students at all but one of 119 colleges surveyed have attended the parties. At some schools, 27 percent of students have attended tobacco bashes (parties),
10 which often include live music and gifts such as T-shirts.

Students who did not smoke before college were almost twice as likely to start if they attended industry-backed parties that included free cigarettes, the article said. The article was based on results from the Harvard School of Public Health College Alcohol Survey, for which nearly 11,000 students were interviewed. Although the
15 study does not prove that such parties directly led people to smoke, the authors say there might be a strong link.

The findings should be a warning to college administrators, says Nancy Rigotti, director of the Tobacco Research and Treatment Center of Massachusetts General Hospital.

"Tobacco-sponsored events aim to link smoking with alcohol, music, and
20 socializing," Rigotti says. Binge drinkers (people who drink large quantities of alcohol at one time) and marijuana users were more likely to attend these parties. The rate of cigarette smoking declined from 1993 to 2000 among all adults, except those ages 18 to 24, according to the study. Researchers note that college students are the youngest legal target for tobacco marketing.

25 Tobacco companies agreed not to market to anyone under 18 as part of the 1998 Master Settlement Agreement. Tobacco companies have since shifted their marketing efforts toward brand-centered social events, Rigotti says.

"The tobacco industry is still clearly marketing to young adults as replacement smokers to replace the ones who die," Rigotti says.

Source: "Smoking Makes the Campus Scene" (Szabo)

E. DISCUSSION In small groups, discuss these questions.

1. Were the predictions that you made in Activity C (page 195) correct? Were you surprised by any of the information in the reading?

2. Is binge drinking, smoking, and/or marijuana use a problem at your school?

3. If there is a problem with alcohol, tobacco, and/or marijuana use at a school or college, what is a possible solution? Do you think that the solution should be the same for all three substances?

4. Even though alcohol and tobacco are legal, do you think they should be banned (not allowed) on college campuses? Explain your answer.

5. Discuss addiction. What is it? What are some things that people become addicted to? How do people become addicted to substances? What are some treatments for addiction? Is it possible to smoke, drink alcohol, or take illegal drugs in moderation (in reasonable amounts) and not become addicted?

6. In your opinion, should illegal addictive substances such as cocaine and heroin be legalized? Explain your answer.

F. RESPONSE WRITING Choose *one* of these topics. Write about it for 10 minutes. Don't worry about grammar and don't use a dictionary. Just put as many ideas as you can on paper.
• Should alcohol and/or tobacco be banned on college campuses?
• Should addictive drugs such as cocaine and heroin become legal or remain illegal?
• Should marijuana be legalized?
• In your opinion, is it possible to try addictive substances and not become addicted?

PART ❷ SOCIAL LANGUAGE Secondhand Smoke

BEFORE LISTENING

A. THINKING AHEAD You are going to listen to Jennifer, Victor, and Brandon complain about people smoking cigarettes. In small groups, discuss these questions.

1. Do you smoke cigarettes? If so, do other people complain about it? If you don't, what do you think about people who smoke?

2. Should smokers have the right to smoke wherever they want? Explain your answer.

3. Is secondhand smoke a health problem? (Secondhand smoke is smoke that other people breathe because someone nearby is smoking.) Explain your answer.

196 **UNIT 4** Health

B. PREDICTING In the conversation, the students give some ideas for why people smoke. What do you think they will say? With a partner, discuss and then write your predictions on the lines.

_____

_____

_____

_____

C. VOCABULARY PREPARATION Read the sentences below. The words and phrases in green are from the conversation. Match the definitions in the box with the words and phrases in green. Write the correct letters on the lines.

a. aim at; appeal to	f. to maintain at a low level
b. dead body	g. removes
c. a disease that affects the brain	h. smokes a lot
d. have doubts about	i. stay
e. a large sign that advertises something	j. understand

_____ **1.** David saw his neighbor die of a heart attack. He was shocked because it was the first time he'd ever seen a **corpse**.

_____ **2.** Sharon **smokes like a chimney**—one cigarette after another!

_____ **3.** I don't **get** why they do that—it just doesn't make any sense to me!

_____ **4.** I exercise **to keep** my weight **down**.

_____ **5.** I can't eat right after I exercise—it **kills** my appetite.

_____ **6.** The **billboard** along Highway 101 with the cigarette advertisement is ugly.

_____ **7.** When you see how foolish people look when they smoke, it makes you **think twice about** starting the habit.

_____ **8.** I was going to go to the library, but the weather is so nice, I think I'll **hang around** outside for a while.

_____ **9.** My grandfather had **Alzheimer's**. This illness caused him to lose his memory, and after a while, he didn't even recognize me.

_____ **10.** Many people complain about the tobacco company that uses a cartoon character in its ads because they believe that the ads **target** kids.

LISTENING

A. LISTENING FOR MAIN IDEAS Listen to the conversation. As you listen, think about these questions:
- Why do some people smoke?
- How do they start smoking?

B. LISTENING FOR SUPPORTING INFORMATION Listen to the conversation again. This time, listen for information that supports the two main ideas. Write the supporting ideas on the lines.

1. How does smoking keep a person's weight down?

Supporting idea 1: _____

_____

Supporting idea 2: _____

_____

2. What are two ways that young people might start smoking?

Supporting idea 1: _____

_____

Supporting idea 2: _____

_____

Listening Strategy

Understanding Sarcasm

People sometimes use sarcasm to be funny when they speak. Sarcasm is using words that are the opposite of what the speaker actually means. That's why it can be difficult even for native speakers to understand sarcasm. You can sometimes recognize sarcasm by the person's intonation pattern. Listen to these "real" opinions followed by sarcastic remarks. Can you hear the difference?

Examples: **Real opinion:** That Professor Taylor is a real smart guy.
Sarcastic remark: That Professor Taylor is a real smart guy.

Real opinion: Hey, smoking sounds like a great way to avoid Alzheimer's!
Sarcastic remark: Hey, smoking sounds like a great way to avoid Alzheimer's!

C. UNDERSTANDING SARCASM Listen to some parts of the conversation again. Listen to each part twice. Then circle *Yes* or *No* to answer the questions.

1. Does Brandon think smoking is a good idea?   **Yes**   **No**

2. Does Victor think smoking is a good idea?   **Yes**   **No**

3. Does Jennifer think being near secondhand smoke is a good idea?   **Yes**   **No**

4. Does Victor think being near secondhand smoke is a good idea?   **Yes**   **No**

D. LISTENING FOR DETAILS Listen to some parts of the conversation again. Listen to each part twice. Listen for the answers to these questions. Write your answers on the lines.

1. Does Jennifer think it is unusual to see people smoking?

_____

_____

2. The students discuss two effects of smoking. What are they?

_____

_____

3. The students imply that one effect of smoking is possibly positive and one is negative. Which is positive? Which is negative?

Possible positive effect: _____

Negative effect: _____

AFTER LISTENING

A. TAKING A SURVEY You are going to interview three classmates about their opinions about smoking.

Step 1
Make predictions about the results of your survey. In small groups, discuss these questions.

1. Do you think most people in your class *do* or *do not* smoke?

2. Do age, gender, and/or culture have anything to do with smoking habits?

Step 2
Think about your answers to the questions in the chart on page 200. Write your own question about smoking in Part 3 of the chart. Then survey three classmates. If possible, try to talk to both males and females from different cultures and of different age groups. Write their answers in the chart. (If they don't want to give their ages, they don't have to answer Question 3.)

Questions	Classmate 1 ☐ Male ☐ Female	Classmate 2 ☐ Male ☐ Female	Classmate 3 ☐ Male ☐ Female
Part 1			
1. Do you smoke now?	☐ Yes ☐ No	☐ Yes ☐ No	☐ Yes ☐ No
2. Have you ever smoked?	☐ Yes ☐ No	☐ Yes ☐ No	☐ Yes ☐ No
3. If you don't mind my asking, how old are you?			
4. Where did you grow up?			
Part 2			
5a. If you don't smoke, why don't you?			
5b. If you do smoke, why do you?			
6a. If you don't smoke, do smokers bother you? How or why?			
6b. If you smoke now, do you think that you bother people? How or why?			
Part 3			
7. Your question:			

B. DISCUSSING SURVEY RESULTS Form small groups. Try not to be in a group with someone that you interviewed. Discuss the results of your survey. Now that you have your results, use them to answer the questions you discussed in Step 1 of Activity A (page 199). Then discuss these questions.

1. Do most people in your class smoke?

2. Do age, gender, and/or culture seem to have anything to do with smoking habits?

3. What are some reasons for smoking among the smokers in your class?

4. Do age, gender, and/or culture seem to have anything to do with reasons for smoking?

5. Do age, gender, and/or culture seem to have anything to do with tolerating (accepting) smoking and smokers?

6. What other information about smoking and smokers surprised or interested you?

PART ③ THE MECHANICS OF LISTENING AND SPEAKING

LANGUAGE FUNCTIONS

Agreeing and Disagreeing

In a conversation when people give their opinions, it is polite to agree (say that you think the same way) or disagree (say that you don't think the same way). There are several ways to express agreement with someone else's ideas.

Examples: **A:** I think there's too much advertising, especially on billboards.

B: | Yeah.   **Less Formal**
| Yeah. I agree.
| Well, you're right.
| You've got a good point.
| Yes, I know what you mean.   **More Formal**

There are also several ways to express disagreement with someone's ideas.

Examples: **A:** Advertising makes young people want to smoke.

B: | No way!   **Less Formal**
| I don't know.
| I don't think so.
| I'm not so sure.
| I disagree.
| I'm afraid I disagree with you   **More Formal**

 A. AGREEING AND DISAGREEING Practice agreeing and disagreeing with a partner. Student A says one of the statements in the box below. Student B agrees or disagrees.

If you agree, answer with one of the agreement expressions in the box above. If you disagree, answer with one of the disagreement expressions. Then exchange roles.

Examples: **A:** People who smoke in public are a danger to others.
B: I disagree with you.

A: People who smoke in public are a danger to others.
B: You've got a good point.

Smoking is a good way to lose weight.
Tobacco should be illegal, like other drugs.
It's impossible to smoke and not become addicted.
People should not be allowed to smoke in any public place.
People should be allowed to buy alcohol at the age of 18.
If tobacco and alcohol are legal, other drugs should be legal, too.

Degrees of Agreement/Disagreement

You can express degrees (weak, neutral, or strong) of agreement or disagreement. To do this, add one of the following words or expressions to your statement.

Examples:

Weak	**Neutral**	**Strong**
I **sort of** (dis)agree with you.	I (dis)agree with you.	I **really** (dis)agree with you.
I **kind of** (dis)agree with you.		I **totally** (dis)agree with you.
I don't **really** agree with that.		I **completely** (dis)agree with you.
I'm **not sure** I agree with that.		I (dis)agree **a hundred percent**.
I **don't know if** I agree.		

B. HEARING DEGREES OF AGREEMENT/DISAGREEMENT Listen to these statements of agreement and disagreement. Decide if they are weak, neutral, or strong. Circle the correct answers.

1.	Weak	Neutral	Strong	**4.**	Weak	Neutral	Strong
2.	Weak	Neutral	Strong	**5.**	Weak	Neutral	Strong
3.	Weak	Neutral	Strong	**6.**	Weak	Neutral	Strong

C. EXPRESSING DEGREES OF AGREEMENT/DISAGREEMENT Practice degrees of agreement and disagreement with a partner. Student A says each of the statements below. Student B responds to each statement with his or her own opinion, but expresses the degree indicated by the cue. Then exchange roles.

Examples: **A:** Pop art is great.
Cue: (Strong)
B: I totally agree.

1. Bribes are unethical. (Strong)

2. The government should help the poor. (Neutral)

3. Andy Warhol was a great artist. (Weak)

4. People study too much ancient Greek art and not enough African or Asian art. (Weak)

5. A person's dreams can predict his or her future. (Neutral)

6. Paranoia is normal. (Strong)

7. I think smoking is a cool habit. (Strong)

8. Alzheimer's is a terrible disease! (Strong)

Expressing an Opinion

People rarely agree or disagree without expressing an opinion as well. If you agree, your opinion might include the following:
- a restatement of the other person's idea
- an extension of the idea
- an additional idea that supports the same point

Example: **A:** I think tobacco companies shouldn't advertise to children.
 B: Yeah, I agree. **Their ads should not be allowed to target kids.**

If you disagree, your opinion might include the following:
- the opposite of the other person's idea
- an explanation of why you disagree

Example: **A:** I think smokers should be allowed to smoke wherever they want.
 B: I totally disagree with you. **Smokers should not be able to smoke in public places.**

Since your opinion follows your agreement or disagreement statement, certain expressions help make this transition.

Examples: **A:** Advertising makes young people want to smoke.
 B: **Oh, I don't know.** I think kids are smarter than that.

 A: Advertising makes young people want to smoke.
 B: I agree. **In my opinion,** advertising is the main reason kids start smoking.

 D. EXPRESSING AN OPINION Practice agreeing or disagreeing and expressing an opinion with a partner. Student A says one of the statements in Activity A on page 201. Student B agrees or disagrees and gives his or her opinion. Then exchange roles.

PRONUNCIATION

∩ Reduced Forms of Words: *a* and *of*

When people speak quickly, some words become reduced, or short. Often the words *a* and *of* are reduced.

Examples:	**Long Forms**		**Reduced Forms**
	What a choice!	→	Whatta* choice!
	Get a drink for me, O.K.?	→	Getta* drink for me, O.K.?
	Want a snack?	→	Wanna snack?
	Let's get **out of** here!	→	Let's get **outta*** here!
	A **couple of** my friends smoke.	→	A **coupla** my friends smoke.
	Some of them smoke.	→	**Somma** them smoke.
	I **kind of** disagree.	→	I **kinda** disagree.
	I **sort of** disagree.	→	I **sorta** disagree.

 *What sound is the *t* in "whatta," "getta," and "outta" most like?

A: A _____ my friends and I are going to that new pizza place.

1

B: _____ my friends went there last week. They have 20 kinds of pizza.

2

_____ choice!

3

A: _____ snack? I can _____ pizza for you.

4   5

B: Um, I think I'll go with you guys.

A: O.K. I'm hungry! Let's get _____ here!

6

WORDS IN PHRASES

The Language of Smoking

You may have noticed that when you talk about starting, stopping, or trying smoking, you have to use some confusing combinations of the main verb + a gerund or an infinitive. Verbs such as *stop*, *start*, and *try* require either a gerund (verb + *-ing*) or an infinitive (*to* + verb) depending on what you want to say. Compare these sentences with *stop*. Try to memorize the structures and their meanings.

She **stopped smoking**. (She doesn't smoke anymore.)
She **stopped to smoke**. (She stopped what she was doing so that she could smoke a cigarette.)

Compare these sentences with *start* and *try*.

Sentences		Meanings
She **started smoking**.	→	She wasn't a smoker before, but now she is.
She **started to smoke**.	→	She lit a cigarette and smoked it.
She **tried smoking**.	→	She never did it before; she experimented with it.
She **tried to smoke**.	→	She attempted it, but she failed.
She **tried stopping**.	→	She attempted to stop.
She **tried to stop**.	→	She attempted it, but she failed.

F. WORDS IN PHRASES Go back to your survey results in Part 2 on page 200. In small groups, discuss the results using the expressions for smoking in the box above.

PUT IT TOGETHER

FORMING AN OPINION You are going to agree or disagree with your partner and add an opinion. Before you start, look at the following list of topics from this book and write an opinion about each one.

1. Offering bribes to get business (Chapter 1)

Opinion: _____

_____

2. Government assistance for the poor (Chapter 2)

Opinion: _____

_____

3. Pop art (Chapter 3)

Opinion: _____

_____

4. The importance of Greek art (Chapter 4)

Opinion: _____

_____

5. The purpose of dreaming (Chapter 5)

Opinion: _____

_____

6. What is "normal" (Chapter 6)

Opinion: _____

_____

7. Smoking in public places (Chapter 7)

Opinion: _____

_____

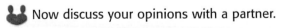 Now discuss your opinions with a partner.

1. Student A gives an opinion about one of the topics.

2. Student B agrees or disagrees. Express weak, neutral, or strong agreement or disagreement, depending on how you really feel. Use the expressions in the box on page 202. Follow with an opinion statement.

3. Then exchange roles.

BEFORE LISTENING

An anti-smoking billboard

A. THINKING AHEAD You are going to listen to a radio program about whether smoking is a **gateway drug**, a drug that makes the user want to take other drugs. Before you listen, discuss these questions in small groups.

1. This program discusses the idea that tobacco (or specifically nicotine, one of the chemicals in tobacco) is a drug. Do you agree with this? If yes, in what way is it a drug?

2. Do you think that taking one drug can lead to taking other drugs? Why or why not?

B. PREDICTING Before you listen, make a prediction about what you are going to hear. Discuss this question with a partner.
• Do you think the program will say that smoking *is* or *is not* a gateway drug? Why?

👥 **C. GUESSING THE MEANING FROM CONTEXT** Read the sentences below. The words and phrases in green are from the radio program. Guess their meanings from the context. Write your guesses on the lines. Then compare your answers with a partner's answers.

1. Some researchers **hypothesize** that tobacco is a gateway drug; they believe that smoking cigarettes leads to taking other kinds of drugs.

   Guess: _____

2. **Substance abuse** is a growing problem on college campuses. Studies show that students are drinking more alcohol and taking more drugs than students did in the past.

   Guess: _____

3. Many kids start smoking because they like the **notion** of taking a risk. They think that being risky will make them more "cool."

   Guess: _____

4. Lloyd Johnston believes that cigarette smoking is one of the **causal factors** of marijuana smoking. He believes that cigarette smoking can lead to marijuana use.

   Guess: _____

5. Greg was in prison for possessing marijuana, but now he's **on probation**. That means he's free, as long as he follows certain rules and meets regularly with his probation officer.

   Guess: _____

6. Jason was very **rebellious** as a teenager; as an adult, he's quite different—now he enjoys following the rules of society.

   Guess: _____

D. VOCABULARY PREPARATION Read the sentences below. The words and phrases in green are from the radio program. First, guess their meanings from the context. Then match the definitions in the box with the words and phrases in green. Write the correct letters on the lines.

a. become addicted to	c. a part of a process	e. serious enforcement of a law or policy
b. illegal	d. risking getting arrested	

_____ 1. There's recently been a **crackdown** on people driving through red lights. The police have put cameras at intersections to catch drivers who do it.

_____ 2. Learning academic English is **a step along the way** to success in an American university.

_____ 3. Some people think that if you are addicted to nicotine, you are more likely to **get hooked on** illegal drugs such as heroin later on.

_____ 4. Many kids start smoking before they start **illicit** drugs because cigarettes are easily available.

_____ 5. If you have marijuana, you're **flirting with the law**, because it's illegal.

LISTENING

A. LISTENING FOR MAIN IDEAS Listen to the radio program. As you listen, think about this question:
- The program presents two sides of the question: Are cigarettes a gateway drug? What are the two sides of the argument presented?

After listening, complete the sentences.

1. Cigarettes *are* a gateway drug because _____

_____

2. Cigarettes *aren't* a gateway drug because _____

_____

B. LISTENING FOR TWO SIDES OF AN ARGUMENT Listen to a section of the radio program again. Vicky Quay interviews four researchers. Listen for information that answers the questions below. Then complete the graphic organizer.
- Which researchers believe that there is a direct connection between smoking and using illegal drugs? Which of them do not?
- What reasons do they give for their beliefs?

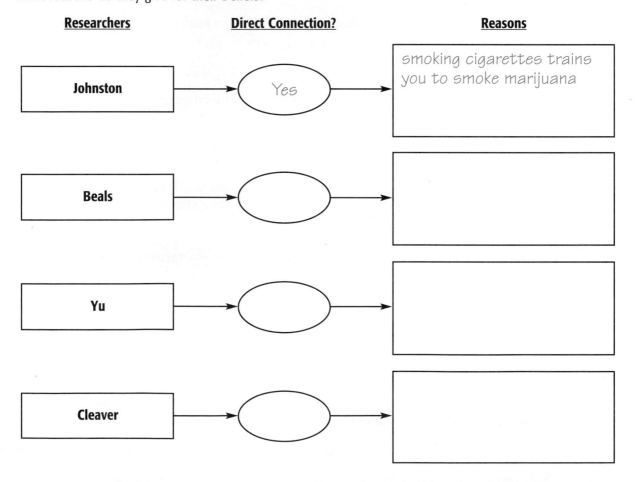

Researchers	Direct Connection?	Reasons
Johnston	Yes	smoking cigarettes trains you to smoke marijuana
Beals		
Yu		
Cleaver		

Critical Thinking Strategy

Evaluating the Source of Information

It's important to pay attention to the qualifications of people who are expressing their opinions about scientific or social scientific ideas. To effectively evaluate their opinions, you often need to know:
• their job title
• their degrees
• their **affiliations** (the institutions they work for or represent)
• their research

For example, a biology professor at a well-known university might say that milk is good for you. However, if the Milk Advisory Board pays the same professor for consulting services, this **affiliation** (connection) might influence her opinions.

C. EVALUATING THE SOURCE OF INFORMATION Listen to sections of the program again. You will hear each expert's qualifications (job title and/or affiliations) twice. Match qualifications with the experts. Write the letters of the correct qualifications on the lines. (There may be more than one for each person.)

_____ **1.** Lloyd Johnston

_____ **2.** Howard Beals

_____ **3.** Jian Yu

_____ **4.** Herbert Cleaver

a. psychologist

b. University of Michigan

c. R. J. Reynolds Tobacco Company

d. George Washington University

e. sociologist

f. Columbia University

g. professor

Now answer these questions with a partner. Write your answers on the lines.

1. Which expert has both a job title and a university affiliation?

_____

2. Which expert does not have a university affiliation?

_____

3. Which expert has an affiliation with a university and a company?

_____

4. Which expert has an affiliation that might influence his opinions?

_____

Listening Strategy

Understanding Latin Terms

People often use Latin terms (terms that come from Latin) in formal speaking situations. Using them in academic speaking situations can make you sound more fluent. Memorize them and try to use them. Below are examples of some common Latin terms and their meanings.

Examples:

Latin Terms		Meanings
modus operandi	→	way of doing something; method or procedure
per se	→	by itself, by himself or herself, by themselves
pro forma	→	made or done in a routine manner
quid pro quo	→	you do something for me, and I'll do something for you
verbatim	→	word for word; literally

D. UNDERSTANDING LATIN TERMS Complete the sentences with Latin terms from the box above.

1. The detective recognized who the thief was by the clues that he left behind at the three crime scenes. The clues helped the detective to figure out the thief's _____, which then helped her to solve the crime.

2. The company has a _____ agreement that all consultants must sign. The agreement doesn't take into consideration consultants' individual circumstances.

3. Warren's not a bad kid _____. He just hangs around with the wrong kind of friends, and they get him into trouble.

4. Becky wrote a speech then read it _____. She read every word exactly as she wrote it.

5. "This is a _____ arrangement," the lawyer told the accountant. "I'll give you advice on this contract. You advise me on how to pay fewer taxes next year."

E. LISTENING FOR LATIN TERMS Listen to a section of the program. You'll hear it twice. The speaker uses a Latin term. First, write the term he uses. Then paraphrase the speaker's statement by translating the Latin term and completing the sentence.

Latin term: _____

What he's saying is that cigarette smoking _____ _____

_____

AFTER LISTENING

DISCUSSION In small groups, discuss these questions.

1. The radio program presents two sides of the question: Are cigarettes a gateway drug? What are the two sides of the argument? Which side of the argument do you agree with? Why?

2. Evaluate the experts who were interviewed in the program. Were they qualified to speak on this subject? Does anything about any of these experts make you question their authority or reliability?

3. Think of an advertisement for smoking and describe it to the group. Whom does it target? How does it make smoking look attractive?

4. Think of movies that portray smoking, drinking, or illegal drug use. Describe one movie that makes using addictive substances look attractive. Then describe a movie that makes it look unattractive.

PART ⑤ ACADEMIC ENGLISH Nicotine Addiction

BEFORE LISTENING

A. THINKING AHEAD You are going to listen to a lecture about how people become addicted to nicotine. In small groups, discuss these questions.

1. What are the health risks of cigarette smoking?

2. What do cigarettes contain that is bad for you?

3. What other tobacco products are bad for your health?

4. If you had a friend who was addicted to nicotine, would you try to help your friend stop smoking? If so, what would you do? If not, why not?

B. PREDICTING The lecture contains statistics on smoking in the United States. Make a prediction with a partner. What will the lecturer say are some of the reasons that people become addicted to nicotine?

C. HAVING QUESTIONS IN MIND Look at the outline for the lecture on pages 215–217 and think about your discussion in Activity A. What would you like to know about tobacco addiction? Write three questions about the subject on the lines.

Question 1: _____

Question 2: _____

Question 3: _____

D. GUESSING THE MEANING FROM CONTEXT Read the sentences below. The words and phrases in green are from the lecture. Guess their meanings from the context. Write your guesses on the lines.

1. I **crave** chocolate. My desire for it is so strong that sometimes I just have to have it.

Guess: _____

2. Jennifer, Victor, and Brandon were exposed to **passive smoke**; that's almost as bad for you as smoking itself.

Guess: _____

3. Many people smoke because it gives them a feeling of **alertness**; this helps them pay attention and stay awake while they work.

Guess: _____

4. You can have a **psychological dependence** on a drug if it has positive effects on your behavior and attitude.

Guess: _____

5. Morgan wanted to stop smoking, but he was afraid that the **withdrawal** from cigarettes would make him feel bad.

Guess: _____

6. Smoking is a health **hazard**. It's dangerous because it causes many serious diseases.

Guess: _____

7. Sandy started smoking **casually**—just one or two cigarettes every once in a while—but soon she became addicted.

Guess: _____

8. Jack wanted to stop smoking, but he didn't have the mental strength to control his behavior—he just didn't have the **willpower**.

Guess: _____

Now compare your answers with a partner's answers.

Listening Strategy

Taking Notes: Numbers

When you are taking notes and you hear numbers, you can write them using numerals or words. Sometimes it's faster to write the numeral (*18*). Other times, it's faster to write the word (*a million*). In some cases, there's a **shortcut**—an abbreviation—for the number (*1 m*) that might be the easiest to write. Choose the method that works best for you.

Examples:	Words		Numerals		Abbreviations
	one million; a million	→	1,000,000	→	1 mill; 1 m
	one thousand	→	1,000	→	1 k
	forty thousand	→	40,000	→	40 k
	sixty percent	→	60 percent	→	60%
	six to eight	→	6 to 8	→	6–8

A. TAKING NOTES: NUMBERS Listen to some parts of the lecture. You'll listen to each one twice. Listen for numerical information—numbers, percents, and quantities—about smoking. Write the numbers you hear on the lines. Use words, numerals, or abbreviations.

1. _____ of people throughout the world smoke cigarettes. But despite the fact that cigarette smoking has declined in the United States over the past _____ years, there are still over _____ Americans who smoke.

2. Now, let's, let's take a look at the health risks of smoking. Smoking cigarettes *is* dangerous. In fact, it's the leading cause of preventable death in the United States. Every year over _____ Americans die as a result of cigarette smoking, and another _____ people suffer from smoking-related diseases.

3. The symptoms of nicotine withdrawal can appear within _____ hours after the last cigarette is smoked.

4. Of people who quit smoking, only about _____ remain smoke-free for more than one year.

B. TAKING NOTES: USING AN OUTLINE Listen to the lecture. It's in four sections. You will listen to each section twice. Fill in as much of the outline as you can. Don't worry if you can't fill in everything. (You'll listen to the whole lecture again later.) Remember to use key words and abbreviations.

Note: There are fewer cues in this outline; you will take more notes on your own than in previous chapters.

Nicotine Addiction

Section 1

I. Introduction

  A. Cigarette smoking is _____ & _____

     1. "Addictive" means:

       a. _____

       b. When you crave something, _____

       c. Once you become dependent, _____

  B. Statistics on smoking

     1. # in world: _____

     2. in U.S. smoking has _____

       but # is _____

     3. Higher rates among _____

  C. Health risks

     1. # who die: _____

     2. # who suffer from diseases: _____

     3. Smoking related diseases and risks:

       a. _____

       b. _____

       c. _____

       d. _____

       e. _____

     4. Non-smoking risks: _____

_____

_____

Section 2

II. Why People Smoke

    A. Reasons young people often start:

        1. _____

        2. _____

        3. _____

        4. _____

        5. Advertising targets _____

            _____

        6. Pleasure: smoking _____

        7. When people attempt to stop, _____

            _____

Chewing tobacco

Section 3

    B. Why cigarettes are addictive

        1. Cigarette smoke contains: _____

            _____

        2. These chemicals cause: _____

            _____

        3. The stimulating effects of nicotine: _____

            _____

            _____

        4. The short-term effects of nicotine: _____

            _____

        5. The long-term effects of nicotine: _____

            _____

        6. The psychological effects of nicotine: _____

            _____

        7. Effects of nicotine withdrawal

          a. Appear w/ in _____

          b. Symptoms include: _____

              _____

              _____

          c. Percent who remain smoke-free after 1 yr.: _____

Section 4

III. Strategies for Treating Nicotine Addiction

    A. Quitting on own: _____

        _____

        _____

    B. Other methods:

        1. _____

        2. _____

    C. Benefits of quitting: _____

        _____

        _____

A nicotine patch

Source: Adapted from a lecture by Deborah E. Blocker, D.Sc., M.P.H., R.N.

Listening Strategy

Listening for Comparisons

Sometimes statistical information includes comparisons of two groups. Some words and expressions that signal comparisons include the following:

more than	higher than	greater than	more + (adjective/adverb) + than
less than	lower than	lesser than	less + (adjective/adverb) + than

Examples: Rates of smoking are **higher** among women **than** among men.
As a group, women smoke **more frequently than** men.

C. LISTENING FOR COMPARISONS Listen to part of the lecture. Listen for comparisons and answer these questions. Write your answers on the lines.

1. Who smokes more, men or women? _____

2. Who smokes more, whites or non-whites? _____

3. Who smokes more, people with a high school education or people without a high school education?

D. CHECKING YOUR NOTES Listen to the lecture again. This time, fill in any information missing on your outline.

AFTER LISTENING

A. USING YOUR NOTES With a partner, use your notes to discuss these questions about the lecture.

1. How do people start smoking?

2. What are the health risks of cigarette smoking?

3. Why is smoking addictive?

4. What are some treatments for nicotine addiction?

5. What are the benefits of stopping smoking?

B. MAKING CONNECTIONS Think about the reading on tobacco-industry parties you read in Part 1, the radio program you listened to in Part 4, and the lecture you just heard. In small groups, discuss this question:
• Should cigarettes and other tobacco products be illegal? Explain your answer.

PUT IT ALL TOGETHER

MAKING A PERSUASIVE ARGUMENT In small groups, you are going to discuss a controversial issue—an issue that has two sides.

Step 1
First, as a group, choose an issue that interests you. Decide on your position and do research. You can use your own idea or argue for or against one of the following issues:
• Alcohol (or tobacco products) should/shouldn't be banned on college campuses.
• Cigarette smoking should/shouldn't be illegal.
• Illegal drugs should/shouldn't be legalized.
• Cigarettes are/aren't a gateway drug.
• Marijuana should/shouldn't be legal.
• Marijuana/tobacco/another drug is/isn't addictive.
• It's possible/impossible to experiment with addictive substances and not become addicted.
• Your own controversial issue on the subject of addictive substances:

_____

Step 2

Do Internet or library research, or find information in an introductory health textbook.

If you do Internet research, try finding current research on addictive substances. Find at least three reasons that support your argument. One way to do this is to decide on different questions for each group member to answer. For example, for the position, "Alcohol should be banned on college campuses," you might get information on the following.

1. How does alcohol affect the physical health of college-aged people?

2. How does alcohol affect the mental health of college-aged people?

3. How does alcohol affect the quality of schoolwork?

4. Is there a relationship between alcohol use and college **drop-out** (leaving school) rates?

5. Is there a relationship between alcohol use and college graduation rates?

Do a key word search using a search engine. To do this, choose the most important words—the key words—in your question and put them in the search engine search box. For example, for Question 1, you might try the key words: *alcohol + physical health + college student.*

Note that you can join key words with a plus sign (+) and you do not need capital letters or *–s* endings for plural nouns.

Share your results with your group members. Choose the best reasons to support your side of the issue.

You are going to present your ideas from notes (see Chapter 4, page 125), so as you do your research, take notes on index cards, or use a form like the example below.

The issue: _____

Your side of the issue: _____

Reason 1: _____

_____

Reason 2: _____

_____

Reason 3: _____

_____

More reasons or other information: _____

_____

_____

Step 3

Go over your notes and organize your information.

Speaking Strategy

Listing Reasons

When you support an opinion, you usually have a list of reasons or arguments. You can present these arguments in order from most important to least important. You can also present them in the opposite order, giving the most important reason last.

Certain expressions help you clearly present your arguments:

First of all . . .   Most importantly, . . .
The main argument for . . . is . . .   Finally, . . .
Secondly, . . .   Finally and most importantly, . . .
Another reason is/that . . .

Example: There are many reasons why cigarettes should be illegal. Cigarette smoking can cause many diseases including lung disease. **Secondly,** smokers can harm the health of people around them with secondhand smoke. **Finally,** some research shows that cigarettes are a gateway drug—they can lead to other types of substance abuse.

Step 4

Form small groups. Decide on a time limit for each speaker. A good length is from three to five minutes. In your groups, present your issue. Follow these guidelines:
• Paraphrase information from your research.
• Use your notes; don't read.
• Present your arguments clearly.
• Make eye contact with your group members.
• Stay within the time limit.
• Take and answer questions from your group members when you are finished.

Step 5

After each person has presented his or her issue, take a few minutes to discuss the issue using agreement and disagreement expressions and opinion statements.

Step 6

In your groups, evaluate each other's presentations. Use the questions below in your evaluation.
• Were the presentations easy to understand?
• Were the issues interesting?
• Did the speakers use notes and make good eye contact?
• Did the speakers use signals or questions to help the audience?
• Did the speakers support their positions with good reasons?

CHAPTER 8

Secrets of Good Health

Discuss these questions:

- What are the benefits of exercise?
- What are some things that you do to stay healthy?
- What other behaviors can lead to good health?

 A. THINKING AHEAD You are going to read about students and health. In small groups, look at the photos and discuss these questions.

1. What's happening in each photo? How might it be connected to good health?

2. Are you concerned with your health? What do you do to stay healthy?

3. Is there a connection between what you eat and maintaining good health? Explain your answer.

4. Do you exercise regularly? Why or why not?

5. How many hours do you sleep each night? How much sleep is healthy for you?

6. Do you try to avoid risky (possibly dangerous) behavior (for example, smoking cigarettes or driving without wearing your seatbelt)?

B. PREDICTING The reading gives advice to college students so that they can avoid stress and stay healthy. With a partner, make predictions about what you will read by discussing the questions.

1. What are some health problems related to living in a dormitory (a place where students live while they go to school)?

2. What are some bad health habits that some college students have?

3. What are some bad safety habits that some students might have?

4. What are some dangerous habits that some college students have?

5. What should students do to avoid stress and to stay healthy?

C. READING Read about staying healthy in college. As you read, think about this question:
• What special stress and health issues do college students have?

The College Transition: Managing Stress and Maintaining Health

The switch from living at home to going away to college can be difficult. Students have a great deal to learn—not only in the classroom, but also in the dormitory and at campus social functions. To safeguard their health, they need to:

Get enough sleep.

Not getting enough sleep can lead to depression, anxiety, poor concentration,
5 memory loss, lowered resistance to illness, and increased drug and alcohol use. College students need to go to bed and get up at regular hours. Many students view all-night study sessions as a normal part of college, but often the practice is a result of poor study habits or weak time-management skills—that is, some students take on more tasks than they should.

10 If noise or roommate conflicts create a sleep problem, student housing or student services can help mediate (solve conflicts). Additional options to encourage sleep include using travel earplugs and eyeshades, or perhaps a fan for a steady background sound. Remember that an alarm clock is also an essential part of college life—no more relying on parents for awakening in time for class.

Maintain good habits.

15 Away from home, students may eat poorly and stop exercising, a combination that saps (reduces) energy and promotes weight gain. Late-night pizza, a tradition in many dorms, does nothing to help. At the other extreme, an eating disorder such as anorexia (an extreme reduction in caloric intake) may appear when a person is away from home for the first time.

20 Pay attention to car and bicycle safety, too. Long before they go to college, people should be in the habit of wearing seat belts in cars and helmets on bikes.

Avoid drugs and alcohol.

Even though most college students are well below the legal drinking age, alcohol is a prominent feature of social life on most campuses. Underage drinking is against the
25 law, as is the recreational use of drugs—and the police don't always ignore violations. There are also physical and emotional hazards of drugs and alcohol. Drinking and drug use can cause depression, anxiety, memory problems, difficulty concentrating, and a host of dangerous behaviors and destructive thought patterns. Students worried about their own or their friends' drinking and drug use should consult their campus student
30 health service for treatment or referral.

Source: MayoClinic.com Special

D. COMPREHENSION CHECK In small groups, discuss these questions.

1. Were the predictions that you made in Activity B correct? Were you surprised by any of the information in the article?

2. Find details in the reading that support the statements at the beginning: "The switch from living at home to going away to college can be difficult. Students have a great deal to learn—not only in the classroom, but also in the dormitory and at campus social functions."

Critical Thinking Strategy

Making Comparisons

Making comparisons between two things helps you to understand both of them better. When you make comparisons, you discuss similarities and differences and give reasons for the similarities and differences. For example, here's a comparison a student made between living at home and living alone.

Living with Family	Living Alone
eat healthy food	eat at fast-food restaurants
eat with other people	eat alone
spend more time with parents	spend more time with friends from school
talk more; watch less TV	talk less; watch more TV
share a bathroom	have a private bathroom

E. MAKING COMPARISONS In small groups, discuss these questions.

1. Compare the ideas about student life that the reading describes with ideas about student life in your culture or another culture that you are familiar with.

2. Compare the ideas about managing stress and maintaining health in the article with ideas about managing stress and maintaining health in your culture or another culture that you are familiar with. Think about:
   • eating habits
   • exercise
   • maintaining weight
   • attitudes about smoking, drinking, and taking drugs
   • use of prescription medicines
   • interest in alternative remedies and therapies

F. RESPONSE WRITING Choose *one* of these topics. Write about it for 10 minutes. Don't worry about grammar and don't use a dictionary. Just put as many ideas as you can on paper.
• Do you think that you are in good health? Why or why not?
• What do you think is the secret to good health?
• Are there cultural differences in **approaches** (methods) to maintaining good health, in your opinion? Explain your answer.

PART ② SOCIAL LANGUAGE Tips for Good Health

BEFORE LISTENING

A. THINKING AHEAD You are going to listen to Evan interview people on the street. He's going to ask them for their **tips** (advice) for good health. In small groups, discuss these questions.

1. What's your definition of good physical health (health of the body)?

2. How do you define good mental health (health of the mind)?

B. PREDICTING You are going to listen to people give their tips for good health. Discuss what you think they will say with a partner. Write your predictions on the lines.

_____

_____

_____

Read the sentences below. The words and phrases in green are from the interviews. Match the definitions in the box with the words and phrases in green. Write the correct letters on the lines.

a. become	e. regular
b. consuming food that is good for you	f. vegetable or animal fat in food
c. good mental idea	g. worried; anxious
d. most important part of	

_____ **1.** Dan has a **positive image** of himself. He knows that he is smart and that people like him.

_____ **2.** Jason has got a **steady** job now, so he'll be able to save some money.

_____ **3.** I think you fried those potatoes in too much cooking oil—they're sitting in a pool of **grease**.

_____ **4.** If you continue to eat junk food like cookies and potato chips, you'll **end up** sick and overweight.

_____ **5.** **Eating right** is the key to staying healthy.

_____ **6.** I'm really **stressed out**—I'm really restless, and I can't sleep at night.

_____ **7.** The **key to** good health is exercising regularly.

LISTENING

🎧 **A. LISTENING FOR MAIN IDEAS** Listen to the interview. As you listen, think about this question:
• Do more students give advice about physical or mental health?

B. LISTENING FOR DETAILS Listen to the interviews twice. The first time you listen, decide if the speaker gives a physical health tip, a mental health tip, or both. Check (✓) the correct boxes in the chart. The second time you listen, write the advice that the speaker gives in the chart.

Speakers	Physical Health Tips?	Mental Health Tips?
1	✓ exercise, eat well	✓ have positive image, think healthy
2	☐	☐
3	☐	☐
4	☐	☐
5	☐	☐
6	☐	☐
7	☐	☐
8	☐	☐

Listening Strategy

Guessing the Meaning of Proverbs

Every language has **proverbs**—well-known sayings that express some wisdom about life. If you hear a proverb that is new to you, you can sometimes guess its meaning from the context.

Example: **You hear:** Since the economy is bad and you already have a job, I don't think you should look for a new one right now. Remember, **a bird in the hand is worth two in the bush**.

You guess: This proverb means that **something you have right now is more valuable than something you might find later.**

C. GUESSING THE MEANING OF PROVERBS Listen to parts of the interviews again. Guess the meanings of the proverbs below by paying attention to their contexts. Write your guesses on the lines.

1. **An apple a day keeps the doctor away.** _____

_____

2. **You are what you eat.** _____

_____

D. LISTENING FOR SPECIFIC INFORMATION Listen to some of the speakers' advice again. Listen for answers to these questions. Write your answers on the lines.

1. **Speaker 4:** How many times a week should you exercise, according to this speaker?

   _____

   _____

2. **Speaker 6:** What are examples of getting "stressed out," according to this speaker?

   _____

   _____

3. **Speaker 7:** This speaker suggests specific activities for maintaining good health. What are they?

   _____

   _____

AFTER LISTENING

A. TAKING A SURVEY Think about your answers to the question in the chart. Write your own question. Then interview three classmates about their tips for good health. Write their tips in the chart.

Questions	Classmate 1	Classmate 2	Classmate 3
1. What do you think is the key to good health?			
2. Your question:			

B. DISCUSSING SURVEY RESULTS Form small groups. Try not to be in a group with someone that you interviewed. Discuss the results of your survey. Did any of the advice surprise you? Were there any unusual suggestions?

LANGUAGE FUNCTION

Giving Health Advice

Many people like to get advice about their health. Usually, people will ask for advice; in fact, they often don't want it *unless* they ask. If someone asks you for advice, here are some ways to give it.

Examples: You **ought to** get a lot of rest.   **Less Formal**
You **should** get a lot of rest.
It's **a good idea** to get a lot of rest.
I suggest that you get a lot of rest.   **More Formal**

WORDS IN PHRASES

Health Advice

Here are some verb phrases for talking about good health habits:

get	a lot of rest
avoid	stress
eat	healthy food
follow	an exercise program
have	a positive image
see	your doctor once a year

A. WORDS IN PHRASES Work with a partner. Practice asking for and giving health advice. Student A asks for health advice. Student B gives the advice. Combine the advice expressions with the verb phrases from the boxes on page 229 or use your own ideas. Then exchange roles.

Examples: **A:** How can I improve my health?
B: You should avoid stress.

B: I'm tired all the time. What should I do?
A: I suggest that you get a lot of rest.

LANGUAGE FUNCTION

Degrees of Advice

Often when you give advice, you want to soften it so that it doesn't sound like you are ordering the person to do something. You can soften advice by adding *perhaps* or *I think*.

Examples: **Perhaps** you should get more rest.
I think you ought to get a lot of rest.

You can make advice a little stronger by adding *really*.

Example: You **really** ought to get more rest.

You can be very strong or direct by making your suggestion an order.

Examples: **Get more rest.**
Just get a lot of rest.

B. HEARING DEGREES OF ADVICE Listen to speakers giving advice. Decide if the advice is soft, strong, or direct. Circle the correct answers.

1. Soft	Strong	Direct	**4.** Soft Strong Direct
2. Soft	Strong	Direct	**5.** Soft Strong Direct
3. Soft	Strong	Direct	

C. EXPRESSING DEGREES OF ADVICE Work with a partner. Practice giving different degrees of advice. Student A doesn't feel well and asks for advice. Student B chooses a suggestion from the box below and uses it to give soft, strong, or direct advice. Then exchange roles.

Examples: **A:** I don't feel well. What should I do?
B: I think you should get more rest. (soft)

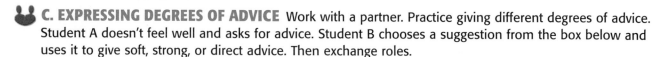

avoid stress	get more rest	see your doctor
eat better	follow an exercise program	

PRONUNCIATION

🎧 /θ/ vs. /t/

It's important to hear the difference between these two sounds: /θ/ and /t/. Listen to these examples. Do you hear the difference?

/θ/	/t/
thank	tank
theme	team
thin	tin
myths	mitts
bath	bat
path	pat
Do you know what he thought?	Do you know what he taught?

🎧 **D. HEARING THE DIFFERENCE BETWEEN /θ/ AND /t/** In each pair of words, circle the one that you hear.

1. thank	tank	**5.** bath	bat	**9.** fourth	fort		
2. eighth	eight	**6.** myths	mitts	**10.** math	mat		
3. thought	taught	**7.** thin	tin	**11.** theme	team		
4. tenth	tent	**8.** thick	tick	**12.** path	pat		

E. PRONOUNCING /θ/ AND /t/ Say 10 of the words from the box below to a partner. Don't say the words in order. Your partner will circle the words in the box. Check each word your partner circles to see if it is what you said. If your partner didn't circle the correct word, try again. Then exchange roles.

tank	tin	bath	eight	fourth	team
tenth	math	tick	mitts	theme	pat
tent	eighth	thick	myths	thought	thank
thin	bat	mat	fort	taught	path

Listening Strategy

Using Context to Distinguish Sounds

You can use context to distinguish similar sounds. In other words, a word with a /θ/ sound usually won't have the same context as a similar word with a /t/ sound.

Example: **You hear:** The baseball **team** played well.
You know: You didn't hear "The baseball **theme** played well" because it doesn't make sense.

 Why doesn't the second sentence make sense?

 F. PRONOUNCING /θ/ AND /t/ IN SENTENCES Now use words with the /θ/ and the /t/ sounds in conversations. Interview your classmates. Ask the questions in the chart. If a classmate answers *yes*, write his or her name on the chart. Think about the context if necessary.

Example: **A:** Do you think it's unhealthy to be thin?
B: Yes, I think it's unhealthy.
A: Great! How do you spell your name?

Questions	Names
Do you have advice for maintaining good health?	
Do you brush your teeth three times a day?	
Are you good at math?	
Do you think it's important to exercise regularly?	
Do you think it's unhealthy to be thin?	
Can you retell some Greek myths?	
Do you write thank you notes when you get birthday presents?	

PUT IT TOGETHER

A. GIVING ADVICE Read the situations below and think of advice for each one. Then write your own situation on the line.

1. Michael wants to see the movie *Alien*.
2. Tim is under a lot of stress.
3. Pam is having trouble sleeping.
4. Harry wants to stop smoking.
5. Brandon has to write a paper about modern art.
6. Dan wants to get a better score on the TOEFL exam.
7. Nina needs information about cultural differences in attitudes towards health.

Your situation: _____

 Now discuss your advice for each situation with a partner. Do you agree with your partner's advice? Follow these directions:

Student A gives advice for one of the situations. Use the expressions in the boxes on pages 229 and 230. Remember to give degrees of advice, depending on what you actually think.

Student B agrees or disagrees with Student A's advice. Use the expressions in the box in Chapter 7 on page 201, and then give your own advice. Express degrees of advice and degrees of agreement or disagreement. (See the expressions for degrees of agreement in Chapter 7, page 202.)

Then exchange roles.

PART ④ BROADCAST ENGLISH Fighting Global Obesity

BEFORE LISTENING

 A. THINKING AHEAD You are going to listen to a radio program about **obesity** (abnormally high body weight). In small groups, discuss these questions.

1. What is your definition of obesity? In other words, what is an abnormally high body weight, in your opinion? Do the definitions in your group differ?

2. In your opinion, do people give too much, too little, or the right amount of attention to obesity?

An obese person

B. PREDICTING Before you listen, make predictions about what you are going to hear. Discuss these questions with a partner.

1. What part of the world has had the greatest problem with obesity?

2. Is obesity becoming a problem in other parts of the world?

3. What are some causes of obesity? What might be some cures for it?

C. GUESSING THE MEANING FROM CONTEXT Read the sentences below. The words in green are from the radio program. Guess their meanings from the context. Write your guesses on the lines. Then compare your answers with a partner's answers.

1. Obesity has a **multitude** of causes. One of the many causes is lack of exercise.

   Guess: _____ _____

2. My grandmother has had a **chronic** disease for many years. She will have it for the rest of her life, and she cannot recover from it.

   Guess: _____

3. Stella's illness is a great **burden**. It's a difficult problem that she must deal with all the time.

   Guess: _____

4. No one in my family has had **cardiovascular disease**, so I'm pretty sure that I have a healthy heart.

   Guess: _____

5. **Processed** food isn't considered natural because it has things added to it such as sugar and salt.

   Guess: _____

6. Sugar is **controversial**. Some people believe that it leads to obesity and others do not.

   Guess: _____

7. James gained weight, and he thinks that sugar is the **culprit**, but I think the cause is not enough exercise.

   Guess: _____

8. James is going to **implement** his diet plan next week. He thinks it will be easier to start it when he gets back from his vacation.

   Guess: _____

9. **Diabetics** must be careful about their diet because they have a disease; their pancreas creates little or no insulin, an important hormone.

   Guess: _____

D. VOCABULARY PREPARATION Read the sentences below. The phrases in green are from the radio program. First, guess their meanings from the context. Then match the definitions in the box with the phrases in green. Write the correct letters on the lines.

a. as much as	d. leaving the house and doing things
b. easy to blame	e. move
c. in addition; also	f. putting in danger

_____ **1.** Obesity is **putting** people **at risk** for many serious illnesses.

_____ **2.** I eat too much. **On top of that**, I don't get any exercise.

_____ **3.** Now that he has a car, Sam doesn't walk **to the extent that** he used to.

_____ **4.** Gail isn't **getting out** as much as she used to. She stays home most of the time.

_____ **5.** Chris is **an easy target**. It's easy to say that he caused the problem because he is not here.

_____ **6.** It's time to get some exercise! Let's **pick up our feet** and get started!

LISTENING

A. LISTENING FOR MAIN IDEAS Listen to the radio program. As you listen, think about this question:
• What recommendations is the WHO (World Health Organization) making to help end global obesity?

B. LISTENING FOR CAUSES Listen to part of the radio program. Use the graphic organizer below to answer this question:
• What are the causes of worldwide obesity, according to Mr. Porter of the WHO?

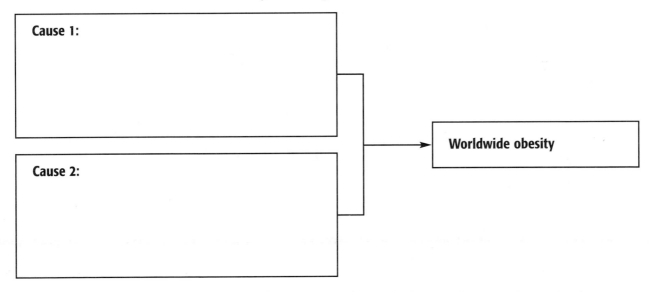

Cause 1:

Cause 2:

Worldwide obesity

C. LISTENING FOR NUMERICAL INFORMATION Listen to parts of the radio program again. You'll hear each part twice. Listen for numerical information that answers these questions. Write the answers on the lines.

1. What percent of deaths from cardiovascular disease is in developing countries?

   _____

2. How many people worldwide are obese, according to the WHO? _____

3. How much sugar does the average person in the United States consume? (In other words, what percent of his or her daily calories is sugar?) _____

D. MAKING INFERENCES Listen to a part of the program. You'll hear it twice. As you listen, try to answer the following question by making an inference. Write your answer on the line.

• How might a reduction in sugar consumption affect Mr. Briscoe or the people whom he represents?

_____

_____

_____

_____

_____

AFTER LISTENING

DISCUSSION In small groups, discuss these questions.

1. In terms of health issues, how are developing countries becoming more like Western nations?

2. Did any of the information in the program surprise you? Why or why not?

3. Have you noticed a higher incidence of heart disease and/or diabetes among people in your area?

4. Do you believe that eating sugar contributes to obesity? Explain your answer.

BEFORE LISTENING

Students eating at the cafeteria

A. THINKING AHEAD You are going to listen to a lecture about maintaining good health. Before you listen, discuss this question with a partner:
• What is your personal approach to maintaining good health?

B. PREDICTING The lecture contains information about how to develop a personal approach to good health in the following areas.

diet	weight	addictive substances
exercise	stress	relationships with others

In small groups, discuss what you think the speaker will say about each one.

C. HAVING QUESTIONS IN MIND Look at the outline for the lecture on pages 239–240 and think about your discussion in Activity A. What would you like to know about maintaining good health? Write three questions about the subject on the lines.

Question 1: _____

Question 2: _____

Question 3: _____

D. GUESSING THE MEANING FROM CONTEXT Read the sentences below. The words in green are from the lecture. Guess their meanings from the context. Write your guesses on the lines.

1. Doctor Wu practices **holistic** medicine, so she will ask you many questions about your lifestyle as well as give you a physical examination.

   Guess: _____

2. Some people believe that **harmony**—feeling comfortable with other people and your environment—is good for physical and mental health.

   Guess: _____

3. Before Sue was sick all the time. Now she feels great. The **adoption** of a healthier lifestyle was the key.

   Guess: _____

4. Gina wants to **enhance** her appearance, so she's going to get a fashionable haircut.

   Guess: _____

5. Ken has the ability to become a successful doctor because in medical school he showed a great deal of **potential** for understanding the causes of and cures for disease.

   Guess: _____

6. Since it's impossible to get money for preventive healthcare at the government level in Xenrovia, ordinary people often work at the **grassroots level** to raise their own money.

   Guess: _____

Now compare your answers with a partner's answers.

LISTENING

A. TAKING NOTES: USING AN OUTLINE Listen to the lecture. It's in four sections. Listen to each section twice. Fill in as much of the outline as you can. Don't worry if you can't fill in everything. (You'll listen to the whole lecture again later.) Remember to use key words and abbreviations.

Notice that this lecture is shorter than those in previous chapters, but there are fewer cues in the outline. You will take more notes on your own than in previous chapters.

What Is Good Health?

Section 1

I. The Meaning of Health

  A. Simple definition of health: _____

    _____

      1. Reflects _____

      2. Limited because _____

  B. WHO view: _____

    _____

      1. Takes into account _____

      2. Good health described as _____

Section 2

II. Achieving and Maintaining Good Health: Individual & Society

  A. Process for individual involves _____ ;

    factors include: _____

  B. Health needs for society: _____

    _____

      1. Poverty: _____

      _____

      2. Health maintenance involves _____

      _____

      groups must ensure _____

      _____

Section 3

III. Global Health Promotion

  A. Must be adapted to _____

    _____

WHO worker giving medical help to children

  B. WHO: _____

    _____

      1. In order to be effective _____

      2. Problem: _____

Section 4

IV. What Individuals Can Do to Achieve and Maintain
Good Health

   A. Diet: _____

       _____

   B. Exercise: _____

       _____

   C. Weight: _____

       _____

   D. Stress: _____

       _____

   E. Drug & alcohol use: _____

       _____

   F. Interpersonal relationships: _____

       _____

One way to reduce stress

Source: Adapted from a lecture by Deborah E. Blocker, D.Sc., M.P.H., R.N.

B. CHECKING YOUR NOTES Listen to the lecture again. This time, fill in any information missing on your outline.

AFTER LISTENING

A. USING YOUR NOTES In small groups, use your notes to answer these questions about the lecture.

1. What does it mean to be healthy? Is there more than one way to define "healthy"?

2. What are five examples of the basic elements that an individual requires for good health?

3. What is the greatest threat to good health worldwide?

4. What is the result when different sectors of a society (such as government, business, healthcare, and schools) all work together?

5. Do you disagree with any of the information in the lecture? What do you disagree with? Why?

6. Is anything missing from the lecture? Is there something important for maintaining health that the lecture did not cover?

B. MAKING CONNECTIONS Think about the article you read about stress management and health maintenance for students in Part 1, the radio program about the WHO's recommendations for greater health worldwide, and the lecture you just heard. Then in small groups, do the following:

• Create a health improvement plan for yourself that you can live with; that is, one that isn't too difficult for you to follow. Share ideas with your group members.

PUT IT ALL TOGETHER

GIVING A PRESENTATION You are going to give a short presentation on a cultural aspect of health. Your presentation will consist of a comparison on how important the issues below are in two cultures or countries.

• diet
• exercise
• weight control

• stress
• addictive substances
• social and personal relationships

• Your topic: _____

 Step 1

First, choose a topic that interests you. Then do Internet or library research, or find information in an introductory health textbook.

If you do Internet research, try doing searches using key word combinations such as the following:

exercise + _____ (country)

exercise + _____ (country) + _____ (country)

importance of exercise + _____ (country)

exercise comparison + _____ (country) + _____ (country)

You are going to present your ideas from notes (see Chapter 4, page 125), so as you do your research, take notes on index cards or use a form like the following.

Your Topic: _____	
Country A: _____	**Country B:** _____
Examples:	**Examples:**

Step 2

Go over your notes and organize your information. Decide on a time limit for each presentation.

Test-Taking Strategy

Making Comparisons

Many standard tests include speaking sections. In these sections you are often asked to compare two or more things. There are several words and expressions to use when you make comparisons. Some emphasize similarities. Others emphasize differences. Some do either. Here are a few words and expressions:

Similarities	Differences	Either
Both . . . and . . .	Although . . .	more . . . than
Neither . . . nor . . .	. . . but . . .	less . . . than
Similarly . . .	However . . .	

Examples: Studies show that citizens of **both** Country X **and** Country Y tend to be about 15 percent overweight.

Citizens of Country X feel that alcoholism is the most serious public health issue. **However**, citizens of Country Y think that poor nutrition is the most serious public health problem that they face.

Citizens of Country Y are **more** likely to visit a doctor regularly **than** are citizens of Country X.

Step 3

Present your information. Follow these guidelines:
• Paraphrase information from your research.
• Stay within the time limit.
• Use your notes; don't read.
• Make eye contact with your group members.
• Use expressions for making comparisons.
• Take and answer questions from your group members when you are finished.

Speaking Strategy

Giving Constructive Criticism

When you evaluate a classmate's work, it's important to use neutral language and to make positive suggestions for improvement. When you do this, you are avoiding hurt feelings, and you are giving real help.

Example: "Dan, **I think** you could look at the audience more. **Perhaps you could try to** look at your notes, memorize one or two points, and then look up at the audience as you say them."

Step 4

Evaluate each other's presentations. Use the following questions in your evaluation:
• Were the presentations easy to understand? Were the issues interesting?
• Did the speakers use notes and make good eye contact?
• Did the speakers support their opinions with good reasons?
• Did the speakers make clear comparisons?
• Are you giving constructive criticism to your classmates?

UNIT 4 VOCABULARY WORKSHOP

Review vocabulary items that you learned in Chapters 7 and 8.

A. MATCHING Match the definitions with the words and phrases. Write the correct letters on the lines.

Words and Phrases	Definitions
_____ **1.** billboard	**a.** removes
_____ **2.** corpse	**b.** illegal
_____ **3.** an easy target	**c.** vegetable or animal fat in food
_____ **4.** end up	**d.** become addicted to
_____ **5.** get hooked on	**e.** leaving the house and doing things
_____ **6.** getting out	**f.** someone who is easy to blame
_____ **7.** grease	**g.** dead body
_____ **8.** illicit	**h.** become
_____ **9.** kills	**i.** regular
_____ **10.** steady	**j.** a large sign that advertises products

B. TRUE OR FALSE? Read the statements below. Circle *T* if the sentence is true. Circle *F* if the sentence is false.

1. An example of **substance abuse** is drinking too much alcohol.	T	F
2. If someone is **on probation**, they're in prison.	T	F
3. If you tell a story **verbatim**, you tell it in your own words.	T	F
4. A person has a **psychological dependence** on alcohol if the alcohol has positive effects on his or her behavior and attitude.	T	F
5. If something is a **hazard**, it's probably good for you.	T	F
6. **Cardiovascular disease** affects the heart.	T	F
7. A **chronic** problem lasts only a short time.	T	F
8. **Alzheimer's** can cause the loss of memory.	T	F
9. A **rebellious** person follows the rules of society.	T	F
10. If you **crave** something, you have a strong desire for it.	T	F

C. THE ACADEMIC WORD LIST In the boxes below are some of the most common *academic* words in English. Fill in the blanks with words from these boxes. When you finish, check your answers in the readings on page 195 (for Items 1–10) and page 223 (for Items 11–18).

administrators	authors	legal	percent	survey
adults	findings	link	researchers	surveyed

Smoking on Campus

Nearly one in 10 college students have gone to an industry-sponsored party, according to an article in a recent edition of the *American Journal of Public Health*. Students at all but one of 119 colleges

_____ have attended the parties. At some schools, 27
  1

_____ of students have attended tobacco bashes (parties), which often include
  2

live music and gifts such as T-shirts.

Students who did not smoke before college were almost twice as likely to start if they attended

industry-backed parties that included free cigarettes, the article said. The article was based on results

from the Harvard School of Public Health College Alcohol _____, for
  3

which nearly 11,000 students were interviewed. Although the study does not prove that such parties

directly led people to smoke, the _____ say there might be a strong link.
  4

The _____ should be a warning to college _____,
  5   6

says Nancy Rigotti, director of the Tobacco Research and Treatment Center of Massachusetts General

Hospital.

"Tobacco-sponsored events aim to _____ smoking with alcohol, music, and
  7

socializing," Rigotti says. Binge drinkers (people who drink large quantities of alcohol at one time) and

marijuana users were more likely to attend these parties. The rate of cigarette smoking declined from

1993 to 2000 among all _____, except those ages 18 to 24, according to the
  8

study. _____ note that college students are the youngest
  9

_____ target for tobacco marketing.
  10

The College Transition: Managing Stress and Maintaining Health

The switch from living at home to going away to college can be difficult. Students have a great deal to learn—not only in the classroom, but also in the dormitory and at campus social

_____. To safeguard their health, they need to:
11

Get enough sleep.

Not getting enough sleep can lead to _____, anxiety, poor concentration,
12

memory loss, lowered resistance to illness, and increased drug and alcohol use. College students need to

go to bed and get up at regular hours. Many students view all-night study sessions as a

_____ part of college, but often the practice is a result of poor study habits or
13

weak time-management skills—that is, some students take on more _____
14

than they should.

If noise or roommate conflicts _____ a sleep problem, student housing or
15

student services can help _____ (solve conflicts). Additional
16

_____ to encourage sleep include using travel earplugs and eyeshades, or
17

perhaps a fan for a steady background sound. Remember that an alarm clock is also an essential part of

college life—no more _____ on parents for awakening in time for class.
18

Information Gap Chart for Activity A, page 103

STUDENT A

Greek Names	Roman Names	Main Characteristics/Activities
Aphrodite	Venus	Goddess of _love and beauty_
Apollo	_____	God of archery, music, prophecy, light, medicine, and poetry
_____	Mars	God of war
Artemis	Diana	_____
Athena	_____	Goddess of crafts, wisdom, and warfare
Demeter	_____	Goddess of agriculture
Dionysus	Bacchus	_____
_____	Cupid	God of love
Hera	_____	Goddess of marriage; protector of women
Hephaestus	Vulcan	_____
_____	Mercury	God of commerce; the gods' messenger
_____	Pluto	God of the underworld

Information Gap Chart for Activity A, page 103

STUDENT B

Greek Names	Roman Names	Main Characteristics/Activities
Aphrodite	Venus	Goddess of love and beauty
Apollo	Phoebus Apollo	_____
Ares	_____	God of war
Artemis	_____	Goddess of the moon, hunting, and childbirth
Athena	Minerva	_____
Demeter	Ceres	_____
_____	Bacchus	God of wine and fertility
Eros	_____	God of love
_____	Juno	Goddess of marriage; protector of women
Hephaestus	_____	God of fire and metalworking; the blacksmith of the Gods
Hermes	Mercury	_____
Hades	_____	God of the underworld

AUDIO SCRIPT

Chapter 1: Doing Business Internationally

Part 2 Social Language
A. Listening for the Main Idea (page 9)

Victor: . . . that was the first time I ever even left the country. Man, I had a great time!

Tanya: Did you visit any ruins?

Victor: Yeah, I spent a few days exploring the Mayan ruins.

Jennifer: I remember going to Germany a few years ago. I was amazed at how strange things seemed, even though I speak German and all.

Victor: Hmm. Yeah, it's more than the language though. In, in Mexico, there are a lot of little things, like, like going to the bank or, or buying fruit at a market, you know, that, well, if you don't know the culture that well, can be pretty challenging.

Tanya: Yeah, that reminds me of when I went to France last summer. I went to the bank to exchange some cash, and there were no lines. You had to get up to the counter real fast and get the teller's attention before anyone else did. Man, that gave me a headache!

Victor: Well, the trouble I had was negotiating stuff at the market—you know like little trinkets and presents for friends and family back home.

Jennifer: Oh, yeah, you're not supposed to pay the asking price, right?

Victor: Right. But even though I'm fluent in Spanish, I didn't know *how* to bargain. I never did it before. I always thought that I was paying too much.

Jennifer: It's just a game. Like playing poker, but I guess if you don't know the rules, it can be kinda tough.

Victor: Yeah, and the rules change depending on what country you're in.

Tanya: Yeah, 'cause you sure can't bargain for trinkets in a store in the U.S.

Jennifer: But you *can* at a flea market, right?

Victor: I dunno.

Tanya: Yeah, you can. And you can also bargain for new cars, didja know that?

Jennifer: Yeah.

Victor: No.

Tanya: Yeah, I watched my father do it last fall. He and the salesman went back and forth for about an hour. Each time my dad proposed something, the salesman went into his boss's office, like they were consulting.

Jennifer: He was probably just having a cup of coffee.

Victor: So did your dad get the car at the price he wanted?

Tanya: Yeah, no problem. They had to get rid of the car anyway, and my dad knew it. That's the key. They were probably gonna sell it at the price he wanted anyway, they just had to go through the ritual.

Victor: I wonder how big corporations do business overseas.

Tanya: Oh darn! It's getting late. I'm gonna hafta turn in.

Jennifer: What, and leave us here to ponder the mysteries of big business?

Victor: Actually, I should be going home. I've gotta get up early tomorrow. See ya.

All: Bye!

B. Listening for Examples (page 9)

Victor: Hmm. Yeah, it's more than the language though. In, in Mexico, there are a lot of little things, like, like going to the bank or, or buying fruit at a market, you know, that, well, if you don't know the culture that well, can be pretty challenging.

Tanya: Yeah, that reminds me of when I went to France last summer. I went to the bank to exchange some cash, and there were no lines. You had to get up to the counter real fast and get the teller's attention before anyone else did. Man, that gave me a headache!

Victor: Well, the trouble I had was negotiating stuff at the market—you know like little trinkets and presents for friends and family back home.

Jennifer: Oh, yeah, you're not supposed to pay the asking price, right?

Victor: Right. But even though I'm fluent in Spanish, I didn't know *how* to bargain. I never did it before. I always thought that I was paying too much.

C. Listening for Details (page 9)

Jennifer: It's just a game. Like playing poker, but I guess if you don't know the rules, it can be kinda tough.

Victor: Yeah, and the rules change depending on what country you're in.

Tanya: Yeah, 'cause you sure can't bargain for trinkets in a store in the U.S.

Jennifer: But you *can* at a flea market, right?

Victor: I dunno.

Tanya: Yeah, you can. And you can also bargain for new cars, didja know that?

Jennifer: Yeah.

Victor: No.

D. Listening for an Anecdote (page 10)

Tanya: Yeah, you can. And you can also bargain for new cars, didja know that?

Jennifer: Yeah.

Victor: No.

Tanya: Yeah, I watched my father do it last fall. He and the salesman went back and forth for about an hour. Each time my dad proposed something, the salesman went into his boss's office, like they were consulting.

Jennifer: He was probably just having a cup of coffee.

Victor: So did your dad get the car at the price he wanted?

Tanya: Yeah, no problem. They had to get rid of the car anyway, and my dad knew it. That's the key. They were probably gonna sell it at the price he wanted anyway, they just had to go through the ritual.

Part 3 The Mechanics of Listening and Speaking

A. Asking for Confirmation (page 12)

1. I heard a great lecture about negotiating in different cultures.
2. I saw a Mexican movie last night.
3. I had a hard time at a bank in Paris.
4. My host looked embarrassed when I talked about politics.
5. I had a nice conversation with an older woman at a bus stop.

B. Asking for Confirmation (page 13)

1. Tanya's majoring in business, right? *[Real Question]*
2. Jennifer doesn't speak Spanish, right? *[Real Question]*

3. You like working overseas, right? *[Confirmation]*
4. The professor doesn't speak very clearly, right? *[Confirmation]*
5. You've been to France, right? *[Confirmation]*
6. Jennifer hasn't seen the ruins yet, right? *[Real Question]*

D. Confirming Understanding (page 14)

1. You like studying English, right? *[Not Real Question]*
2. You've been working hard, right? *[Real Question]*
3. You're majoring in business. Isn't that true? *[Real Question]*
4. You speak Spanish, right? *[Not Real Question]*
5. You like to make small talk. Isn't that right? *[Real Question]*
6. You're studying Italian, right? *[Not Real Question]*

E. Reduced Forms of Words (page 15)

A: Do you wanna try bargaining in the market?

B: You mean you're not supposta pay the asking price?

A: No way! You hafta know the rules of the culture. C'mon . . . let's try it!

B: Uh, I'm not sure.

A: Are you afraid? Well, I'm not! I'm gonna give it a try.

Part 4 Broadcast English

A. Listening for the Main Idea (page 19)
G. Using Graphic Organizers (page 21)

Ford: When 200 of the world's experts on business ethics get together, some of the topics sound like Sunday sermons. For example, one speaker delivered a paper on the intimate intertwining of business, religion, and dialog. Another spoke on cultivating moral courage in business. Most experts seem to agree that international business would be much better off if participants simply followed the Golden Rule: Do unto others what you would have them do unto you. But when you sit down and talk about specifics, the ethicists don't always agree on what's right and wrong. Take for example bribery.

Salim: Cultural factors do play a role here.

Ford: Hiwan Salim is one of Indonesia's leading experts on business ethics.

Salim: What may be considered a bribe in a, uh, a nation may not be considered a bribe in others. Or it may be the other case around.

Ford: In Salim's eyes, paying a lobbyist in Washington isn't too different from paying an insider in the Indonesian government to help facilitate a project. James Spillane, a Jesuit priest and 20-year resident of Indonesia, who teaches business ethics at a regional university, is somewhat sympathetic with Salim.

Spillane: Bribery is more difficult to define in Indonesia because, uh, personal relationships are very important in everything you do. Uh, so gift giving is an accepted part of the culture and, uh, if you really want to do business with people, you have to try and become their friends, and gift-giving is part of the friendship relationship.

Ford: Another concept that caused some trouble at the conference was the "F" word—what's considered fair in one country is sometimes considered unfair in another. For example, some Japanese at the conference considered it unfair that, on average, American CEOs rake in a hundred times more money than their employees. Even more unethical, said Professor Takaiwao, who teaches business ethics, is what happens when CEOs decide to cut costs.

Takaiwao: Layoff, you know, the custom of "layoff," you know, depends on the corporation's situation, you know, executives can fire or layoff you know, workers, uh, so easily.

Ford: The glue of the conference was the common concern that as international business opportunities expand, there's a greater need to identify common values. Kenneth Goodpastor is a professor at the University of St. Thomas in Minnesota.

Goodpastor: There's a concern on the part of many, uh, business, uh, leaders that, uh, as business becomes increasingly global, uh, it is also increasingly, uh, experiencing, uh, different business practices in different parts of the world and being challenged, uh, uh, by, uh, other cultures as well as one's own culture about the appropriate forms of behavior, uh, when it comes to human rights and caring about the noneconomic effects of business, uh, in the community.

Ford: Goodpastor said that getting together with business ethicists from around the world was a first step toward moving away from today's parochial view of what's right and wrong and toward a more universal approach. In Tokyo, this is Jocelyn Ford for Marketplace.

B. Listening for Supporting Ideas: Section 1 (page 19)

Ford: When 200 of the world's experts on business ethics get together, some of the topics sound like Sunday sermons. For example, one speaker delivered a paper on the intimate intertwining of business, religion, and dialog. Another spoke on cultivating moral courage in business. Most experts seem to agree that international business would be much better off if participants simply followed the Golden Rule: Do unto others what you would have them do unto you. But when you sit down and talk about specifics, the ethicists don't always agree on what's right and wrong. Take for example bribery.

Salim: Cultural factors do play a role here.

Ford: Hiwan Salim is one of Indonesia's leading experts on business ethics.

Salim: What may be considered a bribe in a, uh, a nation may not be considered a bribe in others. Or it may be the other case around.

C. Listening for Examples: Section 1 (page 20)

Salim: What may be considered a bribe in a, uh, a nation may not be considered a bribe in others. Or it may be the other case around.

Ford: In Salim's eyes, paying a lobbyist in Washington isn't too different from paying an insider in the Indonesian government to help facilitate a project. James Spillane, a Jesuit priest and 20-year resident of Indonesia, who teaches business ethics at a regional university, is somewhat sympathetic with Salim.

Spillane: Bribery is more difficult to define in Indonesia because, uh, personal relationships are very important in everything you do. Uh, so gift giving is an accepted part of the culture and, uh, if you really want to do business with people, you have to try and become their friends, and gift-giving is part of the friendship relationship.

D. Listening for Supporting Ideas: Section 2 (page 20)
E. Listening for Examples: Section 2 (page 20)

Ford: Another concept that caused some trouble at the conference was the "F" word—what's considered fair in one country is sometimes considered unfair in another. For example, some Japanese at the conference considered it unfair that, on average, American CEOs rake in a hundred times more money than their employees. Even more unethical, said Professor Takaiwao, who teaches business ethics, is what happens when CEOs decide to cut costs.

Takaiwao: Layoff, you know, the custom of "layoff," you know, depends on the corporation's situation, you know, executives can fire or layoff you know, workers, uh, so easily.

F. Listening for the Main Idea: Section 3
(page 21)

Ford: The glue of the conference was the common concern that as international business opportunities expand, there's a greater need to identify common values. Kenneth Goodpastor is a professor at the University of St. Thomas in Minnesota.

Goodpastor: There's a concern on the part of many, uh, business, uh, leaders that, uh, as business becomes increasingly global, uh, it is also increasingly, uh, experiencing, uh, different business practices in different parts of the world and being challenged, uh, uh, by, uh, other cultures as well as one's own culture about the appropriate forms of behavior, uh, when it comes to human rights and caring about the noneconomic effects of business, uh, in the community.

Ford: Goodpastor said that getting together with business ethicists from around the world was a first step toward moving away from today's parochial view of what's right and wrong and toward a more universal approach. In Tokyo, this is Jocelyn Ford for Marketplace.

Part 5 Academic English
A. Listening for the Meaning of New Words and Phrases (page 24)

1. Culture is the set of beliefs and values that the members of a particular society share.

2. Personal distance, um, how close people stand to each other when they talk, also varies from culture to culture.

B. Organizing Your Notes (page 26)
C. Listening for Differences (page 27)
Section 1

Lecturer: Hey! Good morning. How are you? All right, well, let's get started. Today we're talking about ethics and doing business internationally. And, uh, let's start with a definition of culture.

Culture [writes on board]. Culture is the set of beliefs and values that, uh, the members of a particular society share. So, beliefs and values [writes on board]. Now, uh, a country's culture includes the primary beliefs and practices that define socially acceptable behavior in that particular country. Uh, in spite of such things as widespread global travel and the emergence of

huge multinational organizations, the world remains far from homogeneous. Many different cultures exist in the world today. So, therefore, there are differences in, uh, socially acceptable business behavior throughout the world. There are several ways in which business behavior varies from culture to culture.

Now, saying "No" is one area of difference. In some countries it is socially unacceptable to say "No," even when that is the ultimate answer. O.K. Japanese [writes on board] business people, Japanese businesspersons rarely say no to each other or to businesspeople from other countries. So, [writes on board] rarely say no. O.K., this can result in some, uh, prolonged discussions, uh, until the other party finally realizes that the answer is truly negative, and then, uh, they state it. Then the Japanese person can agree by saying "Yes," and negotiations can resume.

Americans, however, value decisiveness [writes on board]. The quicker an American can arrive at a decision, uh, and move on, the more effective he or she feels. So, Americans will say "No" rather quickly. And this can offend people in other cultures where saying "No" is undesirable. Saying, no, quickly [writes on board]. O.K.

Section 2

Lecturer: Personal distance, how close people stand to each other when they talk, also varies from culture to culture. In some countries people tend to move physically closer to each other as they become more familiar with each other. Frequently, uh, when two business people move closer together physically they are also coming closer [brings hands together] together in their business negotiations. Uh, businesspeople in Japan [writes on board] and in some Latin American countries, uh, they like to stand close together as they talk. These people partially judge how close they are to agreement in their business negotiations by how physically close they are standing or sitting next to each other. So, [writes on board] close together, close together.

Now, Americans, on the other hand. Not close [writes on board], O.K. Americans do *not* want other people invading their personal space. This is especially important to American men. If an American businessman were negotiating with a Japanese man, and the Japanese man began to move towards the American [motions away from himself], the American would most likely begin to back away [motions towards himself]. O.K., this could result in both the men becoming suspicious of each other, and it could result in poor communications between them.

Section 3

Lecturer: O.K., now, business cards. Business cards also have different significance in various cultures. In Japan, exchanging business cards is an important ritual. The most important people at a business gathering exchange business cards first. The managers study each other's cards, carefully noting every detail on the card. It may take two people, uh, ten or fifteen minutes to exchange business cards, discuss each other's qualifications and experience, answer questions and compliment each other. Right, so, [writes on board] in Japan discuss and study business cards.

All right, but American [points to board], American businesspeople tend to collect business cards. Uh, O.K., Americans view the information on business cards as important to have in their possession, but, uh, not important to know [writes on board]. Americans pocket business cards. O.K. They accept the cards quickly, and, uh, in a process that takes only two or three seconds, frequently put them into a coat pocket with just a glance. O.K. Then they take the cards from the coat pocket, later, back at the office, and examine them in greater detail.

Now, let's look at ethical behavior. What one culture feels is ethical behavior, uh, another culture may consider unethical. For example, [erases board] there's bribery [writes on board] within the United States, bribes are both unethical and illegal. O.K., people who offer and accept bribes can be charged with criminal activity, and can be jailed for these crimes. Companies whose employees are caught paying bribes can be fined large amounts of money.

Other countries have different attitudes toward what would be considered bribes in the U.S. In Europe, for example, "business gifts" are a more acceptable part of conducting business, but the details of what is and isn't acceptable vary from country to country within Europe. For example, in Spain, [writes on board] in Spain bribes are a regular part of doing business. While bribes are illegal, in the eyes of the law nothing takes place. Right? In Spain, [writes on board] you're O.K. Now, on the other hand, in Germany, people who pay bribes to conduct business can deduct the amounts from their income taxes. O.K., so [writes on board], Germany bribes are tax free. O.K., in Russia bribes are a necessary expense in dealing with most business organizations. In addition, bribes and personal connections are necessary in order to do business with the government in Russia. So, [writes on board] Russia, bribes are necessary.

Section 4

Lecturer: O.K. Now, as we've seen in the case of bribery [points to board], some unethical behavior can also be illegal. In such situations, employees must be aware of what is and is not acceptable behavior. Other ethically unacceptable behavior, while not illegal, may be offensive. Organizations have developed ways to help their employees cope with the many different cultural practices and beliefs.

So, first, in order to [erases board] avoid confusion, [writes on board] code of ethics. An organization might clearly state, in writing, what types of behavior are and are not ethically acceptable [points to board] in that particular organization. This, uh, so-called "code of ethics" can serve as a guideline to employees, eliminating much confusion over what specific types of behavior are and are not acceptable in that particular organization.

A second way, [writes on board] a second way in which organizations promote ethically acceptable behavior is to encourage workers to report unethical behavior in their organizations. In the United States, many states have "whistle-blower" laws [writes on board] whistle blower, whistle blower laws, to prevent organizations from terminating or discriminating against employees who report unethical behaviors. Many organizations have toll-free numbers where employees can report unethical behavior anonymously, hence, uh, protecting their identity.

A third way in which organizations deal with ethically important issues is, uh, to train employees to be aware of such concerns. In many organizations, this is a part of the on-going training of employees O.K. [writes on board] ongoing training, in acceptable business practices. All right, for example, a firm that has a large, international sales force might conduct "how-to" training sessions on, uh, shaking hands, exchanging business cards, right, um, properly addressing men and women in other societies and other ethically-important issues that salespersons might encounter in their everyday jobs.

The fourth and final method used in organizations that, uh, operate in multiple cultures [writes on board] is to think global and act local, O.K. Using this approach, companies can incorporate many of the ideas and procedures that are useful in the rest of the world, while at the same time, uh, remaining sensitive to the values of the local culture, O.K. Think global, act local [writes on board], all right. Many large international companies use this approach uh, to, incorporate effective business practices used in other parts of the world, while at the same time retaining sensitivity to the ethical issues of the local country.

O.K. That's it for today. Are there any questions?

Chapter 2: International Economy

Part 2 Social Language
A. Listening for the Main Idea (page 37)
B. Listening for Details (page 37)

Evan: What, if anything, should the government do to help the poor?

Speaker 1: Um, I think that helping the poor should start with their children, probably, because, um, sometimes the poorest children don't have good schools to go to and if they got a better education then they would be able to help themselves once they get older.

Speaker 2: I think that the government could supply them with jobs to get them back on their feet and educate them. Not just handouts because then they won't learn any skills, but, um, you know, little jobs to get them back to where they want to go.

Speaker 3: Well, I think it's a responsibility on the part of society and government to work together to, uh, to end it.

Evan: Um, I'm doing an interview for a story for Campus TV. Can I ask you a question?

Speaker 4: Sure.

Evan: What, if anything, should we do to help the poor?

Speaker 4: Huh, that's a big question. That's a very big question. O.K., however, I think that, uh, the poor, um—government programs is, is fine but that in itself will not solve the problem. There have to be some sort of a, a do-it-yourself type approach to it and, um, education is basically the key.

Speaker 5: Ah, I think the government should work at the local level to develop programs for people so that they can get off welfare and get jobs.

Speaker 6: I think there should be more programs, you know, more art programs, more business programs, you know. I think schools, I think we need to improve in our schools, especially in the inner cities.

Speaker 7: Um, I think that the, uh, those who are poor need a chance to learn how to help themselves, but I think the government has a significant role. I'm particularly concerned about childcare for working mothers, uh, who are actually being required to work and for whom very few childcare provisions have been made.

C. Listening for Specific Ideas (page 37)

1. I think that the government could supply them with jobs to get them back on their feet and educate them. Not just handouts because then they won't learn any skills, but, um, you know little jobs to get them back to where they want to go.

2. Huh, that's a big question. That's a very big question. O.K., however, I think that, uh, the poor, um—government programs is, is fine but that in itself will not solve the problem. There have to be some sort of a, a do-it-yourself type approach to it and, um, education is basically the key.

3. I think there should be more programs, you know, more art programs, more business programs, you know. I think schools, I think we need to improve in our schools, especially in the inner cities.

4. Um, I think that the, uh, those who are poor need a chance to learn how to help themselves, but I think the government has a significant role. I'm particularly concerned about childcare for working mothers, uh, who are actually being required to work and for whom very few childcare provisions have been made.

Part 3 The Mechanics of Listening and Speaking
C. Reduced Forms of Words (page 41)

1. Couldja help me with this problem?
2. Didja read the last chapter?
3. Wouldja mind if I asked you a question?
4. Didja hear what I just said?
5. Couldja put out that cigarette, please?

Part 4 Broadcast English
A. Listening for the Main Idea: Section 1 (page 45)
B. Listening for Details: Section 1 (page 45)

Omar: In America most people's health insurance is tied to their jobs. The only government provision is for those over 65 and those who are very poor or disabled. If you don't have a job, or if your employer doesn't provide health insurance, you may have to go without. On the other side of the road from SOME's dining room is its free health clinic. The group's director, Father John Adams, is proud of the services it provides.

Adams: This is our eye clinic which is all beautiful new equipment; it was all donated. We have one day a week where we pay an eye doctor to come, and we have other eye doctors that come and volunteer their time from, uh, universities. So this is a godsend to have, an eye clinic.

Omar: It was to a clinic such as this that Dion Lyles decided to go when he became ill. The sad fact is, he says, that if you don't have health insurance, the alternative is to suffer.

Lyles: My friends who, uh, don't have health insurance have to deal with the illnesses that they have, you know, be whatever it might be, you know. Some places do have free clinics, stuff like that, but not a lot of places in D.C. are like that, so they just have to live with it.

C. Listening for the Gist: Section 2 (page 46)

Omar: But why is it that charitable and other non-profit organizations are doing what in many parts of the world governments do—and their people expect as a right? Linda Donaldson believes the answer lies in America's origins, that historically many Americans blamed the poor for being poor.

Donaldson: I think about the Protestant work ethic and the value of work and the value of self sustainability and how that seems to have carried over in many of our American traditions. And we have not integrated a more compassionate stance towards people whose needs arise from their situations, not from personal deficits. I think we still look at personal deficits versus the environmental factors that cause poverty.

D. Listening for Numerical Information: Section 3 (page 47)
E. Listening for Numerical Information (page 47)

Omar: An estimated 44 million Americans are uninsured and the number is growing. Recently the World Health Organization rated the USA thirty seventh in terms of quality of health care. Those countries with universal healthcare systems generally had better results and the USA was ranked fifty-fourth in terms of the fairness of financial contributions towards healthcare. But, says Gail Shearer, the director of health policy at

the Consumers' Union in Washington, health coverage for all Americans is still a long way off.

Shearer: There have been efforts to get national health insurance in the United States ever since the 1930s, but there have been decades and decades of fights over this, and we haven't been able to reach a consensus of how you pay for a national health insurance program. Over the last 20 or 30 years the special interests—the insurance companies, the doctors, the health maintenance organizations, the pharmaceutical companies—have been able to use their power and their money to resist major progressive changes in health policy in the United States.

Part 5 Academic English
A. Listening for the Meaning of New Words and Phrases (page 50)

1. Now, fourth is Swedish policies that ensure full employment and increase the mobility of labor—that is, the ability to change jobs without losing income.

2. The government accomplishes this by offering economic incentives—that is, money that governments give to organizations to help make prices lower or make it cheaper to produce goods—to promote the consumption of goods and services.

C. Taking Notes: Using an Outline (page 50)
D. Checking Your Notes (page 53)
Section 1

Lecturer: Good morning everyone. I hope you all had a nice weekend. Let's get started.

Today we're going to look at the role of social welfare in Sweden. The Swedish economy can be described as a welfare state or democratically controlled socialism. Over time, Sweden has developed a combination of social insurance programs and welfare policies that basically redistribute income. So, the result is that the widespread poverty that most of the world, especially Europe, experienced after World War I, has been eliminated in Sweden. At the same time, Sweden has nurtured free enterprise in the private sector and has created an industrial base that has resulted in a standard of living that many other countries in the world envy.

The Swedes believe in social justice for all. During the 1960s, the slogan *Jamlikhet* began to appear in Sweden. Now, this expression reflects the Swedish belief that, as Scott writes in his book *Sweden: the Nation's History*, quote: "All individuals have an equal right to a rich and evolving life, including security, freedom, happiness, the right to cultural opportunities, employment, and influence in the community." He goes on to say: "This is to be accomplished through an approach to equalization of income. It requires reforms directed against the privileged for the advantage of the underprivileged, with the socially desired outcome of bettering their condition in life." Did everyone get that?

Section 2

Lecturer: O.K. There are five main components of the Swedish social system for equalizing income. The first is a government policy that protects people from the ups and downs of business cycles and unemployment. The government accomplishes this by offering economic incentives—that is, money that governments give to organizations to help make prices lower or make it cheaper to produce goods—to promote the consumption of goods and services. This ensures both earned wages for those working and tax revenue to support those dependent upon social supports.

Section 3

Lecturer: The second component is to allow extensive private ownership and control over production. Although the Swedish government is heavily involved in economic matters, there is no government involvement in either economic planning or production planning. Sweden has an open economy that is highly dependent upon international trade. The Swedish markets are unregulated; as a result, businesses can be competitive in the international economy.

Now, the third component is a wage policy that reduces the differences between the highest and lowest paid workers. Unions negotiate wage agreements that emphasize full employment without inflation. Unions also negotiate wages with the understanding that Swedish products must remain competitive in the international marketplace.

Section 4

Lecturer: Now, fourth is Swedish policies that ensure full employment and increase the mobility of labor—that is, the ability to change jobs without losing income. Swedes have a strong work ethic. This, combined with state-funded programs that minimize unemployment, results in a policy of subsidized employment, which Sweden prefers to high unemployment rates and large welfare expenditures. So, there are a large number of vocational training programs that employers pay for, available to workers in jobs

that have become unnecessary. And there are also subsidies for workers who must change jobs because of changes in the labor market.

Sweden introduced the fifth and final component of their social system just at the end of the 20th century. And this component corrects some of the problems created by the four previously mentioned components. It includes new rules that are designed to improve job stability, such as training programs to help employees learn new skills as their jobs change and become more complex. Also, the government has reduced social insurance and welfare payments.

So, in conclusion, the Swedes are happy with their system. Sweden has achieved more in terms of social equality, economic security and freedom than many other economies. So, as a result, most Swedes aren't interested in reforming the economic system. However, because it is heavily involved in international markets, Sweden must continue to manage its social policies so that it remains competitive in the international marketplace.

O.K. That's about it for today. Any questions?

E. Listening for Causes and Effects (page 53)

1. At the same time, Sweden has nurtured free enterprise in the private sector and has created an industrial base that has resulted in a standard of living that many other countries in the world envy.

2. The Swedish markets are unregulated; as a result, businesses can be competitive in the international economy.

3. Swedes are happy with their system. Sweden has achieved more in terms of social equality, economic security, and freedom than many other economies. So, as a result, most Swedes are not interested in reforming the economic system.

Chapter 3: Art Themes and Purposes

Part 2 Social Language
A. Listening for the Main Idea (page 68)
B. Listening for Examples (page 69)

Rachel: Wow, I am *so* glad we decided to have this study group.

Ashley: Me, too. I'm totally lost.

Mike: Yeah, I did not think that art history was going to be so hard. It's just pictures and all.

Rachel: Yeah, O.K. Well, we've got some serious studying to do.

Ashley: You're right. Well, let's see—this worksheet suggests that we give a definition and an example for each of these types of art.

Mike: Yeah, so, uh, so what'd you guys have for Question 1?

Rachel: Yeah, uh, O.K. Question 1—that's the one about *minimalist* art.

Ashley: What?

Rachel: *Minimalist* art.

Ashley: O.K., I just didn't get that one. I mean, I don't understand what it says in the book.

Rachel: O.K. It says: um, "The purpose of minimalist art is to reduce things to simple elements."

Mike: What does *that* mean?

Rachel: Well, uh, here's an example. On page 203 there's a steel cube. Um, I guess it means using basic shapes.

Ashley: Yeah, geometric shapes, maybe.

Mike: Yeah, that's, that's pretty basic.

Rachel: O.K. Let's move on to the next one.

Ashley: Uh, realism.

Mike: O.K. What kind of art is that?

Rachel: O.K. realism. That's pretty obvious.

Mike: Yeah. Paintings that are realistic. That show things as they really are.

Rachel: Yeah, like those Andy Warhol soup cans that we saw in class.

Ashley: Yeah, isn't that funny? Why is that called *art*? Anybody can copy what's on a can.

Mike: I dunno. It says he was pretty big in the sixties.

Ashley: Talk about realistic, how about that photo, I mean *painting*, of that woman we saw in class today? You could see every line on her face, every hair on her leg. Yuck!

Mike: A painting? I could've sworn that was a photo. It looked just like a photo.

Ashley: That's what you call *photo*realism. Yeah, here it is, on page 244. It's, uh, by Chuck Close. Um, it looks like he got *too* "close" to her!

Mike: Hey, that's a good way to remember his name!

Rachel: Hey, you're right. Anyway, let's get back to work.

C. Listening for Details (page 69)

Rachel: Wow, I am *so* glad we decided to have this study group.

Ashley: Me, too. I'm totally lost.

Mike: Yeah, I did not think that art history was going to be so hard. It's just pictures and all.

Rachel: Yeah, O.K. Well, we've got some serious studying to do.

Ashley: You're right. Well, let's see—this worksheet suggests that we give a definition and an example for each of these types of art.

Mike: Yeah, so, uh, so what'd you guys have for Question 1?

Rachel: Yeah, uh, O.K. Question 1—that's the one about *minimalist* art.

Ashley: What?

Rachel: *Minimalist* art.

Ashley: O.K., I just didn't get that one. I mean, I don't understand what it says in the book.

Part 3 The Mechanics of Listening and Speaking

C. Giving Clarification (page 74)

1. **A:** The painting *Laura* is an example of photorealism.
   B: What?

2. **A:** That's what you call pop art.
   B: What kind of art is that?

3. **A:** My favorite art style is realism.
   B: Can you give me an example of that?

4. **A:** His sculptures are examples of minimalist art.
   B: I'm sorry. What did you say?

5. **A:** One of my favorite works of art is *The Water Lilies.*
   B: Who painted that?

6. **A:** I don't like minimalist art.
   B: I didn't get that.

D. *Wh-* Questions (page 75)

1. Do you like that painting?
2. What's your opinion of minimalist art?
3. Where did you see that poster exhibit?
4. Was pop art a movement from the sixties?
5. Can you give me an example of pop art?
6. Who was Andy Warhol?

F. Hearing the Difference Between /I/ and /i/ (page 75)

1. It's a little beet.
2. The bins are over there.
3. Don't pick at it.

4. Mary's still leaving.

5. The meat is here.

6. I see the ship in the picture.

Part 4 Broadcast English

A. Listening for the Main Idea: Section 1
(page 81)

B. Listening for Details: Section 1 (page 81)

Zwerdling: The next time you wander through an art museum in Los Angeles, or in Trenton, or Tokyo, or Tehran, look for a haunting life-sized human figure, like a ghost in pure white plaster and you'll know it's by sculptor George Segal. We dropped by the Smithsonian's Hirshhorn Museum the other day here in Washington, D.C., to reflect on 40 years of Segal's works. They've just opened a major retrospective. And we caught up with the sculptor as he and the gallery's staff were installing his creations.

Staff: George, we're going to hang Helen here. And then we'll do the, uh, woman behind him.

Segal: Go.

Zwerdling: Sort of fun to see your sculptures, uh, being lifted off tables. And, uh, like right now this bust—it's a bust of a what, of a woman?

Segal: That's no woman; that's my wife.
(Laughter)

Zwerdling: Segal's works aren't sculptures exactly. He makes white plaster casts of real people, surprisingly detailed body casts, textured with the wrinkles on their shirts and the creases in their skin. And then he sets his figures against realistic backdrops to recreate the seemingly mundane moments that make up our lives. In one composition, a white plaster figure sits on a real stool at a real Formica diner counter watching a white plaster waiter fill a real coffee cup. In another work, we seem to spy on a man with long stringy hair, leaning against the counter in a bar, glowing pink under a neon Budweiser sign as the man stares vacantly at the bar's television.

Segal transforms ordinary experience into something universal. And he says it happened almost by accident. Back in 1960, he was teaching art classes and one of the nation's leading medical supply companies hired him to write a booklet selling schools on the idea that the company's new plaster bandages weren't just great for healing broken bones—students would have fun using them for art projects.

Segal: So they gave me three free boxes. I took it home and I had my wife cover me from head to foot. Instead of writing the book—I never wrote the booklet. *(Laughter)*

Zwerdling: You showed them.

Segal: I need—I needed it—I could have used 75 bucks in those days. It was like that. I was looking for a fast way to make a life-size figure because I wanted to use real chairs, real tables, real stuff. I was switching from the idea of making a hand-made sculpture and putting it on a pedestal. And putting it on a pedestal was the same as putting a frame around a painting. You see, this is separated from this nasty, stupid, banal, ordinary, daily world. And I, you know, obviously, I think that daily space is far from banal. I think it's rather miraculous.

Zwerdling: The results of that impromptu experiment shaped what Segal has been creating ever since. For almost four decades now, he's been making his plaster impressions of reality, a rebellion of sorts against all the abstract artists who have been carving stones into random shapes or hurling splotches of paint at a canvas.

C. Listening for the Main Idea: Section 2
(page 81)

D. Identifying Impressions or Opinions: Section 2 (page 83)

Zwerdling: Now, what is it about all your works—the, the woman on the subway, the man standing in a bar, your mother in the butcher shop? There's something about them that always makes . . . I think many people feel almost sad or lonely.

Segal: Well, for years I've been moving through what everybody says is an ordinary day. And, uh, as I walk around, I see glimpses of my own world, you know, the world that you and I live in. Uh, I grew up in the Bronx, went to school in Manhattan. And, uh, I've had this daily experience with city life, and I keep finding myself drawn to the energy of New York.

Zwerdling: But, but in your works I don't get a sense so much of the happy energy of New York. I get a sense, and I think many critics do, of the bleakness of a major city in the same way that Edward Hopper sort of captured in his paintings the bleakness of the all-night diner or the deserted city streets.

Segal: Oh absolutely. Absolutely.

Zwerdling: Do you feel bleak about the city landscapes you're portraying? Do you feel bleak about this lone woman on the rattan seat on the subway car, looking straight ahead?

Segal: Wait a second. We're, we're sitting here looking at her, and she has this beginning of a smile of private delight, pretty much—damn it— the same expression as Mona Lisa. What's the, what's the secret of, uh, the inner life of women? Pretty, pretty extraordinary. All of us are capable of, um, joy, gaiety, ecstasy, suffering, angst, anguish. The loneliness in my head is connected with being introverted or being interior. Or I'm dealing with my own feelings. I'm, um—I can put on a terrific act of being social and friendly, joking. And you know, left to myself, uh, I can—I'll be locked up for endless hours in my studio, not particularly lonely, but absorbed in all my own thoughts.

Zwerdling: Huh. So, your subjects, your sculptures, these white figures, you would like, I think, for them to convey to us a complex mixture of emotions. But to you, they are definitely not gloomy, period.

Segal: You got it. Atta boy.

Part 5 Academic English
A. Listening for the Meaning of New Words and Phrases (page 86)

1. Pop artists were inspired by mass-produced visual media—such as television, magazines, comic books, billboards, and the design of common household objects—and used these things as the starting point for their art.

2. The main difference between Oldenberg's sculptures and the objects that inspire them is that the sculptures are heroic in their size. One example is Oldenberg's 45-foot high *Clothespin* sculpture, which was permanently installed in Center Square in Philadelphia in 1976.

B. Taking Notes: Images (page 87)

Lecturer: Pop art differed from earlier art movements. To understand pop art, it is helpful to know a little bit about the artistic movement that immediately preceded it. This movement was called abstract expressionism. Jackson Pollock is an example of an abstract expressionist. Let's take a look at Pollock's painting entitled *Autumn Rhythm.* Here we see a dense field of overlapping lines that swirl and move all over the surface of the canvas. This painting refers to the process of making the painting more than it refers to anything in the actual world.

Now, Pollock believed that his intuitive approach to making paintings could show his inner self. He said, "Painting is a state of being and self discovery. Every good artist paints what he is."

C. Taking Notes: Key Words (page 88)
D. Checking Your Notes (page 93)
Section 1

Lecturer: Hello, everyone. I hope you've done your reading for today. We have a lot of material to cover. So, if you are ready, let's get started.

Today we're going to be taking a look at pop art. Pop art is an artistic development that began in the late 1950s and really became the most powerful art movement of the 1960s. Although it was a strong cultural force in Europe (especially in England), my presentation today is gonna concentrate on pop art in the United States.

Pop artists were inspired by mass-produced visual media—such as television, magazines, comic books, billboards, and the design of common household objects—and they used these things as the starting point for their art.

Pop art differed from earlier art movements. To understand pop art, it's helpful to know a little bit about the artistic movement that immediately preceded it. This movement was called abstract expressionism. Jackson Pollock is an example of an abstract expressionist. Let's take a look at Pollock's painting entitled *Autumn Rhythm.* Here we see a dense field of overlapping lines that swirl and move all over the surface of the canvas. This painting refers to the process of *making* the painting more than it refers to anything in the actual world.

Now, Pollock believed that his intuitive approach to making paintings could show his inner self. He said quote "Painting is a state of being and self discovery. Every good artist paints what he is."

Abstract expressionism was a highly personal art. It reflected the internal struggles of the individual artists. Pop artists were not at all interested in this internal search. Instead, pop artists believed that art should have a more direct relationship to things in their world.

The economic growth that began in the United States after World War II gained speed in the 1960s. At the same time, television became a primary source of information and entertainment for the American people. In the late 1940s, about 10 thousand Americans owned televisions; by 1957 over 40 million Americans owned them.

Artists of the 1940s and early 1950s used painting and sculpture to understand their own personal states of being. By comparison, the pop artists responded to the intense visual stimulation that the growing consumer culture created.

Section 2

Lecturer: An important pop artist was Robert Rauschenberg, born in Port Arthur, Texas in 1925. He moved to New York City in 1949. Abstract expressionism was very popular at this time, but Rauschenberg had other ideas about what art could say.

Rauschenberg was one of the first pop artists. He wanted to move art away from the personalities of the individual artists and direct it towards the world. The intuitive swirling forms of a Pollock painting said nothing to Rauschenberg about the rapidly changing world that he was experiencing.

By the late 1950s, Rauschenberg was using everyday objects, which he found on the street, as the material for his art. Just imagine taking a long walk around New York and picking up stuff, like old magazines, tires, and crumbled cigarette boxes. What would happen if you tried to make art from this material? That's what Rauschenberg did. He wanted to have his art reflect the world he lived in.

Now take a look at *Canyon,* from 1959. It combines old photographs, cardboard boxes, and even a stuffed bird. Rauschenberg didn't try to impose a unified symbolic meaning on this collection of materials. Instead he wanted the work to reflect the randomness of the things you might see if you were to walk around a densely populated area.

By the early 1960s Rauschenberg was concentrating less on the *objects* and more on the images he found. He was fascinated by how a single photograph could be distributed through a magazine or newspaper across the country virtually immediately. He thought that these printed photographs could comment on the speed at which information was being given to people living in the TV age.

O.K. Now look at *Skyway,* which Rauschenberg made in 1964. This is a classic example of Rauschenberg's image-based work. This painting combines an array of images: President Kennedy giving a political speech, an astronaut landing on the moon—Can you see that?—and a section from a classical painting of the Greek goddess Venus. *Skyway* looks as if Rauschenberg found a few newspapers and a magazine, took one image from each, and then combined and repeated them to make one single artwork. Looking at this work, the viewer might have the sensation of rapidly flipping through a magazine or changing the channels on his or her TV set.

Rauschenberg's use of found objects and images from everyday life was innovative and it set the stage for further developments in pop art.

Pop artists were interested in *visual* communication because they believed that these images reflected the cultural values of contemporary society.

Section 3

Lecturer: O.K. Let's turn now to Andy Warhol, another important pop artist. Warhol was born near Pittsburgh, Pennsylvania in 1928. He received a college degree in graphic design and then moved to New York City and began working as a commercial illustrator. His illustrations became popular and a variety of magazines and newspapers used them, including the *New York Times.* Even though Warhol was successful with commercial illustration, he wanted to make the kind of art that he could show in a fine art gallery.

In the late 1950s, Warhol began making fine art paintings that mirrored the streamlined style of advertising and design for household products. In his group of paintings entitled *200 Campbell's Soup Cans,* which he made in 1962, Warhol painted a series of 200 Campbell's soup cans, which were identical except that many of them had different flavors. He arranged these paintings one next to the other as they might appear on the shelf in a supermarket. Warhol was fascinated by the sameness of a culture that relied on mass production as well as by the powerful role that advertising plays in selling mass-produced products.

This quote by Andy Warhol helps illustrate his fascination with mass produced products. Quote: "What's great about this country is America started the tradition where the richest consumers buy essentially the same things as the poorest. You can be watching TV and see Coca-Cola, and you can know that the President drinks Coke, Liz Taylor drinks Coke, and just think that you can drink Coke, too."

Andy Warhol became the most famous of the pop artists. He was fascinated by the concept of fame. He associated with people who, like himself, came from common backgrounds and achieved fame. To Warhol, television changed the relationship that American culture had with fame. People could become famous very quickly if they were on television.

Throughout the 1960s and into the 1970s, Warhol painted portraits of famous people, including Marilyn Monroe, Elvis Presley, uh, the Chinese leader Mao Tse-Tung, and himself. As he did with *200 Campbell's Soup Cans*, Warhol painted numerous, nearly identical portraits of his subject and then arranged them side-by-side in a grid. Warhol's portraits are fascinating because he painted them with the same detachment as he painted his Campbell's soup cans. Warhol wasn't interested in the individual personality of the people he painted. He was interested in how mass culture could endlessly reproduce images.

Warhol became the first artist to use the culture of television, fast food, and advertising as the subject of fine art. Warhol's work presents interesting ideas about the cultural changes that were happening as the U.S. became a consumer society that spent its leisure time watching TV.

Section 4

Lecturer: O.K. The pop art movement included many other artists, such as Claes Oldenberg and Roy Lichtenstein, who were also influenced by mass culture.

Oldenberg makes large-scale public sculptures that look like common, everyday objects. The main difference between Oldenberg's sculptures and the objects that inspire them is that the sculptures are heroic in their size. One example is Oldenberg's 45-foot high *Clothespin* sculpture, which was permanently installed in Center Square in Philadelphia in 1976.

Roy Lichtenstein, another pop artist, was inspired by the graphic style of comic book illustration. This is *Wham,* which Lichtenstein made in 1963. As you can see, it shows a plane being shot down. Because this work is painted with bold, simplified colors, the viewer tends to focus more on the technique that Lichtenstein used to make this painting than on the tragedy of the event that is shown.

So, in conclusion, from the late 1950s and into the 1970s, American pop artists used the world around them for artistic inspiration. When they went outside, they found a world that wasn't natural but was *manmade.* Instead of seeing trees, they saw billboards.

Well, I see we're about out of time, but before we go, are there any questions? We have time for a couple. Yes, Ethan?

Chapter 4: Ancient Greek Art

Part 2 Social Language
A. Listening for the Main Idea (page 102)

Doug: Oh sorry Tim, I gotta go. Someone's here and it's my office hours. O.K. Bye-bye. Talk to you later. Hi, there.

Tanya: Hi, Doug. Sorry to interrupt.

Doug: No problem! It *is* office hours, after all. Have a seat. Well, what can I do for you?

Tanya: Uh, you know that paper that's due next Friday?

Doug: Yeah. Which assignment did you choose?

Tanya: I chose the one where you hafta explain how Greek art illustrates the ideals of the culture and all.

Doug: Yeah, that's the more challenging one. Good for you.

Tanya: Except I'm having a hard time finding source information at the library. Do you have any suggestions?

Doug: Good question! What you need are good photos of the pottery.

Tanya: Excuse me, but why is that?

Doug: Well, 'cause that's about all we have to go on. Most of the other art the ancient Greeks may have done—painting, sculpture—didn't survive.

Tanya: So why pottery?

Doug: Well they were all made of terracotta.

Tanya: What's that?

Doug: It's baked clay. It's a very durable material. We have thousands of Greek pots dating back to the 8th century, B.C.

Tanya: Wow.

Doug: Yeah, and the great thing is they painted incredibly detailed scenes on them. That's where we get all this information on ancient Greek civilization.

Tanya: So that's why I need good photos.

Doug: Right. Now Chapter 15 has a few, but I think you'll find even better ones in some of these books. Oh, this is the reading list from Art History 290. I'll make a copy of it for you.

Tanya: O.K., thanks.

Doug: No problem. I'll have to do it for you later though. Can you come by around 5:00 to pick it up?

Tanya: Sure. Oh, no, wait, I've got a class from 4:00 to 5:30.

Doug: Oh, I'll be outta here by 5:30 . . . um, I know, I'll leave it with the department secretary. She said she was staying late today.

Tanya: That'll work.

Doug: All right.

Tanya: Thanks, Doug.

Doug: You're welcome. Good luck on that paper.

Tanya: See you later.

B. Listening for Details (page 102)

Tanya: Except I'm having a hard time finding source information at the library. Do you have any suggestions?

Doug: Good question! What you need are good photos of the pottery.

Tanya: Excuse me, but why is that?

Doug: Well, 'cause that's about all we have to go on. Most of the other art the ancient Greeks may have done—painting, sculpture—didn't survive.

Tanya: So why pottery?

Doug: Well they were all made of terracotta.

Tanya: What's that?

Doug: It's baked clay. It's a very durable material. We have thousands of Greek pots dating back to the 8th century, B.C..

Tanya: Wow.

Doug: Yeah, and the great thing is they painted incredibly detailed scenes on them. That's where we get all this information on ancient Greek civilization.

Tanya: So that's why I need good photos.

C. Listening for the Meanings of New Phrases (page 102)

1. **Doug:** Oh sorry Tim, I gotta go. Someone's here and it's my office hours. O.K. Bye-bye. Talk to you later. Hi, there.

    Tanya: Hi, Doug. Sorry to interrupt.

    Doug: No problem! It *is* office hours, after all. Have a seat. Well, what can I do for you?

2. **Tanya:** So that's why I need good photos.

    Doug: Right. Now Chapter 15 has a few, but I think you'll find even better ones in some of these books. Oh, this is the reading list from Art History 290. I'll make a copy of it for you.

    Tanya: O.K., thanks.

3. **Tanya:** Sure. Oh, no, wait, I've got a class from 4:00 to 5:30.

Doug: Uh, I'll be outta here by 5:30 . . . um, I know, I'll leave it with the department secretary. She said she was staying late today.

Tanya: That'll work.

Doug: All right.

Tanya: Thanks, Doug.

Part 3 The Mechanics of Listening and Speaking

B. Understanding Interjections (page 106)

1. **A:** Come back around 5:00 PM.
   B: Huh? [Meaning *What?*]
2. **A:** Can you come back at 5:00 PM?
   B: Uh-huh. [Meaning *Yes*]
3. **A:** Do you like Greek art?
   B: Uh-uh. [Meaning *No*]
4. **A:** Thanks for your help.
   B: Uh-huh. [Meaning *You're welcome.*]
5. **A:** I think you forgot to turn in your paper.
   B: Uh-oh. [Meaning *There's a problem!*]

D. Hearing the Difference Between /θ/ and /s/ (page 107)

1. thank	7. thick
2. tenth	8. seem
3. sing	9. sigh
4. think	10. saw
5. eighth	11. fourth
6. some	12. path

Part 4 Broadcast English

A. Listening for the Main Idea (page 112)

Lyden: We have a sad truth to announce: The ancient Greek bronze statues—say of Aphrodite or the head of Dionysus—may have come off an ancient assembly line. For years, archaeologists thought the classical bronzes of Greek gods and goddesses that they unearthed were unique pieces, principally because they were discovered one at a time. However, in a new exhibit, The Fire of Hephaestus, at the Toledo Museum of Art, Carol Mattusch, an authority on classical bronze sculpture explains that, no, indeed the bronzes were mass-produced in workshops and smelted together from different parts. Ancient Greeks even placed custom orders. Mattusch began to suspect all this when she studied fragments of statues as a graduate student in Greece.

Mattusch: The way to find anything is to look inside the bronze, and I began to find out just how they were cast, how they were pieced together, and it made a really different picture from what I had learned at school about the uniqueness of these original Greek bronzes. They weren't original. They were made by a technology—lost wax casting—that's still used today, and that is, essentially, reproduction.

Lyden: As exciting as your finding is—and it's, uh, a marvelous discovery—does it in some way undercut the appreciation that we've historically had for these statues?

Mattusch: It certainly need not. It adds a new dimension to our understanding of these statues, but at the same time, they were all finished separately. They were all detailed as individual pieces.

Lyden: I love the story about—this is this, uh, earthenware vase that shows a man lying on the ground, his, his head's to one side and it was, it was thought to represent cannibalism, yes?

Mattusch: Yeah, when it was first discovered, in, oh, the early 1800s, people thought, "Hmm, these guys are dismembering this young man and they've got his head on the ground—they're cannibals." Now we know these are not cannibals, but this is a bronze workshop. It's really our best illustration of how this process was conducted in antiquity.

Lyden: Tell me how you find out, uh, how these things are patched or put together.

Mattusch: For this, we need the endoscope. This is something that some people probably know from bitter medical experiences, but they're fabulous inside of statues—fiber-optic tubes with lights on the ends and cameras, so you can photograph or videotape what you find inside these bronze statues, which you wouldn't be able to see just by peeping through a broken arm hole.

Lyden: Hmm, and of course, they don't have to be sedated.

Mattusch: *(laughs)* No, no.

Lyden: What were some of your other important discoveries?

Mattusch: Well, in three different collections, there are large statuettes of Aphrodite that look just alike.

Lyden: The goddess of love.

Mattusch: The goddess of love. One has a gold necklace. One has her arm adjusted differently from another one. They were all finished a little differently, but they were all made from the same basic model. If you choose the gold necklace over the silver for your statuette, you probably have to pay more for it. But, essentially, these are

produced in assembly lines to meet public demand.

Lyden: What were some of the ancient Greeks' most popular choices? What did they like to order?

Mattusch: Well, in the 5th and the 4th centuries, B.C.., in what we would call high classical times, the most popular type of statue was a naked male, either an athlete, a victor in one of the games, say at Olympia, or Delphi, or a political figure, who would have looked like an older individual. He would have his, as his attributes, he would have a shield, a spear, a helmet. But similarly, naked. This was the way, in classical times, to show what—by someone's physical abilities and perfection, to show that he was also a good leader. And so the cities of antiquity were filled with nude males—bearded, for more mature leaders, unbearded for athletes—young men.

Lyden: Carol Mattusch is a professor of art history at George Mason University, in Fairfax, Virginia.

B. Listening for Details: Section 1 (page 112)

Lyden: We have a sad truth to announce: The ancient Greek bronze statues—say of Aphrodite or the head of Dionysus—may have come off an ancient assembly line. For years, archaeologists thought the classical bronzes of Greek gods and goddesses that they unearthed were unique pieces, principally because they were discovered one at a time. However, in a new exhibit, The Fire of Hephaestus, at the Toledo Museum of Art, Carol Mattusch, an authority on classical bronze sculpture explains that, no, indeed the bronzes were mass-produced in workshops and smelted together from different parts. Ancient Greeks even placed custom orders. Mattusch began to suspect all this when she studied fragments of statues as a graduate student in Greece.

Mattusch: The way to find anything is to look inside the bronze, and I began to find out just how they were cast, how they were pieced together, and it made a really different picture from what I had learned at school about the uniqueness of these original Greek bronzes. They weren't original. They were made by a technology—lost wax casting—that's still used today, and that is, essentially, reproduction.

Lyden: As exciting as your finding is—and it's, uh, a marvelous discovery—does it in some way undercut the appreciation that we've historically had for these statues?

Mattusch: It certainly need not. It adds a new dimension to our understanding of these statues, but at the same time, they were all finished separately. They were all detailed as individual pieces.

Lyden: I love the story about—this is this, uh, earthenware vase that shows a man lying on the ground, his, his head's to one side and it was, it was thought to represent cannibalism, yes?

Mattusch: Yeah, when it was first discovered, in, oh, the early 1800s, people thought, "Hmm, these guys are dismembering this young man and they've got his head on the ground—they're cannibals." Now we know these are not cannibals, but this is a bronze workshop. It's really our best illustration of how this process was conducted in antiquity.

C. Listening for Details: Section 2 (page 113)

Lyden: Tell me how you find out, uh, how these things are patched or put together.

Mattusch: For this, we need the endoscope. This is something that some people probably know from bitter medical experiences, but they're fabulous inside of statues—fiber-optic tubes with lights on the ends and cameras, so you can photograph or videotape what you find inside these bronze statues, which you wouldn't be able to see just by peeping through a broken arm hole.

Lyden: Hmm, and of course, they don't have to be sedated.

Mattusch: *(laughs)* No, no.

Lyden: What were some of your other important discoveries?

Mattusch: Well, in three different collections, there are large statuettes of Aphrodite that look just alike.

Lyden: The goddess of love.

Mattusch: The goddess of love. One has a gold necklace. One has her arm adjusted differently from another one. They were all finished a little differently, but they were all made from the same basic model. If you choose the gold necklace over the silver for your statuette, you probably have to pay more for it. But, essentially, these are produced in assembly lines to meet public demand.

Lyden: What were some of the ancient Greeks' most popular choices? What did they like to order?

Mattusch: Well, in the 5th and the 4th centuries, B.C., in what we would call high classical times, the most popular type of statue was a naked

male, either an athlete, a victor in one of the games, say at Olympia, or Delphi, or a political figure, who would have looked like an older individual. He would have his, as his attributes, he would have a shield, a spear, a helmet. But similarly, naked. This was the way, in classical times, to show what—by someone's physical abilities and perfection, to show that he was also a good leader. And so the cities of antiquity were filled with nude males—bearded, for more mature leaders, unbearded for athletes—young men.

Lyden: Carol Mattusch is a professor of art history at George Mason University, in Fairfax, Virginia.

E. Listening for Time Periods (page 114)

Mattusch: Well, in the 5th and the 4th centuries, B.C., in what we would call high classical times, the most popular type of statue was a naked male.

Part 5 Academic English
A. Listening for the Meaning of New Words (page 117)

1. A standing male figure from the Archaic period is known as a *kouros*.
2. And a standing female figure from this period is known as a *kore*.
3. To achieve this, sculptors used a technique known as *contrapposto*. In *contrapposto*, the weight of the figure is carried on one leg and the other leg is relaxed somewhat.

   Items 4 and 5. When their tombs were excavated, people found a number of pieces of Greek jewelry. And, uh, these include armbands or torques, diadems or crowns, and earrings—all of exquisite quality.

B. Using Phonetic Symbols (page 118)

1. A standing male figure from the Archaic period is called a *kouros*.
2. Nude female figures were introduced during the 4th century B.C.E.. in depictions of Aphrodite, the uh, the goddess of love.
3. The earliest known example was sculpted by Praxiteles for the city of Knidos in Asia Minor.
4. The earliest known example was sculpted by Praxiteles for the city of Knidos in Asia Minor.

C. Getting the Main Idea from the Introduction (page 119)

Lecturer: Good morning. I hope everyone had a restful break. O.K. good. Well, let's get started. Today, I'm going to give you an overview of Greek art. I'm going to be covering sculpture, vases, and jewelry.

D. Taking Notes: Timelines (page 119)

Lecturer: Now, when you think about the art of ancient Greece, what comes to mind? Most people think of the Parthenon. There's a nice shot of it in your book. The Parthenon was built between the years 490 and 432 B.C.E., that is, *Before the Common Era*. It was dedicated to the goddess Athena Parthenos That is P-A-R-T-H-E-N-O-S. Did everybody get that? Sorry, let me put that up here, [writes on board] P-A-R-T-H-E-N-O-S. It stands on the Acropolis, which is basically a rocky hill in Athens and the most important site in the city. Now, Greek art began about 500 years before the Parthenon was built and lasted approximately 400 more years.

Scholars have identified several different periods, each with its own special characteristics. The period when the Parthenon was built is known as the *Classical* period. It lasted for about 160 years, from around 480 B.C.E. to 320 B.C.E. Did everyone get those dates? Now, there were three different artistic periods *before* the Classical period. They were the Geometric Period, from about 900 to 700 B.C.E; the Orientalizing Period, from about 700 to 600 B.C.E.; and the Archaic Period, from about 600 to 480 B.C.E. I think you got the first one, "geometric", yes O.K.—the others are Orientalizing [writes on board]—that's O-R-I-E-N-T-A-L-I-Z-I-N-G—and the third was Archaic [writes on board] A-R-C-H-A-I-C. The word "Hellenistic", that's [writes on board] H-E-L-L-E-N-I-S-T-I-C—that covers around 330-320 B.C.E.—is used to describe Greek art made *after* the Classical Period.

E. Taking Notes: Using an Outline (page 120)
F. Checking Your Notes (page 123)
Section 1

Lecturer: Good morning. I hope everyone had a restful break. O.K., good. Well, let's get started. Um, today, I'm going to give you an overview of Greek art. I'm going to be covering sculpture, vases, and jewelry.

Now, when you think about the art of ancient Greece, what comes to mind? Most people think of the Parthenon. There's a nice shot of it in your book. The Parthenon was built between the years 490 and 432 B.C.E., that is, *Before the Common*

Era. It was dedicated to the goddess Athena Parthenos That is P-A-R-T-H-E-N-O-S. Did everybody get that? Sorry, let me put that up here, [writes on board] P-A-R-T-H-E-N-O-S, It stands on the Acropolis, which is basically a rocky hill in Athens and the most important site in the city. Now, Greek art began about 500 years before the Parthenon was built and lasted approximately 400 more years.

Scholars have identified several different periods, each with its own special characteristics. The period when the Parthenon was built is known as the *Classical* period. It lasted for about 160 years, from around 480 B.C.E. to 320 B.C.E. Did everyone get those dates? Now, there were three different artistic periods *before* the Classical period. They were the Geometric Period, from about 900 to 700 B.C.E.; the Orientalizing Period, from about 700 to 600 B.C.E.; and the Archaic Period, from about 600 to 480 B.C.E. I think you got the first one, "geometric", yes O.K.—the others are Orientalizing [writes on board]—that's O-R-I-E-N-TA-L-I-Z-I-N-G— and the third was Archaic [writes on board] A-R-C-H-A-I-C. The word "Hellenistic", that's [writes on board] H-E-L-L-E-N-I-S-T-I-C— around 330-320 B.C.E.—is used to describe Greek art made *after* the Classical Period.

Section 2

Lecturer: Now, the sculpture found in the Parthenon reveals the Greek admiration for the human body. From early in the history of Greek art, male and female figures were depicted in a variety of different positions: standing, sitting and walking. Now, usually male figures were shown naked and women were clothed. But as time passed, artists carved thinner and thinner drapery. This allowed the shape of the female body to become more apparent. Nude female figures were introduced during the 4th century B.C.E. in depictions of Aphrodite, the goddess of love. The earliest known example was sculpted by Praxiteles for the city of Knidos in Asia Minor.

O.K. Now, a standing male figure from the Archaic period is called a *kouros*. Take a look at the example in your book. And a standing female figure from this period is known as a *kore*. The face is always oval. The eyes are large, and the face wears a smile known as the Archaic smile, [points to board] archaic. Notice how in male figures, the arms are held rigidly by the sides. The fists are clenched and one leg is placed slightly in front of the other. Um, can everyone see that? Good.

Now, take a look in your book at the picture of *The Spear Bearer*. Everybody got that? Careful study of the statue, *The Spear Bearer,* shows that during the Classical period, artists began to depict the athletic musculature of their figures much more clearly. As you can see here, the body is less rigid, the arms are held much more loosely, and the head is turned to one side. To achieve this, sculptors used a technique known as *contrapposto.* In *contrapposto,* the weight of the figure is carried on one leg and the other leg is relaxed somewhat. Can everyone see that? O.K., um, the figure's left leg is relaxed here. And in this type of pose, the body is rotated slightly in one direction.

In the Hellenistic period, [points to board] which of course, followed, some figures began to show even more movement and emotion.

Section 3

Lecturer: Well, um, let's turn now to vase painting. Vase painting was a very popular form of art among the Greeks. Illustrations of the lives of the gods, goddesses, and heroes—both fictional and real—usually decorated the vases. The vases were made of red-colored clay by people called potters. The vases had a utilitarian function. That is, people used them to hold dry things such as grain, or liquids like wine or oil.

Now, the artists who decorated the vases perfected different techniques of glazing. They painted glazes on the vases, and then fired them in an oven or a kiln to make them waterproof. Artists illustrated the stories on them in different ways. They did this by decorating them in bands that wrapped around the pots [makes circular motion]. Now, at times, many bands with small figures were popular, and at other times fewer bands with larger figures were more popular. As with architecture and sculpture, many examples of this art form have disappeared.

Now, the earliest vases date back to the Geometric period. These vases had abstract geometric designs. In the *late* Geometric period, figures start to appear on the vases. Now, during the *Archaic* period, [points to board] the black-figure technique was popular. In black-figure technique, the figures are outlined in black against the natural red background of the clay. Later, a painter known as Andokides [writes on board]—that's A-N-D-O-K-I-D-E-S—Andokides developed a reverse technique, called red-figure technique. An example of red-figure technique can be seen in a *krater,* which is a type of vase. Take a look at the example in your book. As you can see, it's decorated with scenes from the lives of the gods. In the scene we can see here, Artemis, the goddess of hunting, kills Actaeon after he accidentally sees her bathing.

Section 4

Lecturer: Now, let's turn to jewelry. That's one of my favorite subjects. Jewelry design was a popular form of Greek art. Both men and women wore gold jewelry. Unfortunately, though, both because of the value of the gold and because of its delicate character, very little has survived. But fortunately, there was a thriving export market, so many of these items ended up in other places. And people in other cultures were often buried with their valued possessions. When their tombs were excavated, people found a number of pieces of Greek jewelry. And these include arm bands or torques, diadems or crowns, and earrings—all of exquisite quality. There's a good example of a 4th century diadem in your books. Everybody find that illustration? O.K.

Now, in conclusion, as a result of trade and conquest, Greek art was carried throughout the Mediterranean world and as far east as India. And Greek art had a remarkable influence on later art in Europe, Asia Minor, and India. When the Europeans went to the Americas and everywhere else, they carried the ideals of Greek art with them. So Greek art has fascinated people for many years and we can feel its impact even today in the art and architecture that surround us.

Well, that's it for today. Are there any questions? Yes, Kana.

Chapter 5: States of Consciousness

Part 2 Social Language

A. Listening for the Main Idea (page 135)

B. Listening for Details (page 135)

Chrissy: Hi. I'm Chrissy, and your name is . . . ?

Speaker 1: Crystal.

Chrissy: O.K., I'm doing an interview for Campus TV. Can I ask you a few questions?

Speaker 1: Sure.

Chrissy: Great. Do you remember your dreams?

Speaker 1: Yeah.

Chrissy: Uh, can you describe one?

Speaker 1: Uh, the one I had last night was, huh, I walked to Japan, and when I got there, I ran in a three-day marathon, and I won.

Chrissy: But you walked there?

Speaker 1: Yeah.

Chrissy: How did you manage that? Did you walk on the water or anything?

Speaker 1: I don't remember. I guess so. There's like a bridge or something. I don't know.

Speaker 2: Yes, actually I do remember my dreams a lot. I usually have a couple dreams a night that I remember.

Chrissy: Can you describe one?

Speaker 2: Well, one was when I was walking to a supermarket, and I saw one of my favorite, uh, actresses from television. Uh, her name is Helen Hunt and she's on, uh, a sitcom, and I got to speak to her, and talk to her, and she's really nice.

Speaker 3: I remember most of them. I don't think I can describe them right now. Usually I just remember the scary ones, so I try not to think about it.

Chrissy: Can you maybe grasp—grab a scary one out from the blue?

Speaker 3: Um, probably my most recent scary one was my alarm going off, and it just kept going off all night, but when I woke up it actually wasn't a dream. It was going off but that was pretty scary.

Chrissy: Do you remember your dreams?

Speaker 4: Sometimes.

Chrissy: Can you describe one?

Speaker 4: Oh, lately I haven't had a lot. I had one where actually a bunch of papers on my desk turned into snakes one time. That was the scariest one I've had in a long time.

Chrissy: Do you remember your dreams?

Speaker 5: Most of the time, yes.

Chrissy: Can you describe one?

Speaker 5: I remember dreaming once about an airliner that was landing in New York City and crashed.

Speaker 6: Um, I remember 'em.

Chrissy: Can you describe one?

Speaker 6: I'd rather not.

C. Listening for Details (page 136)

1. **Chrissy:** O.K., I'm doing an interview for Campus TV. Can I ask you a few questions?

   Speaker 1: Sure.

   Chrissy: Great. Do you remember your dreams?

   Speaker 1: Yeah.

   Chrissy: Uh, can you describe one?

   Speaker 1: Uh, the one I had last night was, huh, I walked to Japan, and when I got there, I ran in a three-day marathon, and I won.

2. **Speaker 3:** I remember most of them. I don't think I can describe them right now. Usually I just remember the scary ones, so I try not to think about it.

   Chrissy: Can you maybe grasp—grab a scary one out from the blue?

   Speaker 3: Um, probably my most recent scary one was my alarm going off, and it just kept going off all night, but when I woke up it actually wasn't a dream. It was going off but that was pretty scary.

3. **Chrissy:** Do you remember your dreams?

   Speaker 4: Sometimes.

   Chrissy: Can you describe one?

   Speaker 4: Oh, lately I haven't had a lot. I had one where actually a bunch of papers on my desk turned into snakes one time. That was the scariest one I've had in a long time.

4. **Chrissy:** Do you remember your dreams?

   Speaker 5: Most of the time, yes.

   Chrissy: Can you describe one?

   Speaker 5: I remember dreaming once about an airliner that was landing in New York City and crashed.

Part 3 The Mechanics of Listening and Speaking

B. Hearing the Difference Between *Can* and *Can't* (page 139)

1. You can ask me that.
2. I can't see over your head.
3. She can't come with us.
4. Mike can sing very well.
5. I can understand French.
6. They can't hear you.

Part 4 Broadcast English

A. Understanding Scientific Terms (page 145)

Items 1 and 2: The energy reserves come in the form of something called glycogen that's stored in special cells in the brain called glial cells. So, to restore the energy reserves, you need to restore the glycogen, and to do that, you've got to reduce the activity of nearby nerve cells that are demanding it as they do the brain's work.

Items 3 and 4: Now, sleep is divided into stages, and at first it seemed like Heller and Bennington's theory only explained the stage of sleep known as non-REM sleep. We spend the bulk of the night in non-REM sleep, and non-

REM is the sleep stage we go into when we first fall asleep. But they think their theory also explains REM, or rapid-eye movement sleep. REM is the stage of sleep where dreams occur.

B. Listening for the Main Idea (page 145)

Palca: Stanford sleep researcher Craig Heller says it's not hard to understand why scientists are fascinated by sleep.

Heller: We spend one-third of our lives sleeping and we don't know why, and we don't know how, and that seems like a pretty important question to be answered. Uh, one-third of our existence is unexplained.

Palca: The answer to the question "Why do we sleep?" might seem obvious, but it's not. There have been many theories from reorganizing memory to restoring some bodily function depleted while we're awake. But none of these theories has been proven.

It seems as if sleep has to be restorative in some way, but no one has been able to find exactly what, if anything, is restored. If sleep were simply to restore tired muscles, you'd predict that football players would all want to go to sleep right after a big game, but generally, that's not what happens. Scientists do know that sleep is essential. If you deprive an animal of sleep, it will die.

Now Craig Heller and his colleague, Joel Bennington, have proposed an explanation for why there's such a powerful need for sleep. As Heller explains, their new theory suggests that sleep does have something to do with restoring the body after a long day awake, but the need for sleep is quite literally all in our heads.

Heller: Perhaps what is happening during wake is that we are running down our energy reserves in the brain. The brain doesn't have much in the way of energy reserves. Uh, muscles can use fat as fuel. Uh, everything, of course, uses glucose from the blood as fuel, but when muscles run out of glucose in the blood coming through, they just burn fat. Well, the brain can't do that. The brain has to have glucose, and if the supply of glucose in the blood isn't adequate, then it has to use up whatever reserves it has within the cell or nearby the cell.

Palca: The energy reserves come in the form of something called glycogen that's stored in special cells in the brain called glial cells. So, to restore the energy reserves, you need to restore the glycogen, and to do that, you've got to reduce the activity of nearby nerve cells that are demanding it as they do the brain's work. But Heller says, because of the way the brain is organized, it's impossible to renew those glycogen stores while you're awake.

Heller: You can't take a region of the brain offline to replace it during wake, or else you'll compromise information processing, and the brain is a parallel processor. It's processing lots of sources of information all the time, and you can't take one section of it offline to give it a chance to recover its energy supply. So during sleep, you take the whole brain offline at the same time. You shut down its information processing while energy reserves are replenished and replaced.

Palca: Heller and Bennington have some experimental evidence that supports their theory. There's a chemical in the brain called adenosine that's released when brain energy stores are depleted. When the researchers injected a compound that mimics the effect of adenosine into rats, the rats immediately went into a deep sleep.

Now, sleep is divided into stages, and at first it seemed like Heller and Bennington's theory only explained the stage of sleep known as non-REM sleep. We spend the bulk of the night in non-REM sleep, and non-REM is the sleep stage we go into when we first fall asleep.

But they think their theory also explains REM, or rapid-eye movement sleep. REM is the stage of sleep where dreams occur. During REM, the brain's electrical activity looks just like it does when someone's awake, so it was hard to argue that the brain was "offline," as Heller puts it, during REM.

In fact, Heller and Bennington believe that glycogen is only restored during non-REM sleep, but that process takes the brain out of electrical balance. REM sleep, then, is necessary to restore that balance. So dreaming is not so much a road to the unconscious as a road to continued restorative sleep.

If they are on the right track, it could open up entirely new ways of manipulating sleep and treating the tens of millions of people in this country for whom getting a good night's sleep is a nightmare.

This is Joe Palca in Washington.

C. Listening for Details: Section 1 (page 146)

Palca: Stanford sleep researcher Craig Heller says it's not hard to understand why scientists are fascinated by sleep.

Heller: We spend one-third of our lives sleeping and we don't know why, and we don't know how, and that seems like a pretty important question to be answered. Uh, one-third of our existence is unexplained.

Palca: The answer to the question "Why do we sleep?" might seem obvious, but it's not. There have been many theories from reorganizing memory to restoring some bodily function depleted while we're awake. But none of these theories has been proven.

It seems as if sleep has to be restorative in some way, but no one has been able to find exactly what, if anything, is restored. If sleep were simply to restore tired muscles, you'd predict that football players would all want to go to sleep right after a big game, but generally, that's not what happens. Scientists do know that sleep is essential. If you deprive an animal of sleep, it will die.

Now Craig Heller and his colleague, Joel Bennington, have proposed an explanation for why there's such a powerful need for sleep. As Heller explains, their new theory suggests that sleep does have something to do with restoring the body after a long day awake, but the need for sleep is quite literally all in our heads.

Heller: Perhaps what is happening during wake is that we are running down our energy reserves in the brain. The brain doesn't have much in the way of energy reserves. Uh, muscles can use fat as fuel. Uh, everything, of course, uses glucose from the blood as fuel, but when muscles run out of glucose in the blood coming through, they just burn fat. Well, the brain can't do that. The brain has to have glucose, and if the supply of glucose in the blood isn't adequate, then it has to use up whatever reserves it has within the cell or nearby the cell.

Palca: The energy reserves come in the form of something called glycogen that's stored in special cells in the brain called glial cells. So, to restore the energy reserves, you need to restore the glycogen, and to do that, you've got to reduce the activity of nearby nerve cells that are demanding it as they do the brain's work. But Heller says, because of the way the brain is organized, it's impossible to renew those glycogen stores while you're awake.

Heller: You can't take a region of the brain offline to replace it during wake, or else you'll compromise information processing, and the brain is a parallel processor. It's processing lots of sources of information all the time, and you can't take one section of it offline to give it a chance to recover its energy supply. So during sleep, you take the whole brain offline at the same time. You shut down its information processing while energy reserves are replenished and replaced.

D. Listening for Supporting Information: Section 2 (page 147)

Palca: Heller and Bennington have some experimental evidence that supports their theory. There's a chemical in the brain called adenosine that's released when brain energy stores are depleted. When the researchers injected a compound that mimics the effect of adenosine into rats, the rats immediately went into a deep sleep.

Now, sleep is divided into stages, and at first it seemed like Heller and Bennington's theory only explained the stage of sleep known as non-REM sleep. We spend the bulk of the night in non-REM sleep, and non-REM is the sleep stage we go into when we first fall asleep.

But they think their theory also explains REM, or rapid-eye movement sleep. REM is the stage of sleep where dreams occur. During REM, the brain's electrical activity looks just like it does when someone's awake, so it was hard to argue that the brain was "offline," as Heller puts it, during REM.

In fact, Heller and Bennington believe that glycogen is only restored during non-REM sleep, but that process takes the brain out of electrical balance. REM sleep, then, is necessary to restore that balance. So dreaming is not so much a road to the unconscious as a road to continued restorative sleep.

If they are on the right track, it could open up entirely new ways of manipulating sleep and treating the tens of millions of people in this country for whom getting a good night's sleep is a nightmare.

This is Joe Palca in Washington.

E. Separating Fact from Theory (page 148)

1. Perhaps what is happening during wake is that we are running down our energy reserves in the brain.

2. . . . when muscles run out of glucose in the blood coming through, they just burn fat.

3. But they think their theory also explains REM, or rapid-eye movement sleep.

4. In fact, Heller and Bennington believe that glycogen is only restored during non-REM sleep, but that process takes the brain out of electrical balance.

Part 5 Academic English

A. Listening for the Meaning of New Words and Phrases (page 149)

1. Now, to begin with, let's take a look at consciousness. Consciousness—uh, this is the state of being aware.

2. Sleep is a different state of consciousness. This is known as an altered state of consciousness.

3. And with prolonged sleeplessness, people tend to become incoherent. They have difficulty thinking and talking clearly.

4. There's a name for this natural rhythm—the natural rhythm known as sleep cycle or, circadian rhythm. Some researchers describe circadian rhythms as two internal clocks. One internal clock controls the sleep cycle.

5. Researchers have discovered by observing eye movement and using EEGs—that's electroencephalographs, those are machines that measure brain wave patterns—that there are four stages of sleep.

B. Listening for Topic Change Signals (page 150)

1. By the way, in case you're interested, uh, the record for one person staying awake is 11 days. A 17-year-old boy, I think his name is Randy Gardner, set it at a state fair back in, uh, January, 1964. Experts studied him during and after the 11 days of sleeplessness.

2. So, moving on—sleep is a natural biological need. Our bodies have a biological need to rejuvenate.

C. Taking Notes: Using an Outline (page 150)
D. Checking Your Notes (page 155)
Section 1

Lecturer: Hi everybody! We're gonna get started, so I want you to shut off your cell phones, and let's get started.

Today, I'm going to discuss what goes on in the brain during sleep. Now, to begin with, let's take a look at consciousness [points to board]. Consciousness—this is the state of being aware. Human beings have the capacity, like all living things, to be aware of our environmental surroundings. So, we use our senses to hear, see, and feel what's around us. We can use any, or all, of our senses to be aware of our environment. For example, even with our eyes closed [closes eyes], we know that we're near the ocean by the sound of the waves and the smell of the salt in the air.

Now, human consciousness is different from that of all other living beings, such as plants and animals and fish. And one area of difference is that human beings have the capacity to be self-conscious. That is, humans can be aware of themselves. This is known as self-awareness. Humans can focus their attention and awareness on themselves.

Sleep is a different state of consciousness. This is known as an altered state of consciousness [points to board]. We are alive, but we're not consciously aware. Our consciousness is altered, that is, it's changed when we sleep. We're not self-aware.

There are many theories on why we sleep. We'll take a look at those in a moment. However, experts have stated what many people already know—the longer someone goes without sleep, the more moody and irritable they become. Without sleep, people have difficulty focusing their eyes. They have mood swings: one moment they're pleasant, and the next moment they're angry.

People also get irritable, uncooperative. They're very easily annoyed. They get angry easily. And with prolonged sleeplessness, people tend to become incoherent. They have difficulty thinking and talking clearly. By the way, in case you're interested the record for a person staying awake is 11 days. A 17-year-old boy, I think his name is Randy Gardner, set it at a state fair back in January, 1964. Experts studied him during and after the eleven days of sleeplessness.

Section 2

Lecturer: So, moving on—sleep is a natural biological need. Our bodies have a biological need to rejuvenate. After a certain number of hours, our bodies need to rest. This natural biological need for rest is regulated. At approximately the same time each day, we get sleepy, and we need approximately the same amount of sleep to be rested. There's a name for this natural rhythm—the natural rhythm known as sleep cycle or, circadian rhythm [writes on board]. Some researchers describe circadian rhythms as two internal clocks. One internal clock controls the sleep cycle.

A second internal clock controls our physiology, our bodily functions—for example, our body temperature. There are some researchers who describe circadian rhythms as one clock with two different functions.

Circadian rhythms have these features:

- One, they, they function even if we are in 24 hours of daylight or 24 hours of darkness without knowing the time.
- Two, they help control our, our bodily rhythms.
- Three, they control our sleep patterns.
- And four, they also control temperature.

Our natural circadian rhythms may be disturbed by a daily work schedule that isn't regular, such as the schedule of, uh, an airline pilot, or a fire fighter. Jet lag, or traveling from one time zone to another, that can also disrupt our circadian rhythms.

So, why do we sleep? Well, researchers have been trying to discover whether sleep is a process of rest or recovery. So, let's look at three perspectives on this issue. One perspective is the physical restoration view [points to board]. Those who support this theory believe that sleep is a natural state, and that it allows the body to recover from a day of expending energy.

Now, other researchers view sleep as hibernation [points to board]. They believe that sleep evolved from the need to conserve energy during the night, when people couldn't hunt or search for food. This group sees sleep as a process similar to the hibernation of bears in the winter. There's a third theory. That's the cerebral restoration theory [points to board]. Now, this view is that sleep is a time when the brain's cortex recovers from exhaustion. Researchers who have this view believe that sleep aids the cortex in recovering. They also believe that sleep has little effect on basic bodily processes. They believe that the remainder of the body can find better ways to rest, such as conscious meditation or biofeedback.

We often wonder why some people need more sleep than others do. We know that everybody requires some sleep, and that most people require an average of up to eight hours' sleep. Now, the amount of sleep an individual needs varies from oh, say, four hours to up to 10 hours. Age has some effect on the amount of sleep a person needs: teenagers tend to sleep longer than college students, and the elderly sleep less than young people do. Activity levels don't influence the amount of sleep people need. In fact, active people may need less sleep.

Section 3

Lecturer: Now, what are the cycles and stages of sleep? Our sleep cycles are repetitive. Each day we go to sleep approximately the same time. A full sleep cycle lasts approximately 90 minutes. Then the cycle begins again. The average sleep pattern, eight hours, has five cycles of sleep.

Researchers have discovered by observing eye movement and using EEGs [points to board], that's, electroencephalographs, those are machines that measure brain wave patterns—that there are four stages of sleep. Stage 1 occurs upon first falling asleep: this stage, the sleep is light and people can be awakened easily. In Stages 2 and 3, there are increasingly deeper levels of sleep, which last about 30 to 40 minutes each. Finally, there is Stage 4, a very deep sleep, where it's difficult to wake people up.

Rapid eye movement or REM [points to board] is the sleep that occurs in the transitions from one stage to another. The rapid movement of the eyes makes it easy to identify REM sleep. REM sleep occurs when we dream. It begins after going through the four stages. REM sleep is necessary for normal bodily and behavioral functioning. Non-rapid eye movement sleep or "NREM" sleep [points to board] occurs during the four stages of sleep, where there is no rapid eye movement.

The brain emits alpha waves, slow waves that can be seen on an EEG, during rest just prior to sleep. The brain emits delta waves during Stage 4, this is the deep sleep stage. The brain emits intense wave activity during REM sleep, which is similar to the wave activity recorded when a person is awake.

People who are denied REM sleep, even for just a couple of hours, are very tired the next day. They become irritable, anxious, and agitated. People who are denied REM sleep for a considerable amount of time suffer from many symptoms, some of which can be psychologically damaging. People who sleep, but are denied REM sleep, will feel as if they haven't slept at all.

Section 4

Lecturer: Now, let's turn to the subject of dreaming. What is a dream? A dream is an altered state of consciousness that occurs during REM sleep. Dreams begin approximately 90 minutes after falling asleep. A dream includes visual imagery. It can also include smells, sounds, physical sensations, especially for people who are blind. During dreams, heart rate increases, rapid eye movement occurs, changing brain-wave patterns can be identified, and body movement is minimal. Most people have four to five dreams a night. Dreams last from a few seconds to a few minutes. Non-REM sleep is less visual and more like thinking while we're sleeping.

You might wonder why we remember some, but not all of our dreams. We have about five dreams each night, yet only remember one or two, if any.

Some people have the same or similar dreams over and over again. And some people have dreams that continue from one, from the night before. Now, most dreams are about ordinary life events and are difficult to recall because they are so plain and ordinary. And most dreams include people and events that we're familiar with, like friends and family. Many have common themes including sex, aggressive incidents, and misfortunes. Sounds and other sensations that don't wake up a sleeper may get included in a dream. So, for example, if it's raining and thundering outside, a dreamer may dream of baths or swimming or rainstorms.

We tend to remember a dream if we awaken in the middle of it. And, we remember a dream if it was specifically powerful or vivid. You can often remember dreams by altering your pattern of awakening. For example, people who lie in bed for a few minutes before rising remember more dreams. People who get up immediately and get active right away remember fewer dreams.

Sometimes people are aware of dreaming while they're asleep. Now, this is known as lucid dreaming [points to board]. Lucid dreaming makes you feel as if you are both inside and outside the dream simultaneously. So, therefore, lucid dreams are sometimes upsetting and tend to awaken the dreamer.

From the beginning of time, people have wondered what dreams mean. Well, many cultures and traditions have given dream interpretation an important place in their belief systems. In western culture, many researchers have claimed that dreams have personal, hidden meanings. The psychological theorists, Sigmund Freud and Carl Jung [points to board], among many others, have written books on the interpretation of dreams, including dream symbolism and analysis.

Other researchers, however, believe that dreams are nothing more than brain activity. During sleep, the parts of the brain responsible for vision, hearing, and emotions are stimulated during REM sleep. The brain's cortex tries to organize the sensations created by the REM stimulation, creating what we call dreams and what these researchers call activation-synthesis.

O.K. That's all we have time for today. Are there any questions?

Chapter 6 Abnormal Psychology
Part 2 Social Language
A. Listening for the Main Idea (page 164)
B. Listening for Details (page 164)

Chrissy: Hi my name is Chrissy, and your name is?

Speaker 1: Stephanie.

Chrissy: Hi, Stephanie. I'm doing an interview for Campus TV. Can I ask you a few questions?

Speaker 1: Sure.

Chrissy: What are you afraid of?

Speaker 1: I used to be afraid of spiders, but I've sort of gotten over that now. Um, I'm still afraid—I just learned to pretend that I'm not. Um, snakes—those sorts of things.

Speaker 2: Uh, cockroaches and spiders.

Chrissy: Have you ever had like some weird experience or anything?

Speaker 2: Yeah, I was drinking coffee one morning—it was really early, and I went to pick up my cup, and there was a cockroach in it, and it was just, I saw it right before I was ready to drink it.

Chrissy: What are you afraid of?

Speaker 3: Oh, I would say the thing I'm most afraid of is drowning.

Chrissy: Did you, like, have an incident when you were younger or anything?

Speaker 3: I didn't, but I saw a child once actually go under the water and be rescued by a lifeguard and ever since then it's been kinda scary.

Speaker 4: Uh, I'm afraid of wide open spaces.

Chrissy: Is there any particular reason why?

Speaker 4: I just feel safer when there's buildings and people and cars around.

Speaker 5: I don't particularly like earthquakes.

Chrissy: Have you ever been in one?

Speaker 5: Yes, I have.

Chrissy: What are you afraid of?

Speaker 6: Seaweed, ants, and dying.

Chrissy: Wow, seaweed. Is there a specific reason why seaweed?

Speaker 6: I just—It's slimy. I just really don't like it.

Chrissy: What are you afraid of?

Speaker 7: Nothin'.

C. Listening for Specific Information
(page 165)

1. **Chrissy:** Hi, my name is Chrissy, and your name is?

   Speaker 1: Stephanie.

   Chrissy: Hi, Stephanie. I'm doing an interview for Campus TV. Can I ask you a few questions?

   Speaker 1: Sure.

   Chrissy: What are you afraid of?

   Speaker 1: I used to be afraid of spiders, but I've sort of gotten over that now. Um, I'm still afraid—I just learned to pretend that I'm not. Um, snakes—those sorts of things.

2. **Chrissy:** What are you afraid of?

   Speaker 3: Oh, I would say the thing I'm most afraid of is drowning.

   Chrissy: Did you, like, have an incident when you were younger or anything?

   Speaker 3: I didn't, but I saw a child once actually go under the water and be rescued by a lifeguard and ever since then it's been kinda scary.

3. **Speaker 6:** Seaweed, ants, and dying.

   Chrissy: Wow, seaweed. Is there a specific reason why seaweed?

   Speaker 6: I just, it's slimy. I just really don't like it.

4. **Chrissy:** What are you afraid of?

   Speaker 7: Nothin'.

Part 3 The Mechanics of Listening and Speaking
C. Hearing the Difference Between /ɛ/ and /æ/ (page 168)

1. said
2. lend
3. pan
4. trek
5. band
6. sand
7. tan
8. left
9. guess
10. jam

D. Hearing /ɛ/ and /æ/ in Sentences (page 168)

1. Can you send that for me?
2. Can you see the gem?
3. Can I borrow your pan?
4. I bought ten shirts.
5. Keith laughed when he heard the joke.

Part 4 Broadcast English
A. Listening for the Main Idea (page 173)
D. Listening for Details (page 174)

Phillips: Are you paranoid? Just because you say "no" doesn't mean that you can't be. Our guest today is Ronald Siegel. He's associate research professor at the University of California, Los Angeles, School of Medicine, most recently author of *Whispers: The Voices of Paranoia.* He's done numerous other distinguished works. I'm your host, Michael Phillips. Welcome to *Social Thought,* Dr. Siegel. You evoke paranoia very effectively in the book *Whispers.* But before we go into what's evoked, where does this whole function lie in the human brain?

Siegel: The roots of paranoia, both the neurological structures and the chemical pathways, are deep inside everyone's brain. And they're lurking; they're just waiting for the appropriate triggers to activate these systems and to grip you. And anybody can be gripped by this paranoid streak, or what I call this "demon of paranoia." It, uh, gripped Adolph Hitler; it killed Ernest Hemingway; and it's out there waiting for all of us, including you, Michael.

Today, it's particularly relevant because the 1990s are what a lot of theorists and psychiatrists are calling the Age of Paranoia.

There are many reasons for our collective unease. Here in California, we have a lot of earthquakes. We have a lot of street crime, a lot of random, drive-by shootings. There's concern about AIDS, about the resurgence of streptococcus A infection, which eats away flesh at the rate of an inch an hour. So there's a lot of reasons why people get agitated, and it's not surprising that 10 percent of the hospital admissions within the continental United States are for paranoia. It's a very pervasive feeling.

And it makes sense that we, as a species, should feel some paranoia, because it makes survival sense. When our ancestors, uh, first emerged from caves, uh, life was very threatening. Uh, violence, disease, accidents almost always ended life early. And part of the brain evolved, over 200 million years, to give us these kinds of premonitions—these kinds of warning signals— that something was threatening us. This is a part of the brain, deep in the center, that we call the limbic system. And it's concerned with the four "F" words of survival: uh, feeding, fighting, fleeing, and fornicating.

And when you get paranoid, you have a deep-seated feeling in this part of the brain. And people interpret this as a very primitive, raw emotion. And it is primitive. It's 200 million years old. And then this electrical excitation comes up into the thinking areas and you start thinking about it and trying to find an explanation. And your mind starts searching for all kinds of explanations and reasons for this raw feeling. Most of us can handle this in the everyday world, but some individuals can get very, very carried away. And those are the individuals that seek help. Most of them don't seek help and even the ones that do, the sad news is that treatment for paranoia is largely ineffective. We really don't know how to take care of this disorder.

B. Guessing the Meaning from Context
(page 173)

1. There's concern about AIDS, about the resurgence of streptococcus A infection, which eats away flesh at the rate of an inch an hour.

2. And part of the brain evolved, over 200 million years, to give us these kinds of premonitions—these kinds of warning signals—that something was threatening us.

C. Listening for Reasons (page 173)

Siegel: Today, it's particularly relevant because the 1990s are what a lot of theorists and psychiatrists are calling the Age of Paranoia.

There are many reasons for our collective unease. Here in California, we have a lot of earthquakes. We have a lot of street crime, a lot of random, drive-by shootings. There's concern about AIDS, about the resurgence of streptococcus A infection, which eats away flesh at the rate of an inch an hour. So there's a lot of reasons why people get agitated, and it's not surprising that 10 percent of the hospital admissions within the continental United States are for paranoia. It's a very pervasive feeling.

Part 5 Academic English

B. Using Medical Roots to Guess the Meaning of New Words (page 177)

1. The first type of phobic disorder is simple phobia. Two examples of simple phobias are acrophobia—that's A-C-R-O-P-H-O-B-I-A and claustrophobia—that's C-L-A-U-S-T-R-O-P-H-O-B-I-A. Acrophobia is the fear of high places.

2. These therapists believe that people with phobic disorders should be forced to confront what they fear so that they will realize that no real danger exists. For example, a person may be asked to ride in

the elevator a hundred times in order to uh, eliminate claustrophobia.

3. Drug therapies use psychotropic drugs, drugs that primarily affect the brain, to alleviate the symptoms of anxiety disorders.

C. Listening to a Lecture Introduction
(page 178)

Lecturer: All right, I hope that everyone had a nice weekend. Please remember to turn your cell phones off or set them to vibrate. Today, I'm going to be discussing several types of anxiety disorders and various treatments for each one.

Now, anxiety can be defined as a state of fear, apprehension, or worry that affects many areas of functioning. People who are anxious feel tense and preoccupied, even though they might not know the cause. We all experience anxiety as part of everyday life. We can experience symptoms of anxiety in many different situations—for example, when we take a test, when we speak to a group, or when we have to go to the doctor. As a result of these experiences, many of us find ways to cope with our anxiety. The anxiety of taking a test might cause someone to study for several hours. Anxiety about staying healthy leads some people to join a gym and to incorporate regular exercise in their daily lives. Now, all of us experience anxiety in our lives, but some of us experience this uneasiness on a more regular, frequent, and persistent basis. Now, for people like this, anxiety can become very painful and unpleasant. This persistent distressing feeling can turn into an anxiety disorder. Now, three common anxiety disorders are generalized anxiety disorder, phobic disorder, and obsessive-compulsive disorder.

D. Taking Notes: Using an Outline
Section 1 (page 179)
E. Taking Notes: Using a Chart (page 184)

Lecturer: All right, I hope that everyone had a nice weekend. Please remember to turn your cell phones off or set them to vibrate. Today, I'm going to be discussing several types of anxiety disorders and various treatments for each one.

Now, anxiety can be defined as a state of fear, apprehension, or worry that affects many areas of functioning. People who are anxious feel tense and preoccupied, even though they might not know the cause. We all experience anxiety as part of everyday life. We can experience symptoms of anxiety in many different situations—for example, when we take a test, when we speak to a group, or when we have to go to the doctor. As a result of these experiences, many of us find ways to cope with our anxiety. The anxiety of taking a test might cause someone to study for several hours. Anxiety about staying healthy leads some people to join a gym and to incorporate regular exercise in their daily lives. Now, all of us experience anxiety in our lives, but some of us experience this uneasiness on a more regular, frequent, and persistent basis. Now, for people like this, anxiety can become very painful and unpleasant. This persistent distressing feeling can turn into an anxiety disorder. Now, three common anxiety disorders are generalized anxiety disorder, phobic disorder, and obsessive-compulsive disorder.

O.K. A generalized anxiety disorder develops when a person is constantly tense and extremely worried about two or more life problems. These life problems usually center on money, family, health, and employment. Now, persistent worries about these issues can cause the person to become tense and restless all the time. He or she may be constantly waiting for something bad to happen. As a result of such thoughts, the person can develop physical symptoms or reactions, such as stomach problems, extreme fatigue, a racing pulse, continuous blinking, or even stomach ulcers. Because of the tension and the physical symptoms, such people often find it difficult to concentrate, or to make decisions, or to keep promises.

Section 2

Lecturer: All right. A phobia is a constant and unreasonable fear of a particular object, activity, or situation. Phobic fears cause severe anxiety. Physiological symptoms may accompany phobic feelings. Physical reactions include an elevated heart rate, sweating, and sometimes panic attacks. The first type of phobic disorder is simple phobia. Two examples of simple phobias are acrophobia—that's A-C-R-O-P-H-O-B-I-A and claustrophobia—that's C-L-A-U-S-T-R-O-P-H-O-B-I-A. Acrophobia is the fear of high places. Claustrophobia is the fear of closed places, such as elevators or subway cars. O.K., now the second type of phobic disorder is the social phobia. People with social phobias may be afraid to talk or perform in public, or to use a public bathroom, or to eat in public.

Obsessions are unwanted, disturbing, and unreasonable thoughts or ideas that people cannot get out of their minds. An obsession can involve a disturbing concern with dirt and germs, or a strong feeling that something terrible might happen. Compulsions are unchanging, rigid, and repetitive behaviors that are used to reduce the person's anxiety. Compulsions involve behaviors

such as excessive hand-washing or repeatedly checking to see that a door is locked or giving undue attention to one's clothing and personal appearance.

Although there are numerous treatments for anxiety disorders, three major therapies are most widely used. Psychodynamic therapy is based on the view that psychological forces, which the person is unaware of, determine the person's behavior. Psychotherapy concentrates on helping a patient uncover and determine the impact of past events. Two basic techniques of psychotherapy are free association and dream analysis. In free association the patient describes whatever thoughts or feelings come to mind, even if they seem silly or unimportant. In dream analysis, the patient's dreams can reveal unconscious or hidden anxieties and conflicts. Using these techniques, the patient's dreams, thoughts, and feelings are explored with the therapist, and the resulting revelations generally lead to recovery.

Section 3

Lecturer: Now, behavioral therapy identifies a patient's specific unwanted behaviors and applies learning principles to either change these behaviors or replace them with more appropriate ones. This therapy has made a substantial contribution to the treatment of phobias. The major behavioral techniques used are systematic desensitization, flooding, and modeling.

The first one, systematic desensitization, is a process through which a phobic patient learns to relax and react calmly, instead of anxiously, when faced with a fearful object or situation. Systematic desensitization is taught in three phases: one, relaxation training; two, construction of a fear; and three, the pairing of a feared object with a relaxation response. For example, when dealing with a fear of public speaking, a behavior therapist would first train the patient to relax different muscles and use various breathing techniques while imagining a mildly fearful situation. This situation might center around having dinner in a restaurant with a group of friends and feeling afraid to speak up when asked to pay more than his or her share. The therapist would then help the patient make a chart which lists mildly anxiety-causing situations—such as speaking with a small group of friends—along with more fearful situations—such as giving an oral presentation in class. Different fearful situations are then combined with the relaxation technique until the patient feels no trace of anxiety while visualizing these situations.

Now, therapists who use the second technique—called flooding—believe that the patient will stop fearing things when they are exposed to them many times. Doctors think that patients will learn to realize that the supposedly dangerous situation is actually quite harmless. These therapists believe that people with phobic disorders should be forced to confront what they fear so that they will realize that no real danger exists. For example, a person may be asked to ride in the elevator a hundred times in order to eliminate claustrophobia. Flooding can also be useful in eliminating an obsessive-compulsive ritual. The patient who has a fear of being dirty would be made to touch and handle dirt, but prevented from performing a hand-washing ritual.

The third technique is modeling. Now, modeling is a form of learning in which a patient observes and imitates others. In this treatment, the therapist is the one who confronts the feared object while the patient watches. If a patient had a snake phobia, the *therapist* would touch and handle a snake and then encourage the patient to do the same. Or if a patient were fearful of heights, the therapist might climb up a high ladder as the patient watches. When the patient accepts the idea that climbing the ladder isn't really dangerous, he or she will be encouraged to do so.

Section 4

Lecturer: Drug therapies use psychotropic drugs, drugs that primarily affect the brain, to alleviate the symptoms of anxiety disorders. Anti-anxiety drugs, also called minor tranquilizers, lessen tension and anxiety. The most popular of anti-anxiety drugs are benzodiazepines—that's B-E-N-Z-O-D-I-A-Z-E-P-I-N-E-S. Three widely prescribed benzodiazepines are Xanax, Valium, and Librium. Antipsychotic drugs are another example of psychotropic medication. These drugs are used to help relieve or reduce symptoms—such as confused thinking or withdrawal—and are sometimes effective in the treatment of generalized anxiety, social phobia, and obsessive-compulsive disorders. However, if these drugs are overused or *misused*, they can cause physical dependency and mild to severe side effects. And also, these drugs do not provide a permanent solution for most cases of anxiety.

Now, are there any questions? No? O.K., uh, don't forget your midterm is next week. I'll see you on Monday.

Chapter 7: Addictive Substances
Part 2 Social Language
A. Listening for Main Ideas (page 198)
B. Listening for Supporting Information (page 198)

Jennifer: Phew! What's that?

Victor: Those two girls behind you. They've been smokin' like chimneys. You just noticed?

Brandon: I don't get why anybody does that anymore. It's so annoying!

Jennifer: Yeah, you know, you don't really see that many people around here smoking. But back home all my girlfriends smoked.

Victor: Really?

Jennifer: Yeah. You know why girls start smoking?

Brandon: No?

Victor: No, why?

Jennifer: To keep their weight down. To keep from eating.

Brandon: Whaddya mean?

Jennifer: Well, it kills your appetite. Or they smoke instead of eating.

Brandon: Sounds dumb.

Victor: Sounds like a great idea. That way you can be a beautiful corpse!

Brandon: Hey, I remember reading an article in a magazine about how people who smoke have less of a chance of getting Alzheimer's.

Victor: What's the connection?

Brandon: I dunno. Somethin' about blood flow to the brain.

Jennifer: It makes sense.

Victor: I dunno what's worse—dying of lung cancer or Alzheimer's.

Brandon: Whatta choice! I'd rather not have either, thanks!

Victor: So when did all of these friends of yours start smoking, anyway?

Jennifer: A couple of them started when they were 14.

Brandon: Wow! How do kids that young get the idea to smoke, anyway?

Jennifer: I dunno. They see other kids doing it, and they think it looks cool. And in the case of these girls, their mothers and their older sisters smoked. And, and then there's all the advertising, you know, especially billboards.

Victor: Tobacco companies target kids. They wanna get them when they're young.

Jennifer: [Coughing] I've gotta get out of here. This second-hand smoke is gonna kill me. I might as well start smoking myself if I stay here any longer.

Brandon: Yeah, me too. Makes you think twice about trying to enjoy the fresh air. You leaving?

Victor: No, I think I'll hang around and take my anti-Alzheimer's treatment.

Jennifer: Bye, Victor.

Brandon: Yeah, see ya later, man.

C. Understanding Sarcasm (page 199)
Items 1 and 2

Jennifer: Well, it kills your appetite. Or they smoke instead of eating.

Brandon: Sounds dumb.

Victor: Sounds like a great idea that way you can be a beautiful corpse!

Items 3 and 4

Jennifer: [Coughing] I've gotta get out of here. This secondhand smoke is gonna kill me. I might as well start smoking myself if I stay here any longer.

Brandon: Yeah, me too. Makes you think twice about trying to enjoy the fresh air. You leaving?

Victor: No, I think I'll hang around and take my anti-Alzheimer's treatment.

D. Listening for Details (page 199)

1. Jennifer: Phew! What's that?

Victor: Those two girls behind you. They've been smokin' like chimneys. You just noticed?

Brandon: I don't get why anybody does that anymore. It's so annoying!

Jennifer: Yeah, you know, you don't really see that many people around here smoking. But back home all my girlfriends smoked.

Items 2 and 3

Brandon: Hey, I remember reading an article in a magazine about how people who smoke have less of a chance of getting Alzheimer's.

Victor: What's the connection?

Brandon: I dunno. Somethin' about blood flow to the brain.

Jennifer: It makes sense.

Victor: I dunno what's worse—dyin' of lung cancer or Alzheimer's.

Part 3 The Mechanics of Listening and Speaking
B. Hearing Degrees of Agreement/Disagreement (page 202)

People should be allowed to buy alcohol at the age of 18.

1. I completely agree.
2. I disagree.
3. I don't really agree with you.
4. I totally disagree with you about that.
5. I agree.
6. I don't know if I agree with you.

E. Reduced Forms of Words (page 204)

A: A coupla my friends and I are going to that new pizza place.

B: Somma my friends went there last week. They have 20 kindsa pizza. Whatta choice!

A: Wanna snack? I can getta pizza for you.

B: Um, I think I'll go with you guys.

A: O.K. I'm hungry. Let's get outta here!

Part 4 Broadcast English
A. Listening for Main Ideas (page 208)

Adams: Many experts agree that cigarettes are a so-called "gateway" to illegal drug abuse, but as NPR's Vicky Quay reports, the question is far from subtle.

Quay: Lloyd Johnston, at the University of Michigan, has spent the last 22 years surveying America's teenagers about their drug habits. Johnston says studies he's conducted show 8th graders who smoke a pack of cigarettes a day are 26 times more likely to smoke marijuana than teenagers who don't smoke cigarettes.

Johnston: I think it's clear, that, uh, tobacco is, uh, a step along the way, uh, to drug involvement. Uh, it's not hard to hypothesize what it may be. Uh, for one thing, um, a youngster, in learning to smoke cigarettes, uh, is getting perfect training for learning how to consume marijuana, which is also smoked. And I think that helps to account for the, uh, the very strong association between those two drugs.

Quay: Johnston says teenagers who smoke cigarettes are also more likely to smoke crack and use other illicit drugs. That's why many substance abuse experts believe cigarettes, along with alcohol and marijuana, are so-called "gateway" drugs—drugs young people use first, before they get hooked on more serious and dangerous substances. Experts say the younger a person starts smoking, the more likely he or she is to develop a serious drug habit. But some researchers aren't convinced tobacco is a gateway drug. Howard Beals is a professor at George Washington University.

Beals: I have never found the evidence in support of that notion at all persuasive. Um, it is clear that there are some common causal factors, um, and it's not surprising that kids tend to begin with the drugs that, as a practical matter, are more widely available, uh, like, uh, like cigarettes and alcohol, rather than, uh, drugs that are more difficult to find. Um, that simple process, it seems to me, is all it takes to explain the observation, um, that a lot of kids started smoking before they started, uh, other illegal drugs. It doesn't in any way imply that there's any causal connection there.

Quay: Beals says studies he's conducted show family problems and the friends a child chooses are more likely to influence future drug use. Now Beals does do work as a consultant to the R.J. Reynolds tobacco company, but he's not alone. New York sociologist Jian Yu argues it's rebelliousness and risk-taking that lead young people to develop drug habits. Yu interviewed nearly 2,000 young people enrolled in state drug and alcohol programs or on probation. He says while teenagers who smoke marijuana or binge drink are more likely to develop serious drug habits and break the law, the evidence isn't as clear when it comes to cigarettes.

Yu: We're not saying that, uh, smoking cigarettes is not a bad thing for kids. It is a bad thing for kids. But the point is that cigarette smoking, per se, does not have a significant effect on the involvement of criminal behavior in the future because of the different aspects—social aspects of cigarettes, different attitudes towards cigarettes.

Quay: Yu says most teenagers consider smoking cigarettes flirting with the law. Marijuana, he says, is very different. It's much more rebellious, and it's this risk-taking rebelliousness, not smoking itself, that leads to illegal drug use. But psychologist Herbert Cleaver, at Columbia University, says even when researchers account for a variety of delinquent behaviors, teenagers who smoke cigarettes are still more likely to abuse drugs. Cleaver says his research suggests cigarettes cause a physiological change in the brain that makes it more difficult for people to feel pleasure naturally.

Cleaver: So I think that it is more than simply, uh, rebelliousness. I think something really changes in the brain and that when you use these substances, ultimately you change something in

the brain that makes you want bigger and better effects from drugs.

Quay: While researchers may disagree about whether cigarettes really are a gateway to drug abuse, no one disputes the fact that they can cause serious health problems for young people. I'm Vicky Quay in Washington.

B. Listening for Two Sides of an Argument
(page 208)

Quay: Lloyd Johnston, at the University of Michigan, has spent the last 22 years surveying America's teenagers about their drug habits. Johnston says studies he's conducted show 8th graders who smoke a pack of cigarettes a day are 26 times more likely to smoke marijuana than teenagers who don't smoke cigarettes.

Johnston: I think it's clear, that, uh, tobacco is, uh, a step along the way, uh, to drug involvement. Uh, it's not hard to hypothesize what it may be. Uh, for one thing, um, a youngster, in learning to smoke cigarettes, uh, is getting perfect training for learning how to consume marijuana, which is also smoked. And I think that helps to account for the, uh, the very strong association between those two drugs.

Quay: Johnston says teenagers who smoke cigarettes are also more likely to smoke crack and use other illicit drugs. That's why many substance abuse experts believe cigarettes, along with alcohol and marijuana, are so-called "gateway" drugs, drugs young people use first, before they get hooked on more serious and dangerous substances. Experts say the younger a person starts smoking, the more likely he or she is to develop a serious drug habit. But some researchers aren't convinced tobacco is a gateway drug. Howard Beals is a professor at George Washington University.

Beals: I have never found the evidence in support of that notion at all persuasive. Um, it is clear that there are some common causal factors, um, and it's not surprising that kids tend to begin with the drugs that, as a practical matter, are more widely available, uh, like, uh, like cigarettes and alcohol, rather than, uh, drugs that are more difficult to find. Um, that simple process, it seems to me, is all it takes to explain the observation, um, that a lot of kids started smoking before they started, uh, other illegal drugs. It doesn't in any way imply that there's any causal connection there.

Quay: Beals says studies he's conducted show family problems and the friends a child chooses are more likely to influence future drug use. Now Beals does do work as a consultant to the R.J.

Reynolds tobacco company, but he's not alone. New York sociologist Jian Yu argues it's rebelliousness and risk-taking that lead young people to develop drug habits. Yu interviewed nearly 2,000 young people enrolled in state drug and alcohol programs or on probation. He says while teenagers who smoke marijuana or binge drink are more likely to develop serious drug habits and break the law, the evidence isn't as clear when it comes to cigarettes.

Yu: We're not saying that, uh, smoking cigarettes is not a bad thing for kids. It is a bad thing for kids. But the point is that cigarette smoking, per se, does not have a significant effect on the involvement of criminal behavior in the future because of the different aspects—social aspects of cigarettes, different attitudes towards cigarettes.

Quay: Yu says most teenagers consider smoking cigarettes flirting with the law. Marijuana, he says, is very different. It's much more rebellious, and it's this risk-taking rebelliousness, not smoking itself, that leads to illegal drug use. But psychologist Herbert Cleaver, at Columbia University, says even when researchers account for a variety of delinquent behaviors, teenagers who smoke cigarettes are still more likely to abuse drugs. Cleaver says his research suggests cigarettes cause a physiological change in the brain that makes it more difficult for people to feel pleasure naturally.

Cleaver: So I think that it is more than simply, uh, rebelliousness. I think something really changes in the brain and that when you use these substances, ultimately you change something in the brain that makes you want bigger and better effects from drugs.

C. Evaluating the Source of Information
(page 209)

1. **Quay:** Lloyd Johnston, at the University of Michigan, has spent the last 22 years surveying America's teenagers about their drug habits.

2. **Quay:** Howard Beals is a professor at George Washington University.

3. **Quay:** Now Beals does do work as a consultant to the R.J. Reynolds tobacco company, but he's not alone. New York sociologist Jian Yu argues it's rebelliousness and risk-taking that lead young people to develop drug habits.

4. **Quay:** But psychologist Herbert Cleaver, at Columbia University, says even when researchers account for a variety of delinquent behaviors, teenagers who smoke cigarettes are still more likely to abuse drugs.

E. Listening for Latin Terms (page 210)

Yu: But the point is that cigarette smoking, per se, does not have a significant effect on the involvement of criminal behavior in the future because of the different aspects—social aspects of cigarettes, different attitudes towards cigarettes.

Part 5 Academic English
A. Taking Notes: Numbers (page 214)

1. Millions of people around the world smoke cigarettes. But despite the fact that cigarette smoking has declined in the United States over the past 30 years, there are still over 50 million Americans who smoke.

2. Now, let's, let's take a look at the health risks of smoking. Smoking cigarettes *is* dangerous. In fact, it's the leading cause of preventable death in the United States. Every year over 400,000 Americans die as a result of cigarette smoking, and, uh, another 10,000,000 people suffer from smoking-related diseases.

3. The symptoms of nicotine withdrawal can appear within 6 to 18 hours after the last cigarette is smoked.

4. In fact, of people who quit smoking, only about 20 to 25 percent remain smoke-free for more than one year.

B. Taking Notes: Using an Outline (page 214)
D. Checking Your Notes (page 217)
Section 1

Lecturer: Hi everyone! How are you today?

Students: Good.

Lecturer: Now, today I'm going to be discussing nicotine addiction and some strategies for treating it. As you know, cigarette smoking is more than just a bad habit. It's a major public health problem worldwide. Cigarette smoking is also considered to be addictive. Now, that means that once you start smoking cigarettes, even casually, your body will become dependent on cigarettes and you will begin to crave them. Now, when you crave something, you need it, want it, and you feel that you must have it—which causes you to, to use more of that thing. And once you become dependent on cigarettes, it's very difficult to quit smoking.

Millions of people around the world smoke cigarettes. But despite the fact that cigarette smoking has declined in the United States over the past 30 years there are still over 50 million Americans who smoke. Rates of smoking are higher among men than women, higher among non-white people than whites, and people with less than a high school education are more likely to smoke.

Now, let's, let's take a look at the health risks of smoking. Smoking cigarettes is dangerous. In fact, it's the leading cause of preventable death in the United States. Every year over 400,000 Americans die as a result of cigarette smoking, and another 10,000,000 people suffer from smoking-related diseases. Now, cigarette smokers are at higher risk of developing lung disease—also called respiratory disease—heart disease, high blood pressure, and certain cancers—especially lung cancer—than non-smokers. Smoking during pregnancy increases the risk of delivering a low birth weight baby.

Now, you don't have to smoke to be in danger from tobacco. Other forms of tobacco use, including cigar and pipe smoking, and smokeless and chewing tobacco, cause health problems. Smokeless or chewing tobacco is associated with an increased risk of mouth cancer, gum disease, and tooth loss. And studies have shown that even non-smokers who live and work in smoke-filled environments are in danger from passive or second-hand smoke. And of particular concern are children who live in homes where the parents smoke. The health hazard to non-smokers from passive or second-hand smoke has resulted in laws banning cigarette smoking in most public places, including offices, schools, airplanes, trains, and buses.

Section 2

Lecturer: O.K. Why *do* people smoke? People smoke for a number of reasons. Teenagers often smoke because they think that smoking is "cool" and because it makes them feel grown-up. Their friends or their parents may smoke. Young people may also be influenced by seeing movie stars, athletes, and other celebrities who smoke or use other tobacco products. Most of the people who now smoke began when they were teenagers, and tobacco companies often target young people with cigarette advertising. Sadly, larger numbers of children have begun experimenting with cigarette smoking at younger and younger ages. Tobacco companies also target African Americans, Latinos, and women with cigarette advertising.

Now, many people find that smoking is pleasurable. It may relax them, or it may be stimulating. Others consider smoking a habit, and they may enjoy the feel of a cigarette in their hands and the act of smoking. Most people do not consider themselves dependent on cigarettes. However, when they attempt to stop smoking, it's almost always extremely difficult. The fact is, most people who try smoking, indeed, become addicted to it.

Section 3

Lecturer: Now, why are cigarettes addictive? Cigarette smoke contains thousands of chemicals, many of which are dangerous to human health. The two best-known chemicals are tar and nicotine. Tar and other chemicals in cigarette smoke have been shown to cause lung cancer. Lung cancer, the most common form of cancer in the United States, causes over 150,000 deaths each year. Nicotine is a chemical that has several effects on the human body and brain, and is considered to be the drug that is responsible for tobacco addiction.

Now, what effect does nicotine have on the body? When cigarette smoke is inhaled, nicotine enters the bloodstream and then the brain. The nicotine is taken up by the brain very quickly, within ten seconds of inhaling cigarette smoke into the lungs. Nicotine has a stimulating effect on the brain, which causes smokers to experience a feeling of increased well-being—either alertness or relaxation. Smokers have described these positive feelings using terms like "pleasure," "increased alertness," "better concentration," "better mood," "improved ability to accomplish a task," and "stimulation."

Nicotine has other affects on the body, both short-term and long-term [points to board]. Short-term effects include increases in heart rate and blood pressure. Long-term effects include an increasing risk of developing hardening of the arteries and heart attacks.

In addition to a physical dependence on nicotine, smokers often develop a psychological dependence on the drug because of its pleasant effects. This causes smokers to crave cigarettes in specific situations, for example, while drinking coffee, or when under stress.

Now, let's turn to the effects of nicotine withdrawal. When a smoker stops smoking, he or she will experience discomfort due to nicotine withdrawal. The symptoms of nicotine withdrawal can appear within 6 to 18 hours after the last cigarette is smoked. Now, these symptoms include irritability, anxiety, restlessness, difficulty concentrating, headache, sleep disturbances, and depression. Many people find that they eat more and gain weight when they attempt to quit smoking. Because of these physical symptoms of nicotine withdrawal and the psychological dependence on the drug, it usually takes more than willpower to quit smoking. In fact, of people who quit smoking, only about 20 to 25 percent remain smoke-free for more than one year.

Section 4

Lecturer: What are some of the strategies for treating nicotine addiction? Most people who decide to quit smoking do so on their own. For this strategy to work, the person must be highly motivated. For some smokers, however, simply giving up cigarettes will not enable them to quit smoking because the physical and psychological effects of nicotine withdrawal are too great. For these people there are a number of programs available where smokers meet in groups and receive counseling and support to help them quit smoking. These programs emphasize changing behavior, and substituting health habits—like exercise—for cigarette smoking. There are also medical therapies designed to ease the stress of nicotine withdrawal, such as nicotine patches, which the smoker can wear, or nicotine gum he or she can chew. These patches and chewing gums provide the smoker with a small amount of nicotine and this eases the craving for cigarettes.

So, in conclusion, there are health benefits for people who quit smoking, including a reduction in the risk of developing smoking-related diseases. And people who successfully give up smoking report that they feel better, have greater enjoyment of everyday activities, and feel a greater sense of self-esteem.

C. Listening for Comparisons (page 217)

Lecturer: Rates of smoking are higher among men than women, higher among non-white people than whites, and people with less than a high school education are more likely to smoke.

Chapter 8: Secrets of Good Health

Part 2 Social Language
A. Listening for Main Ideas (page 226)
B. Listening for Details (page 227)

Evan: What do you think the secrets are to good health?

Speaker 1: Uh, exercise, eating well and, uh, having a positive image about yourself. Think healthy.

Speaker 2: The secrets to good health—I think definitely, uh, a steady exercise program, uh, and diet and, definitely, uh, leaving stress out of your life.

Speaker 3: Um, I guess it would be exercise and a well balanced diet, 'cause you are what you eat. If you eat grease and stuff that's all you're gonna end up being.

Speaker 4: An apple a day keeps the doctor away. I don't know. I mean just, um, eating well and, um, trying to exercise a coupla times a week and making sure that you go to your doctor's appointments every year.

Evan: What do you think the key to good health is?

Speaker 5: Oh, the key to good health. Um, I would say probably eating right, exercising. You know, the typical things that everybody does on a daily basis.

Speaker 6: Not getting too stressed out. Eating well. You know, staying calm and not overreacting to everything.

Speaker 7: Key to good health. I think mental health and physical health are, are two very important items. I mean, you should try and have, try and have a balance in life so you're not just doing one thing or the other thing. Participate in sports and, uh, in reading and, and just exploring, exploring what the world has to offer. That, that's the key to, to mental and physical health.

Speaker 8: Good health? Brush your teeth everyday. Eat your vegetables. Um, you just gotta take care of your body, you know. It's, it's very simple.

C. Guessing the Meaning of Proverbs (page 227)

1. **Speaker 4:** An apple a day keeps the doctor away. I don't know. I mean just, um, eating well and um, trying to exercise a coupla times a week and making sure that you go to your doctor's appointments every year.

2. **Speaker 3:** Um, I guess it would be exercise and a well balanced diet, 'cause you are what you eat. If you eat grease and stuff that's all you're gonna end up being.

D. Listening for Specific Information (page 228)

1. **Speaker 4:** An apple a day keeps the doctor away. I don't know. I mean just, um, eating well and, um, trying to exercise a coupla times a week and making sure that you go to your doctor's appointments every year.

2. **Speaker 6:** Not getting too stressed out. Eating well. You know, staying calm and not overreacting to everything.

3. **Speaker 7:** Key to good health. I think mental health and physical health are, are two very important items. I mean, you should try and have, try and have a balance in life so you're not just doing one thing or the other thing. Participate in sports and, uh, in reading and, and just exploring, exploring what the world has to offer. That, that's the key to, to mental and physical health.

Part 3 The Mechanics of Listening and Speaking

B. Hearing Degrees of Advice (page 230)

1. You really ought to see your doctor.
2. All you have to do is eat less.
3. Perhaps you should get more exercise.
4. Just have a positive image.
5. I think you should get more rest.

D. Hearing the Difference Between /θ/ and /t/ (page 231)

1. thank	7. tin
2. eight	8. thick
3. taught	9. fort
4. tent	10. math
5. bath	11. team
6. myths	12. pat

Part 4 Broadcast English

A. Listening for Main Ideas (page 235)

Edwards: This is Morning Edition from NPR News. I'm Bob Edwards.

Health officials worldwide are concerned about the numbers of people who are overweight, particularly in childhood, putting them at risk for a multitude of chronic diseases as they age. The World Health Organization last week published its recommendations for a healthier global population. The final plan will be voted on by member nations in May. NPR's Patricia Neighmond reports.

Neighmond: It used to be that extra pounds were the burden of the well-to-do. No more. Health officials are worried about overweight children not only in the U.S., Canada, and Europe but also in countries like India, China, Chile, Egypt, and Zambia. David Porter is an official with the World Health Organization, or WHO, and when it comes to the diseases that are related to obesity, Porter says the rest of the world has become Westernized.

Porter: We're talking about, uh, cardiovascular disease, now the leading killer worldwide, killing about 70 million people every year. Probably 80 percent of those deaths are in developing countries. We've got countries like India with—and China with 20 to 30 million diabetics.

Neighmond: Problems that, as in the U.S., are directly related to the foods we eat.

Porter: What we're eating is food that's increasingly sugary, salty, fatty—food that's increasingly processed.

Neighmond: And on top of that, like in the U.S., people in developing countries are a lot less active than they used to be.

Porter: People who are not working in the fields anymore. They're not planting rice. They're working in factories. They're working in offices. They're taking buses. They're riding little motorcycles. They're not walking to the extent that they used to.

Neighmond: The WHO estimates that 300 million people worldwide are obese, one billion are overweight. The WHO proposal makes a number of recommendations like limiting consumption of high-fat foods, sugars, and salt, and increasing consumption of fruits, vegetables, legumes, whole grains, and nuts and, of course, getting out and getting more active; advice health officials have been giving for years. But in the context of an official international document, the advice becomes controversial, even threatening.

Briscoe: My name is Andrew Briscoe. I'm president and CEO of the Sugar Association here in Washington, D.C.

Neighmond: Sugar, says Briscoe, has been made into a culprit in the debate about obesity. And the industry, he says, is an easy target. The WHO proposal does not suggest actual limits for sugar, salt, or fat, but it does refer to an earlier document that did suggest limits and that very reference is being challenged by Briscoe and other industry officials. That's because that earlier document suggested limiting added sugars to 10 percent of all daily calories.

Briscoe: In the United States, our average consumption figure is 15.7 percent, as calculated by the USDA. Therefore, if we were to implement the figure of 10 percent, we would be asking Americans to reduce their sugar intake by roughly 30 percent. And there's not a scientific justification for that type of restriction.

Neighmond: Many other big food and beverage companies have argued similar points, that there's not enough science to justify restricting certain foods and additives. Nonsense, say health officials, who point to various studies linking obesity to food intake. But Briscoe says there are just as many studies that point to the need for exercise. And he says that's what the WHO should focus on.

Briscoe: Exercise is 50 percent of the equation, folks. We need to understand that and we need to feel good about it and just get up and get out and get moving. We need to move. We need to pick up our feet and, and, and burn some calories. If we did that, none of us would be obese.

B. Listening for Causes (page 235)

Porter: We're talking about cardiovascular disease, now the leading killer worldwide, killing about 70 million people every year. Probably 80 percent of those deaths are in developing countries. We've got countries like India and China with 20 to 30 million diabetics.

Neighmond: Problems that, as in the U.S., are directly related to the foods we eat.

Porter: What we're eating is food that's increasingly sugary, salty, fatty food that's increasingly processed.

Neighmond: And on top of that, like in the U.S., people in developing countries are a lot less active than they used to be.

Porter: People who are not working in the fields anymore. They're not planting rice. They're working in factories. They're working in offices. They're taking buses. They're riding little motorcycles. They're not walking to the extent that they used to.

C. Listening for Numerical Information (page 236)

1. **Porter:** We're talking about cardiovascular disease, now the leading killer worldwide, killing about 70 million people every year. Probably 80 percent of those deaths are in developing countries. We've got countries like India and China with 20 to 30 million diabetics.

2. **Neighmond:** The WHO estimates that 300 million people worldwide are obese, one billion are overweight.

3. **Briscoe:** In the United States, our average consumption figure is 15.7 percent, as calculated by the USDA. Therefore, if we were to implement the figure of 10 percent, we would be asking Americans to reduce their sugar intake by roughly 30 percent. And there's not a scientific justification for that type of restriction.

D. Making Inferences (page 236)

Briscoe: My name is Andrew Briscoe. I'm president and CEO of the Sugar Association here in Washington, D.C.

Neighmond: Sugar, says Briscoe, has been made into a culprit in the debate about obesity. And the industry, he says, is an easy target. The WHO proposal does not suggest actual limits for sugar, salt, or fat, but it does refer to an earlier document that did suggest limits and that very reference is being challenged by Briscoe and other industry officials. That's because that earlier document suggested limiting added sugars to 10 percent of all daily calories.

Briscoe: In the United States, our average consumption figure is 15.7 percent, as calculated by the USDA. Therefore, if we were to implement the figure of 10 percent, we would be asking Americans to reduce their sugar intake by roughly 30 percent. And there's not a scientific justification for that type of restriction.

Part 5 Academic English

A. Taking Notes: Using an Outline (page 238)
B. Checking Your Notes (page 240)

Section 1

Lecturer: Good afternoon, everyone. Today, I'm going to discuss some basic concepts of health and heath maintenance.

First of all, what does it mean to be healthy? Health means different things to different people. The simplest definition of health is "the absence of disease." This definition reflects a medical view of health involving mainly the diagnosis and treatment of illness. This view is limited because it focuses only on physical health and how to go about curing specific physical illnesses. The World Health Organization has a broader view. This organization talks about "the state of complete, physical, emotional, social, intellectual, environmental, and spiritual health." This holistic view of health and wellness takes into account the whole person. Good health can be described as a relationship of harmony with yourself, with others, and with your environment, which allows you to get the most out of life.

Section 2

Lecturer: Now, let's look at how an individual can achieve and maintain good health. This process involves adopting lifestyle habits that promote a state of well-being. An individual's health depends on a variety of factors—food, shelter, clothing, income, and social relationships.

The health needs of the larger society include such additional conditions as peace, safety, social justice, respect for human rights, respect for women's rights, and fairness in general.

Poverty is probably the greatest threat to good healthcare. Health maintenance must become an activity that involves the entire society—government, business and industry, the healthcare system, the media, schools, communities and individual families. These groups must work together to ensure that nutritious food, clean water, decent housing, good schools, and proper health care are accessible to all. When these basic elements are available, people will be able to live longer, healthier, and happier lives.

Section 3

Lecturer: Health promotion is a global issue and basic health promotion strategies must be adapted to meet the unique cultural climate in various countries, and in different regions and communities within each country. The goal is to create conditions that allow each individual to achieve and maintain good health.

The World Health Organization and other international organizations are hard at work around the world. But in order for their work to be effective, it must reach people at the grass roots level. Health education is needed in thousands of settings around the world and this extremely complex task can, at times, seem overwhelming.

Section 4

Lecturer: What can an individual do to achieve and maintain good health? Anyone can embrace the principles of good health, and one of the most important ones is diet. A healthy diet contains a moderate number of calories, is low in fat and salt, and includes a lot of fruits and vegetables.

Oh, and another important factor in maintaining good health is exercise. Being physically active benefits both body and mind. People who exercise regularly feel better and have more energy. They also have healthier hearts and lower blood pressure than less active people. In addition, those who are physically fit feel better about themselves, have less stress, and have a more positive outlook on life.

Maintaining a healthy weight is also important. Being overweight increases the risk of developing heart disease, high blood pressure, and diabetes. By adopting a healthy diet and exercise plan, most people can maintain a desirable body weight.

Another factor in health maintenance is the management of stress. Stress can destroy the quality of a person's life and even cause physical illness. Learning positive ways of coping with stress is one of the best ways to attain wellness. Meditation and relaxation techniques are examples of positive strategies for coping with stress. Drug use, alcohol use, and overeating are examples of ways that people try to cope with stress which damage their health in the long run. Avoiding alcohol and drugs is important in maintaining physical and mental health and in maintaining strong personal and professional relationships.

And finally, developing solid interpersonal relationships contributes to good health. Strong friendships provide you with the enjoyment and support that make life worth living. Also, treating others with kindness and respect usually insures that you will receive the same treatment in return. Studies have shown that people who get along with others and have successful relationships are healthier and live longer than their more isolated peers.

O.K. That's all for right now. Are there any questions?

VOCABULARY INDEX

retrospective
sketch
state of being
streamlined
subjects of sculpture
tableau
yuck

Chapter 4
admiration
antiquity
assembly line
be out of here
blacksmith
cannibal
challenging
chronological order
come to mind
commerce
contrapposto
crafts
custom order
dating from
dedicate
department secretary
detailed
diadems
dismembered
durable
earthenware
endoscope
excavate
fertility
fragment
glazing
good for you
ideals
illustrate
kiln
kore
kouros
lost-wax casting
mass-produced
musculature
nude
office hours
prophecy
reading list
sedate(d)
smelt(ed)
source information

that will work
to go on
tomb
torques
underworld
unearth
utilitarian

Vocabulary Workshop: Unit 2
Academic Word List
assume
classics
coincidence
computer
concepts
contemporary
elements
major
periods
philosophy
produced
proportion
survived
works

UNIT 3
Chapter 5
all in your head
aloft
altered state of consciousness
ask about
brag about
bulk
call up
cerebral
circadian rhythm
consciousness
cortex
crack(ed)
deplete
deprive
digression
dream about
dream scenario
EEGs (electroencephalographs)
emit
from out of the blue
glial cells
glucose

glycogen
head for
hibernation
incoherent
interpretation
manage to
marathon
mimic
moody
non-REM sleep
on the right track
recall
rejuvenate
REM sleep
reserves
restorative
run down
run out
sail across/ to
sitcom
turn into
turn over

Chapter 6
abnormal
acrophobia
activate
agitated
agoraphobia
anxiety disorders
anxious
apprehension
claustrophobia
confront
cope with
deep-seated
demon
diminish
disrupt
drive-by shooting
drown(ing)
eat away at
evoke
figurative
gender
generalized anxiety disorder
get carried away
get over
grip
limbic system
literal

lurk
neurological
obsessive-compulsive disorder
out of my mind
paranoia
pervasive
phobic disorder
physiological
premonitions
preoccupied
psychotropic drugs
raw
rescue
resurgence
side effects
slimy
sort of
speak up
streptococcus A infection
triggers
weird
whatever comes to mind
withdrawal

Vocabulary Workshop:
Unit 3
Academic Word List
abnormal
accompanied
approach
consciously
create
definition
indication
mental
occurs
over
response
so
statistical
symbol
symbolize

UNIT 4
Chapter 7
affiliation
alertness
Alzheimer's disease
billboard
casually

causal factors
controversial issue
corpse
crackdown
crave
drop-out
flirting with the law
gateway drug
get
get hooked on
hang around
hazard
hypothesize
illegal
illicit
kill
modus operandi
notion
on probation
passive smoke
per se
pro forma
psychological dependence
quid pro quo
rebellious
shortcut
smokes like a chimney
start smoking
step along the way
substance abuse
target
think twice about
to keep down
try to smoke
try to stop
verbatim
willpower
withdrawal

Chapter 8
adoption
an easy target
approaches
at risk
burden
cardiovascular disease
chronic
controversial
culprit
diabetics
eating right

end up
enhance
getting out
grassroots level
grease
harmony
holistic
implement
key to
multitude
obesity
on top of that
pick up our feet
positive image
potential
processed (food)
proverbs
steady
stressed out
tips
to the extent that

Vocabulary Workshop:
Unit 4
Academic Word List
administrators
adults
authors
create
depression
findings
functions
legal
link
mediate
normal
options
percent
relying
researchers
survey
surveyed
tasks

SKILLS INDEX

CREDITS

Text

p. 5 Adapted from *Do's and Taboos Around the World, 3e* by Roger E. Axtell, 1993. p. 32 Adapted from "Transformation through Education: The Story of Lalita", UNICEF, www/unicef.org, accessed 2/18/05. p. 65 Adapted from "Michael Cassidy" by Margaret Moore, *Hemispheres Magazine*, November 1997. p. 99: Mark Getlein, "Greece" adapted from *Gilbert's Living with Art, Sixth Edition.* Copyright © 2002 by McGraw Hill, Inc. Reprinted with the permission of the publishers. p. 133 Adapted from *Ask the Dream Doctor by* Charles McPhee. New York: Random House, 2002. p. 161 "Definitions of Abnormal Behavior" adapted from *Introduction to Psychology, 5e* by Rod Plotnik, 1999. p. 195 *Smoking Makes the Campus Scene* by Liz Szabo, which appeared on USA Today online, www.usatoday.com, 12/28/04. p. 223 "The College Transition: Managing Stress and Maintaining Health" as appeared on MayoClinic.com Special to CNN.com February 5, 2004.

Photo

Cover (top right): © Milton Montenegro/Getty Images; (middle left): © PicturePress/Getty Images; (bottom right): © The McGraw-Hill Companies, Inc.

Unit 1. p. 1: © image100/Getty Images; p. 3: © PicturePress/Getty Images; p. 4 (top left) : © Purestock/Age Fotostock; p. 4 (top right): © Kate Abbey/Alamy; p. 4 (bottom left): © Digital Vision; p.4 (bottom right): © Triangle Images/Age Fotostock; p. 9, 12, 14, 24: © The McGraw-Hill Companies, Inc.; p. 26: © David Woolley/Getty Images; p. 31: © Brand X Pictures/Getty Images, p. 33. © Sean Sprague/The Image Works; p. 35, 36, 40: © The McGraw-Hill Companies, Inc.; p.45 (top left): © Brand X Pictures/PunchStock; p.45 (top right): © Steven Rubin/The Image Works; p.45 (bottom): © Mary Kate Denny/ PhotoEdit; p. 51: © Ronnie Kaufman/CORBIS; p. 52: AP/Wide World Photos.

Unit 2. p. 61: © Erin Patrice O'Brien/Getty Images; p. 63: © Grossman/Photo Researchers; p. 64: Michael Cassidy. *Waikiki Surf Festival*, 1996. Seventh Heaven Publishers, Vista, CA; p. 66 (top left): Donald Judd, *Untitled*, (Stack). 1967. Lacquer on glavanized iron. The Museum of Modern Art, New York. Helen Achen Bequest (by exchange) and gift of Joseph Helman. Photograph © 1999 The Museum of Modern Art/ /Licensed by SCALA/Art Resource, NY. Art © Judd Foundation. Licensed by VAGA, New York, NY; p. 66 (top right): Chuck Close,

Linda. 1975-76. Acylic on canvas, 9'x7'. Courtesy Pace Wildenstein, New York; p. 66 (bottom): Andy Warhol: *100 Campbell Soup Cans*, 1962. Albright-Knox Art Gallery, Buffalo, NY (gift of Seymour H. Knox, 1963. © 2007 Andy Warhol Foundation for the Visual Arts/Artists Rights Society (ARS), New York; p. 67: Digital Image © The Museum of Modern Art/Licensed by SCALA/Art Resource, NY. © 2007 Tony Smith/Artists Rights Society (ARS), New York; p. 68: © The McGraw-Hill Companies, Inc.; p. 71 (top left): Frank Stella, *Pergusa*, 1981. © 2007 Frank Stella/Artists Rights Society (ARS), New York; p. 71 (top right): Jasper Johns, *Three Flags*, 1958. Collection, Whitney Museum of American Art, New York. Art © Jasper Johns/Licensed by VAGA, New York, NY; p. 71 (bottom left): George Segal, *Blue Girl on Park Bench*, 1980. Collection Jeanette, Nina and Constance Golder. Art © The George and Helen Segal Foundation/Licensed by VAGA, New York, NY; p. 71 (bottom right): Duane Hanson, *Self-Portrait with Model*. 1979. Art © Duane Hanson/Licensed by VAGA, New York, NY; p. 72: © The McGraw-Hill Companies, Inc.; p. 78 (top left): © Kevin Fleming/CORBIS. Art © The George and Helen Segal Foundation/ Licensed by VAGA, New York, NY; p. 78 (top right): Louise Nevelson. *City on a High Mountain*. 1983. Steel painted black. 246 x 276 x 162 in. Storm King Art Center, Mountainville, N.Y. Purchase Fund, 1984.4. Photo by Jerry L. Thompson, © 2007 Estate of Louis Nevelson/Artists Rights Society (ARS), New York; p. 78 (bottom): Jeff Koons, *Puppy*, 1992. Live flowers, earth, wood and steel. © Jeff Koons. Photo by Dieter Schwerdtle; p. 80: © Christopher Felver/CORBIS; p. 81 (left): © Massimo Listri/ CORBIS; p. 81 (right): © Joe Schuyler/Stock Boston; p. 82: © Don Emmert/AFP/Getty Images. Art © The George and Helen Segal Foundation/VAGA, New York; p. 84 (top left, top right & bottom left): © Royalty-Free/CORBIS; p. 84 (bottom right): The McGraw-Hill Companies Inc./Ken Cavanagh Photographer; p. 88: Jackson Pollock. *Autumn Rhythm*. The Metropolitan Museum of Art, George A. Heam Fund, 1957. (57.92). All rights reserved. © 2007 The Pollock-Krasner Foundation/Artists Rights Society (ARS), New York; p. 89: Robert Rauschenberg. *Canyon*. 1959. Art © Robert Rauschenberg/Licensed by VAGA, New York, NY; p. 90: Robert Rauschenberg. *Skyway*. 1964. Dallas Museum of Art, The Roberta Coke Camp Fund, The 500, Inc., Mr. and Mrs. Mark Shepherd, Jr. and General Acquisitions Fund. Art © Robert Rauschenberg/Licensed by VAGA, New York, NY; p. 91: Andy Warhol, *200 Campbell's soup Cans*. 1962. The Andy Warhol Foundation, Inc./Art Resource, NY. © 2007 Andy Warhol Foundation for the Visual Arts/Artists Rights Society (ARS), New York; p. 92: Claes Oldenberg. *Clothespin*. 1979. Cor-Ten and stainless steel. 45 ft. x 12 ft. 3 1/4 in. x 4 ft. 6 in. (13.72 x 3.74 x 1.37 m). Centre Square Plaza, Fifteenth and Market Streets, Philadelphia. Photo by G. Benson/ Robertstock.com; p. 93: Roy Lichtenstein. *Whaam!* 1963. © Contemporary Arts Services, NY. Tate Gallery, London, Great Britain/Art Resource, NY. © 2007 Estate of Roy Lichtenstein; p. 97: © Milton Montenegro/Getty Images; p. 98: *Dipylon Vase*, Greek, 8th C., B.C. The Metropolitan Museum of Art, Rogers Fund, 1914. (14.130.14). All rights reserved; p. 100: © Reunion des Musees Nationaux/Licensed by SCALA/Art Resource, NY; p.102, 104: © The McGraw-Hill Companies, Inc.; p. 110: © Scala/Art Resource, NY; p. 117: © The McGraw-Hill Companies, Inc.; p. 120: © Milton Montenegro/Getty Images; p. 121 (top right): *Kouros*. c. 600 B.C.E Marble, height 6'4". The Metropolitan Museum of Art, Fletcher Fund, 1932. (32.11.1). All rights reserved; p. 121 (bottom left): © Scala/Art Resource, NY; p. 122 (left): *Dipylon Vase*, Greek, 8th C., B.C. The Metropolitan Museum of Art, Rogers Fund, 1914. (14.130.14). All rights reserved; p. 122 (right): *Bell Krater*, View: (Side A) Artemis. Attributed to the Pen Painter. James Fund and by Special Contribution, Coutresy of Museum of Fine Arts, Boston; p. 123: *Diadem*; Dionysos and Ariadne in relief. The Metropolitan Museum of Art, Rogers Fund, 1906. (06.1217.1). All rights reserved; p. 124 (left): Vatican Museum, Rome; p. 124 (right): © Nimatallah/Art Resource, NY; p. 125: © Art Resource, NY.

Unit 3. p. 129: © Alfred Gescheidt/Getty Images; p. 131: © Image Source Limited/ IndexStock Imagery; p. 132 (top): Salvador Dali. *The Persistence of Memory*, 1931. © The Museum of Modern Art/Licensed by SCALA/Art Resource, NY. © 2007 Salvador Dali, Gala-Salvador Dali Foundation/Artists Rights Society (ARS), New York; p. 132 (bottom): © John Holcroft/Superstock; p. 135, 138: © The McGraw-Hill Companies, Inc.; p.143: © Superstock; p. 150: © The McGraw-Hill Companies, Inc.; p. 153: © Science Photo Library/Photo Researchers; p. 155 (left): © Hulton-Deutsch Collection/CORBIS; p. 155 (right): © Bettmann/CORBIS; p. 159: © Jon Bradley/Getty Images; p. 160: © Andre Rouillard/Superstock; p. 161: © Rick McCarthy/The San Diego Union-Tribune; p. 164: © The McGraw-Hill Companies, Inc.; p. 171: © Erich Lessing/Art Resource, NY. © 2007 Edvard Munch/Artists Rights Society (ARS), New York; p. 179: © Michael Newman/PhotoEdit; p. 181: © Bruce Ayres/Getty Images; p. 182: © Custom Medical Stock Photo.

Unit 4. p. 191: © Neil Beckerman/Getty Images; p. 193: © Rachel Epstein/The Image Works; p.194: © Jim Arbogast/Getty Images; p. 206: © Lee Snider/The Image Works; p. 213: © The McGraw-Hill Companies, Inc.; p. 214: The McGraw-Hill Companies, Inc./Christopher Kerrigan, photographer; p. 216: © Lon C. Diehl/ PhotoEdit; p. 217: © Michael Keller/CORBIS; p. 221: © Steve Cole/Getty Images; p. 222 (top left & bottom):

© Royalty-Free/CORBIS; p. 222 (top right): The McGraw-Hill Companies, Inc./Andrew Resek, photographer; p.226, 229: © The McGraw-Hill Companies, Inc.; p. 233: © Dennis MacDonald/Age Fotostock; p. 237: © David Mendelsohn/Masterfile; p. 239: AP/Wide World Photos; p. 240: © Chris Ware/The Image Works.

Radio

Chap. 1: "Code of Ethics in Business Conference in Tokyo" (Jocelyn Ford, reporter), J8uly 12, 1996. Marketplace. Chap. 2: "I have a right to . . ." (Rageh Omar, correspondent), October 20, 2000, BBC Radio. Chap. 3: "George Segal" from "All Things Considered" (Daniel Zwerdling, host), February 21, 1998, National Public Radio. Chap. 4: "Ancient Greek Statues" from "All Things Considered" (Jackie Lyden, interviewer), December 15, 1996, National Public Radio. Chap. 5: ""New Theory Says Sleep Serves to Restore Brain Energy" from "All Things Considered" (Joe Palca, reporter), January 12, 1996, National Public Radio. Chap. 6: Excerpt from "What Is Paranoia?" (Michael Phillips, interviewer), January 15, 1995, Social Thought. Used with the permission of Dr. Robert Siegel. Chap. 7: Excerpt form "Smoking-The 'Gateway' Drug" (Vicki Quay, reporter), August 23, 1996, National Public Radio. Chap. 8: "WHO, Food Industry at Odds on Obesity" from "Morning Edition" (Patricia Neighmond, reporter), April 26, 2004, National Public Radio.

NOTES

 **NOTES**